2025
교원임용시험 전공영어 대비
최신 출제경향 반영

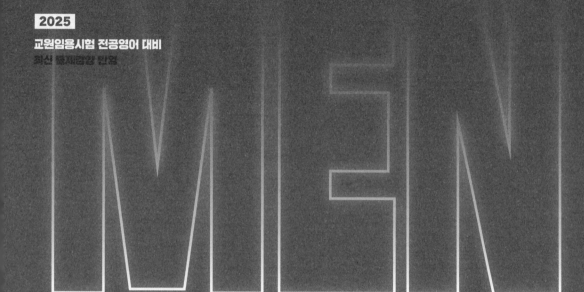

Mentor Linguistics

# 멘토영어학 문제은행

LSI 영어연구소 앤드류 채 편저

박문각 임용    동영상강의 www.pmg.co.kr    박문각

멘토영어학 문제은행은 실제 시험 대비를 위한 종합적 훈련 교재이다.

2022년~2023년까지 2년간 출제된 문제를 주제별로 엄선해서 지금까지 배운 내용학 복습과 문제 적용 훈련 및 답안 작성 연습을 통해 실제 시험 대비를 위한 종합적 훈련이 가능하도록 구성했다. 임용시험 합격을 위해선 지문 분석 능력과 답안 작성의 기술적인 능력 향상이 필요하다.

효과적인 학습을 위해 아래와 같은 학습법을 제안한다.

- 수업 전  수업 진도에 따라 반드시 미리 문제를 풀어보고, 이해되지 않는 부분을 표시한다.
- 수업 중  강의를 통해서 이해되지 않았던 부분을 해결하고, 관련 주제의 핵심 개념을 다시 숙지한다.
- 수업 후  모범답안을 참고하여 본인의 답안을 보완하고, 자주 쓰는 표현을 익숙하게 쓸 수 있도록 연습한다.

임용시험 준비 기간의 후반기로 접어들면서 정신적 · 체력적으로 지쳐가는 시기이다. 7~8월 무더운 날씨에 건강에 유의하여 체력관리를 잘하는 것도 시험 준비에 있어서 중요한 부분이다. 같은 시간이라도 집중력 있게 공부하고 출제 빈도가 높은 주제에 좀 더 시간을 투자해서 학습의 효과를 극대화하길 바란다.

부디, 수험생 예비교사 여러분의 임용시험 합격에 본 교재가 조금이나마 도움이 되었으면 한다.

## 효과적인 **학습전략**

**1  비중이 높은 영역을 공략하라.**

통사론 · 학교문법 · 음운론의 비중이 높고, 기타 형태론 · 의미론 · 화용론이 비중이 상대적으로 낮으므로 효율적인 학습계획과 학습전략을 수립하는 것이 필요하다.

**2  개념이해와 용어정리를 확실히 하라.**

주어진 지문을 정확하게 읽고 이해하기 위해서는 영어학의 개념과 용어를 정확히 숙지하고 있어야 한다.

**3  주어진 자료를 문제 지시내용에 따라 정확하게 분석하라.**

영어학 문제는 주어진 자료(data)에 한정하여 출제자의 의도를 파악하고 지시내용(directions)을 토대로 분석해야만 출제자가 원하는 답을 도출할 수 있다. 지시내용을 무시하고 관련 주제에 관해 자신이 아는 내용을 함부로 적용해서는 안 된다.

**4  기입형 대비: 지문 흐름 따라가기 훈련과 정확한 용어정리를 하라.**

출제자가 요구하는 답은 지문에 정해져 있으므로 평소 지문이 말하고자 하는 바를 파악하는 훈련이 필요하다.

**5  서술형 대비: 주어진 자료를 분석하고 지시내용을 토대로 서술하는 훈련을 하라.**

서술형은 지문을 이해하고 지시내용에 따라 주어진 자료를 분류 · 분석하여 서술하는 문제로 출제된다. 따라서 답안에 포함되어야 할 핵심 용어(key terms)를 찾고 이것들을 정돈해 깔끔하게 기술하는 연습이 필요하다. 자신의 지식이나 생각보다 출제자가 의도하고 요구하는 답을 도출하는 연습이 필요하다.

수험생 예비교사 여러분의 합격을 진심으로 기원하며

2024년 6월

*Andrew Chai*

차 례
# CONTENTS

모범답안

# 01

PART Syntax

# Raising

Answer Key p.03

**01** Read the passage and fill in each blank with the ONE most appropriate word. Write your answers in the correct order. [2 points]

There are four distinct types of embedded non-finite constructions: subject-to-subject raising, subject-to-object raising, subject control, and object control. It should be noted that some verbs allow more than one type of construction. For example, the verb *want* allows either subject control or subject-to-object raising:

(1) a. Jean$_i$ wants [PRO$_i$ to leave].    *subject control*
    b. Jean wants Bill$_i$ [t$_i$ to leave].    *subject-to-object raising*

We can see four types of embedded non-finite constructions and their properties below:

(2) Jean is likely to leave.
    (a) Main clause predicate assigns one theta role (to the proposition) and no external (subject) theta role.
    (b) DP movement of embedded subject to the specifier of TP for EPP and Case.
    (c) Allows idiomatic readings and extraposition.

(3) Jean prefers Robert to leave.
    (a) Main clause predicate assigns ___①___ theta roles.
    (b) Main clause predicate has an Accusative [ACC] Case feature.
    (c) Allows idiomatic readings.

(4) Jean is reluctant to leave.

    (a) Main clause predicate assigns two theta roles.

    (b) No DP movement for Case.

    (c) Does not allow idiomatic readings or extraposition.

(5) Jean ordered Robert to leave.

    (a) Main clause predicate assigns ____②____ theta roles.

    (b) No DP movement for Case.

    (c) Does not allow idiomatic readings or extraposition.

**02** **Read the passage <A> and the sentences in <B>, and follow the directions.**

[4 points]

┤ A ├

Consider the following examples:

(1) a. To understand this lesson is difficult.

    b. → It is difficult to understand this lesson.

    c. → This lesson is difficult to understand.

In English, there are adjectives which allow the transformation of sentences like the examples given in (1). The adjective *difficult* in (1) has to do mainly with the ease or difficulty of the situation described in the infinitival clause or with one's emotional attitude to it.

    However, the adjective *ready* in (2) is semantically and syntactically less homogeneous. A number of adjectives used in this construction are collocationally quite restricted.

(2) a. *To sign the document is now ready.

    b. *It is now ready to sign the document.

    c. The document is now ready for you to sign.

As shown in (2c), in *ready*-type, the subject of the main clause is identified with the object of the infinitive clause. But unlike *difficult*-type in (1), *ready*-type cannot allow the construction with an infinitive clause subject shown in (2a) and an extraposed construction shown in (2b).

    The adjectives like *essential* can allow the transformation of sentences in (3).

(3) a. To spray the trees every year is essential.

    b. It is essential (for you) to spray the trees every year.

The infinitive clause is an extraposed subject. Adjectives in this type express volition, modality, or emotion.

Part 01

---
**| B |**

(a) John is wonderful to work with.

(b) John is impossible to live with.

(c) It is free to borrow these toys.

(d) It is crucial for us to take three meals a day.

(e) To breathe the air was frosty.

(f) To follow this direction is awkward.

---

In <B>, identify TWO ungrammatical sentences, and explain why, specifying the type of the adjective, based on the description in <A>.

_____

_____

_____

_____

_____

# Complements & Adjuncts

Answer Key p.04

**01** Read the passage and fill in each blank with the ONE most appropriate word. (Use the SAME answer for all the blanks.) [2 points]

> In an acceptable coordination the coordinates are syntactically similar. When the coordinates belong to the different category, the coordinate structures in (1) are ungrammatical.
>
> (1) a. *We invited [the Smiths and because they can speak Italian].
>    b. *She argued [persuasively or that their offer should be rejected].
>
> In a large majority of the coordinate structures, the coordinates belong to the same category. But coordinates do not have to be of the same category. Other examples are given in (2):
>
> (2) a. He won't reveal [the nature of the threat or where it came from].
>
>                                                          [NP + Clause]
>    b. I'll be back [next week or at the end of the month]. [NP + PP]
>    c. He acted [selfishly and with no thought for the consequences]. [AdvP + PP]
>
> What makes the coordinations in (2) acceptable despite the differences of category is that each coordinate could occur alone with the same _____.

(3) a. He won't reveal <u>the nature of the threat</u>.

    b. He won't reveal <u>where it came from</u>.

(4) a. I'll be back <u>next week</u>.

    b. I'll be back <u>at the end of the month</u>.

(5) a. He acted <u>selfishly</u>.

    b. He acted <u>with no thought for the consequences</u>.

In each pair here the underlined element in (b) has the same _____ as that in (a): complement of the verb in (3), time adjunct in (4), manner adjunct in (5). Contrast these examples with those in (6):

(6) a. *We're leaving [Rome and next week].     [NP + NP]

    b. *I ran [to the park and for health reasons].     [PP + PP]

Here the coordinates belong to the same category, but don't satisfy the requirement of functional likeness. Therefore, _____ is more important than category in determining the permissibility of coordination.

## 02 Read the passage <A> and the sentences in <B>, and follow the directions.

[4 points]

─────┤ A ├─────

Both syntactic categories (NP, AP, VP, PP, etc.) and grammatical functions (subject, complement, and modifier) play important roles in the analysis of English sentences. We have also observed that the grammatical function and form of each constituent depend on where it occurs or what it combines with.

The combinatory properties of words and phrases involve two aspects of syntax: internal and external syntax. Internal syntax deals with how a given phrase itself is constructed in a well-formed manner whereas external syntax is concerned with how a phrase can be used in a larger construction. Observe the following examples:

(1) a. *John [put his gold].
    b. *John [put under the bathtub].
    c. *John [put his gold safe].
    d. *John [put his gold to be under the bathtub].
    e. John [put his gold under the bathtub].

Why is only (1e) acceptable? Simply, because only it satisfies the condition that the verb *put* selects an NP and a PP as its complements, and it combines with them in the VP. In the other examples, this condition is not fulfilled. This combinatory requirement starts from the internal (or lexical) properties of the verb *put*, and is not related to any external properties of the VP.

In contrast, the external syntax is concerned with the external environment in which a phrase occurs. The well-formed VP in (1e) can be unacceptable, depending on external contexts. For example, consider frame induced by the governing verb *kept* in (2):

(2) a. *The king kept [put his gold under the bathtub].

b. The king kept [putting his gold under the bathtub].

The VP *put his gold under the bathtub* is a well-formed phrase, but cannot occur in (2a) since this is not the environment where such a finite VP occurs. That is, the verb *kept* requires the presence of a gerundive VP like *putting his gold under the bathtub*, and therefore imposes an external constraint on VPs.

---

┤ B ├

(a) This is the box in which John put his gold.

(b) This is the gold that John put under the bathtub.

(c) John placed Kim behind the garage.

(d) John placed behind the counter.

(e) John stayed Kim behind the garage.

(f) John stayed behind the counter.

**Identify TWO ungrammatical sentences in <B>, and explain why, based on the description in <A>.**

_____

_____

_____

_____

_____

**03** Read the passage and fill in each blank with ONE word from the passage. Write your answers in the correct order. [2 points]

> We could distinguish complements and modifiers by tree structures: complements combine with a lexical head (not a phrase) to form a minimal phrase whereas modifiers combine with a phrase to form a maximal phrase. This means that we have structures of the following forms:
>
> (1)
>
>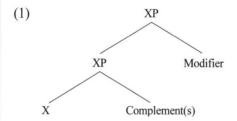
>
> The difference that follows from the structural distinction between complements and modifiers is an ordering difference. As a complement needs to combine with a head first, modifiers follow complements:
>
> (2) a. John met [a student] [in the park].
>
>     b. *John met [in the park] [a student].
>
> A similar contrast can be observed in the following contrast:
>
> (3) a. the student [of linguistics] [with long hair]
>
>     b. *the student [with long hair] [of linguistics]
>
> The PP *with long hair* is a modifier whereas the PP *of linguistics* is the complement of *student*. This is why *with long hair* cannot occur between the head *student* and its complement *of linguistics*.
>
> A modifier can cooccur with a relatively broad range of heads whereas a complement is typically limited in its distribution. Note the following contrast:

(4) a. Kim camps/jogs on the hill.

    b. Kim jogs on the hill/under the hill/over the hill.

(5) a. Kim depends/relies on Sandy.

    b. Kim depends on Sandy/*at Sandy/*for Sandy.


The semantic contribution of the _____①_____ *on the hill* in (4a) is independent of the head whereas that of the _____②_____ *on Sandy* in (5a) is idiosyncratically dependent upon the head.

**04** Read the passage <A> and the sentences in <B>, and follow the directions. [4 points]

---

| A |

Consider the italicized expressions in (1):

(1) a. John put books *in the box*.

   b. John talked *to Bill about the exam*.

These italicized expressions are neither objects nor predicative complements. Since their presence is obligatory, for syntactic well-formedness, they are called oblique complements. Roughly speaking, 'oblique' contrasts with the 'direct' functions of subject and object, and oblique phrases are typically expressed as PPs in English.

   Most ditransitive verbs can also take oblique complements:

(2) a. John gave a book *to the student*.

   b. John bought a book *for the student*.

The PPs here, which cannot be objects since they are not NPs, also do not serve as predicate of the subject or object—they relate directly to the verb, as oblique complements.

   The functions of DO, IO, predicative complement, and oblique complement all have one common property: they are all selected by the verb, and we view them as being present to 'complement' the verb to form a legitimate VP. Hence, these are called complements (COMPS), and typically they cannot be omitted.

   Unlike these COMPS, there are expressions which are truly optional:

(3) a. The bus stopped *suddenly*.

   b. Shakespeare wrote his plays *a long time ago*.

---

The italicized expressions here are all optional and function as modifiers (also called 'adjuncts' or 'adverbial' expressions). These modifiers specify the manner, location, time, or reason, among many other properties, of the situations expressed by the given sentences.

One additional characteristic of modifiers is that they can be stacked up, whereas complements cannot:

(4) a. *John gave Tom [a book] [a record].
   b. I saw this film [several times] [last year] [during the summer].

As shown here, temporal adjuncts like *several times* and *last year* in (4b) can be repeated, whereas the two complements *a book* and *a record* in (4a) cannot. Of course, adjunct NPs do not become the subject of a passive sentence, suggesting that they cannot serve as objects:

(5) a. My uncle visited today.
   b. *Today was visited by my uncle.

---

┤ B ├

(a) Account was taken of his claim.
(b) His claim was taken account of.
(c) I never argue with anyone about anything.
(d) John talked about the exam to Bill.
(e) The wrong way was performed by Mary.
(f) All afternoon is played by few children.

---

Identify TWO ungrammatical sentences in <B>, and explain why, based on the description in <A>.

_____

_____

_____

**05** Read the passage and fill in each blank with the ONE word from the passage. Write your answers in the correct order. [2 points]

---

Complements have to be licensed by the head noun. Consider the following examples:

(1) a. the attack <u>on the Prime Minister</u>
    b. the abolition <u>of taxes</u>
    c. the fact <u>that she's alive</u>

Subordinate clauses may be finite or non-finite, and both types are found as complements to nouns, as in (2)—(3):

(2) a. the claim <u>that he was ill</u>      FINITE
    b. a suspicion <u>that it was a hoax</u>      FINITE
(3) a. her ability <u>to complete the task</u>      NON-FINITE
    b. his eagerness <u>to redeem himself</u>      NON-FINITE

Consider now the following examples, where brackets enclose the NP and underlining marks the complement.

(4) a. We had to put up with [a longer delay <u>than we had bargained for</u>].
    b. He gave [so complicated an explanation <u>that I was completely baffled</u>].
    c. It was [too serious a problem <u>for us to ignore</u>].

We call these indirect complements because although they follow the head noun, it is not the head noun that licenses them. In (4a) the complement is licensed by the word ___①___: if we drop this the NP becomes ungrammatical. Similarly, in (4b) the complement is licensed by the word ___②___. In (4c) it is licensed by the word *too*. This time we could drop *too serious* without loss of grammaticality—but it would have a dramatic effect on the interpretation of the infinitival clause. *A problem for us to ignore* means "a problem that we can/should ignore", whereas the NP in (4c) means "a problem that was so serious that we could/should not ignore it".

---

**06** Read the passage <A> and the sentences in <B>, and follow the directions.

[4 points]

---
### ┤ A ├
---

The dependents of the predicator in the VP are of two main kinds: complements and adjuncts. The admissibility of a complement depends on the predicator belonging to a particular subclass of verbs. The term we use for this is licensing: complements have to be licensed by their head, V, N, A, etc.

The object is one kind of complement, and we can illustrate the concept of licensing by considering the occurrence of an object with the following three verbs:

(1) a. Sue used the cheese.
    b. *Sue used.                 [object obligatory]
(2) a. Sue ate the cheese.
    b. Sue ate.                    [object optional]
(3) a. *Sue disappeared the cheese.
    b. Sue disappeared.           [object excluded]

An object such as *the cheese* is admissible with, hence licensed by, the verbs *use* and *eat,* but not *disappear*: (3a) is ungrammatical. There is a further difference between *use* and *eat*. With *eat* the object is optional whereas with *use* it is obligatory: (2b) is grammatical, but (1b) is not. The status of a dependent as a complement is most obvious when it is obligatory for at least some heads. But this is not essential: the crucial feature of licensing is that the admissibility of the element depends on the presence of an appropriate head.

The occurrence of adjuncts is not restricted in this way. They occur more freely, essentially without regard to what the predicator is. The examples in (4) illustrate the difference between complements (the italicized phrase) and adjuncts (single underlining).

(4) a. I saw *your father* <u>this morning</u>.
    b. They <u>still</u> think *they were right*.

In (4a), *your father* is a complement licensed by *see*. If *see* were replaced by *fall*, we would have an ungrammatical sentence. *This morning* in (4a), by contrast, is an adjunct; a temporal NP of this kind is compatible with any verb. In (4b), *still* is an adjunct, again because it is compatible with any verb. But the subordinate clause *they were right* is a complement, licensed by *think*. Again it is easy to find verbs like *alter* or *lose* or *work* that are incompatible with a subordinate clause of this kind, whatever its particular semantic content.

┤ B ├

Consider the following examples focusing on the underlined PPs:

(a) I cut it <u>with a razor-blade</u>.

(b) She regularly gives us very useful advice <u>on financial matters</u>.

(c) John blamed the incident <u>on Mary</u>.

(d) He declaimed <u>against Syntax</u>.

(e) Max glanced <u>at the falling acrobat</u>.

(f) He will work <u>at the office</u>.

In <B>, identify TWO sentences where the underlined PP has the different function from the rest (i.e., only the two PPs have the same function), and state the function of each PP, based on the description in <A>.

_____

_____

_____

_____

_____

## 07 Read the passage and fill in the blank with the appropriate TWO words.

[2 points]

A phrase normally consists of a head, alone or accompanied by one or more dependents. The category of the phrase depends on that of the head: a phrase with a noun as head is a noun phrase, and so on.

The object is a kind of complement since it satisfies the licensing requirement. The subject is rather different: all canonical clauses contain a subject, so in a sense subjects are compatible with any verb. However, certain syntactic kinds of subject are restricted to occurrence with particular kinds of verb, so the concept of licensing applies here too. Take, for example, the subject of (1a):

(1) a. <u>Whether we will finish on time</u> depends primarily on the weather.

　　b. *<u>Whether we will finish on time</u> ruined the afternoon.

The underlined expression in (1a) is a subordinate clause functioning as subject of the larger clause that forms the whole sentence. It is, more specifically, a subordinate interrogative clause: the main clause counterpart is *Will we finish on time?* A subject of this syntactic form has to be licensed by the verb (or VP). It is admissible with *depend*, but there are innumerable other verbs such as *ruin, see, think, yearn*, etc., that do not accept subjects of this form; so (1b), for example, is ungrammatical.

Therefore, subjects do satisfy the condition for being complements. But they are different from other types of complement in an obvious way: they are not positioned within the VP. We will refer to the subject as a/an _____. The other complements that are internal to the VP will be referred to as internal complements.

_____

_____

**08** Read the passage <A> and the sentences in <B>, and follow the directions.

[4 points]

---

┤ A ├

Not all syntactic ambiguity can be explained in terms of hierarchical structure. Some ambiguities arise in sentences in which material is missing but nevertheless understood. Phrase structure helps us explain why we understand such sentences the way we do.

The following sentence is ambiguous:

(1) The crab is too hot to eat.

Do you understand the sentence as having two meanings? There are no lexical ambiguities here; the noun *crab*, whether the living creature or your dinner, has the same meaning; *hot* indicates temperature, and *eat* means *consume*. In syntactic terms, the ambiguity can be stated in this way: who or what is the subject of *eat* —the crab or someone else? And who or what is the complement of *eat*—crab food or the crab itself? Complements are phrases that combine with heads to form (or "complete") a larger phrase. So, *eat* is a verb that typically is followed by an NP complement because we typically eat *something*. Here, the complement is understood but not overt or pronounced.

What all this boils down to is that in order to interpret this sentence, we must assume that there is an unpronounced subject of the (infinitival) verb *eat* and also an unpronounced complement of that verb. These two "invisible" NPs are represented by the delta symbol, Δ.

(2) The crab is too hot [Δ to eat Δ].
(3) The crab is too hot (for someone) to eat (the crab).
(4) The crab is too hot (for the crab) to eat (something).

We explain the syntactic ambiguity of this sentence by proposing not that the sentence could have two different structures but that there is an "understood" or "silent" subject of *eat* and also a silent complement of *eat*.

Other ambiguities arise in a sentence due to the difference of functions (complement vs. adjunct), of grammatical forms (NP, AP, etc.) or of scope.

---
**B**

(a) George wants the presidency more than Martha.

(b) Tell me when you are ready.

(c) Liz bought a pen.

(d) Nicole saw the people with binoculars.

(e) The tuna can hit the boat.

(f) John couldn't explain last night.

---

In <B>, identify TWO ambiguous sentences due to the difference of functions (*complement* vs. *adjunct*), and explain why, stating the phrase or clause which involves a complement or adjunct interpretation, based on the description in <A>.

_____

_____

_____

_____

_____

**09** **Read the passage and fill in each blank with the appropriate preposition. Write your answers in the correct order.** [2 points]

One striking difference between nouns and verbs is that nouns don't take objects. With nouns that are morphologically related to transitive verbs, as *criticism* is related to *criticise*, the complement of the noun that corresponds to the object of the verb has the form of a PP:

(1) a. I *criticised her decision*.

   b. my *criticism of her decision*

(2) a. He *abandoned his ship*.

   b. his *abandonment of his ship*

(3) a. Sandy *married Pat*.

   b. Sandy's *marriage to Pat*

The preposition is usually *of*, as in (1b) and (2b), but with certain nouns other prepositions are selected, as in (3b).

Dependents with the form of PPs qualify as complements when they are licensed by the particular head noun. The clearest cases have one or more of the following properties.

They correspond to object or subject NPs in clause structure. The object case has been illustrated in (1)—(3), while correspondence with a subject is seen in (4)—(5):

(4) a. The warriors returned.

   b. the return of the warriors

(5) a. The premier attacked.

   b. an attack by the premier

The choice of preposition is specified by the head noun. Many nouns take complements headed by a particular preposition:

(6) a. their belief *in* God

    b. your reply *to* my letter

    c. secession ____①____ the alliance

    d. his disillusionment ____②____ Linguistics

The PP is obligatory because the noun makes little sense without it:

(7) a. the advent of the steam engine

    b. the abandonment of sensible budgetary policies

    c. the feasibility of the proposal

    d. a dearth of new ideas

## 10 Read the passages and follow the directions. [4 points]

┤ A ├

All phrases have something in common, namely the fact that they must minimally contain a Head. In the bracketed phrases in the sentences below, the Heads are shown in bold type:

(1) The defendants denied the charge: they claim that they did [VP not **destroy** the garden]

(2) She proposed [NP an **analysis** of the sentence]

(3) Jack is [AP so **fond** of coffee]

Notice that apart from the obligatory presence of the Heads, there are further similarities between these phrases. First of all, there appears to be a strong bond between the Head and the constituent that follows it in each case. Thus, in (1) the verb *destroy* requires the presence of a Noun Phrase that refers to an entity that is destroyable. Similarly, in (2) the PP *of the sentence* complements the noun *analysis* in that it specifies what is being analysed. We briefly introduced the notion Complement as a general term to denote any constituent whose presence is required by another element.

The phrases we have looked at so far contained only a Specifier, a Head and a Complement. Phrases can, however, be structurally more complicated. Consider first the bracketed VP below:

(4) The defendants denied the charge: they claim that they did [VP not destroy the garden deliberately]

In this sentence the AdvP *deliberately* modifies the sequence *destroy the garden*, and is positioned after the Head *destroy* and its Complement *the garden*. This AdvP functions as an Adjunct. In tree diagrams, the Complement *the garden* is closer to the Head *destroy* than the Adjunct *deliberately*: the Complement is a sister of V, whereas the Adjunct is a sister of the V' that immediately dominates V.

---

**B**

Draw the tree for each sentence or phrase below in your mind, and then decide whether the statements for each sentence or phrase are true or false.

(a) *their realisation that all is lost*: the underlined clause is the Complement and is a sister of N.

(b) *her question whether the expense was worth it*: the underlined clause is the adjunct and is a sister of the N'.

(c) *I served as secretary*: the underlined PP is the complement and is a sister of V.

(d) *He looked at the picture*: the underlined PP is the complement and is a sister of V.

(e) *The tiles on the floor are ancient*: the underlined PP is the complement and is a sister of N.

---

**Identify TWO false statements in <B>, and correct the statements, based on the description in <A>.**

_____

_____

_____

_____

_____

## 11 Read the passage and follow the directions. [4 points]

──────────────────┤ A ├──────────────────

Like verbs, certain adjectives can also select CPs as their complements. For example, *insistent* selects a finite CP, whereas *eager* selects an infinitival CP:

(1) a. Tom is insistent [that the witnesses be truthful].

b. Tom seems eager [for her brother to catch a cold].

We can easily find more adjectives which select a CP complement:

(2) a. I am ashamed that I neglected you.

b. I am delighted that Mary finished his thesis.

Nouns can also select a CP complement, for example, *eagerness*:

(3) (John's) eagerness [for Harry to win the election]

One pattern that we can observe is that when a verb selects a CP complement, if there is a corresponding noun, it also selects a CP, as shown in (4):

(4) a. We believe that the directors were present.

b. the belief that the directors were present

This shows us that the derivational process which derives a noun from a verb preserves the COMPS (complements) value of that verb. A caution here is that not all nouns can of course select a CP complement:

(5) a. *his attention that the earth is round

b. *the expertise that she knows how to bake croissants

These nouns cannot combine with a CP complement, indicating that they do not have CP in the value of COMPS.

┤ B ├

(a) Tom is confident that the elephants respect him.

(b) We are content for the cleaners to return the drapes next week.

(c) his conviction that the operation is safe

(d) the allegation that Fred signed the check

(e) the ignorance that James can play the flute

(f) his article that the earth is flat

In <B>, identify TWO ungrammatical sentences or phrases, and explain why, based on the description in <A>.

_____

_____

_____

_____

_____

## 01 Read the passage and follow the directions. [4 points]

┤ A ├

One reliable test often used to distinguish complements from modifiers is the *do so* or *do the same thing* test. As shown in (1), we can use *do the same thing* to avoid repetition of an identical VP expression:

(1) a. John deposited some money in the checking account and Mary did the same thing (too).

    b. John deposited some money in the checking account on Friday and Mary did the same thing (too).

What we can observe in (1b) is that the VP *did the same thing* can replace either the minimal phrase *deposited some money in the checking account* or the maximal phrase including the modifier *on Friday*. Notice that this VP can replace only the minimal phrase, leaving out the modifier, as shown in (2).

(2) John deposited some money in the checking account on Friday and Mary did the same thing on Monday.

From these observations, we can draw the conclusion that if something can be replaced by *do the same thing*, then it is either a minimal or a maximal phrase. This in turn means that this 'replacement' VP cannot be understood to leave out any _____. This can be verified with more data:

(3) a. *John [deposited some money in the checking account] and Mary did the same thing in the savings account.

    b. *John [gave a present to the student] and Mary did the same thing to the teacher.

Here the PPs *in the checking account* and *to the student* are both complements, and thus they should be included in the *do the same thing* phrase. This gives us the following informal generalization:

(4) Do-so Replacement Condition:

    The phrase *do so* or *do the same thing* can replace a verb phrase which includes at least any _____ of the verb.

---

┤ B ├

(a) John locked the dog in the garage and Mary did so, (too).

(b) John asked a question of the child and Tom did so of the mother.

(c) I will send the letter in a minute and you will do so in an hour.

(d) I will send the letter in a minute and you will do so, (too).

(e) The boy saw the man with the telescope and I did so, (too).

---

**First, fill in each blank with ONE word from the passage <A>. Use the SAME answer for both blanks. Second, identify ALL and ONLY ungrammatical sentence(s) in <B>, and explain why, ONLY based on the description in <A>.**

_____

_____

_____

_____

_____

**02** Read the passage <A> and the sentences in <B>, and follow the directions.

[4 points]

---

┤ **A** ├

English possesses a word that can replace less than a full NP, and this is the proform *one*. The proform *one* replaces N'-constituents. Consider the following sentence:

(1) Mark is a dedicated teacher of language, but Paul is an indifferent one.

In this sentence, *one* replaces *teacher of language*. This proform cannot be a full NP because it is preceded by the determinative *an* and the AP *indifferent*. We can show this more clearly in a tree diagram.

(2)

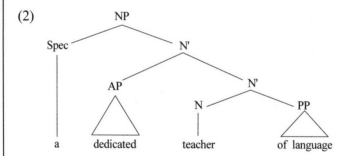

(3)

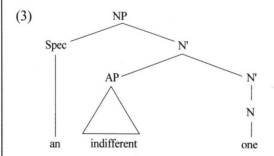

As *one* in (3) replaces *teacher of language* in (2), it must be replacing an N' (N-bar). *One* is a pro-N'. It cannot replace an N by itself unless an N is the constituent of an N'. Consider (4):

(4) *Ben likes the Italian student of English, but not the Spanish one of literature.

---

┤ B ├

(a) Frank believed the claim that Mary made, and he believed another one.

(b) Frank believed the claim that Mary made, and he believed another one that she put forward recently.

(c) Frank believed the claim that Mary made a mistake, and he believed another one.

(d) Frank believed the claim that Mary made a mistake, and he believed another one that she solved the problem.

Identify ONE ungrammatical sentence in <B>, and explain why, stating the corresponding word(s) for the proform *one*, based on the description in <A>.

_____

_____

_____

_____

_____

**03** Read the passage <A> and the sentences in <B>, and follow the directions.

[4 points]

┤ A ├

The fact that complements are more closely related to the verb than adjuncts is reflected in the scope of certain anaphoric expressions, notably *do so*. Anaphoric expressions are those which derive their interpretation from an antecedent. Compare, for example, *Jill signed the petition and Pam did so too* with *Jill visited my mother and Pam did so too*, where the first instance of *did so* is interpreted as "signed the petition" and the second as "visited my mother". The relevance of *do so* to the distinction between complements and adjuncts is seen in the following examples:

(1) a. *Jill keeps her car in the garage but Pam does so in the road.

b. Jill washes her car in the garage but Pam does so in the road.

The antecedent for *do so* must embrace all internal complements of the verb: it therefore cannot itself combine with such a complement. In (1a) *in the garage* is a complement of *keep* (it is obligatory when *keep* has the sense it has here), and therefore must be included in the antecedent for *do so*. This means that *Pam does so* has to be interpreted as "Pam keeps her car in the garage"; we can't add *in the road* as another complement in the second clause. The inclusion of *in the road* to contrast with *in the garage* in the first clause requires the interpretation "Pam keeps her car": the ungrammaticality results from this conflict. But in (1b) *in the garage* is an adjunct in the *wash*-clause, and hence need not be included in the antecedent of *does so*: we interpret it as "Pam washes her car"; with *in the road* added as an adjunct contrasting with *in the garage* in the first clause.

Note that the data in (1) lend support to the position adopted in (1b) above, namely that certain kinds of element can be either complements or adjuncts: locative *in the road*, for example, is a complement in (1a) and an adjunct in (1b). Moreover, in certain case, the added phrase in the second clause does not contrast with anything in the first clause because the added phrase can consist of another complement; it cannot combine with *do so* in the second clause.

---

**┤ B ├**

(a) I didn't read all the reports but I did so most of them.

(b) I didn't cover this topic last time but I shall do so on Tuesday.

(c) She rode her bicycle and she did so to school.

(d) She performed all the tasks and she did so remarkably well.

(e) Mary treated us remarkably well and John did so too.

---

**Identify ALL and ONLY ungrammatical sentence(s), and explain why, specifying the antecedent for do so, ONLY based on the description in <A>.**

_____

_____

_____

_____

_____

## 04  Read the passages and follow the directions. [4 points]

─────────────────┤ A ├─────────────────

According to the X-bar theory, determiners expand N-bar into NP, adjuncts recursively expand N-bar into N-bar, and complements expand N into N-bar.

(1)

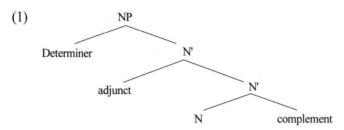

Consider the following Noun Phrase:

(2) an English teacher

(2) is ambiguous; this phrase can be paraphrased as in (3) below:

(3) a. a teacher of English (a teacher who teaches English)

　　b. a teacher from English (a teacher who is from English)

On one reading, (2) has the meaning of (3a) when *English* is interpreted as an NP complement. On the other reading, (2) has the meaning of (3b) when *English* is used as an AP adjunct. The ambiguity arises according to whether the lexical item *English* is interpreted as a complement or an adjunct in terms of function, and the categorial status (form) of *English* can either be a prenominal NP or a prenominal AP in (2).

---

**B**

    The proform *one* replaces N'-constituents; it cannot replace an N. All the words *French* in (4) have the same meaning, and in (5) also have the same meaning.

(4) a. Frank is a French professor and Steve is another one.
    b. Frank is a French professor and Steve is an English one.
    c. a [typically French] professor
(5) a. Frank is a French professor and Steve is another one.
    b. *Frank is a French professor and Steve is an English one.
    c. an [old French] professor

*Note: '*' indicates the ungrammaticality of the sentence.*

---

In <B>, first, state the function AND form of the word *French* in (4b) and (5b), respectively. Second, identify the form of *French* in (4c) and in (5c), respectively, based on the description in <A>.

_____

_____

_____

_____

_____

# UNIT 04 Case Theory

**01** Read the passage <A> and the sentence in <B>, and follow the directions.

[4 points]

┤ A ├

Every NP in a sentence must observe the following two constraints.

(1) The Theta Criterion:

    a. Each noun phrase is assigned one and only one theta role.

    b. Each theta role is assigned to one and only one noun phrase.

(2) The Case Filter: All noun phrases must be assigned a Case.

Consider the following sentences:

(3) a. Tom hit Bill.

    b. *Tom hit Bill John.

Sentence (3a) is grammatical but sentence (3b) is ungrammatical. In (3b) the noun phrase *John* doesn't get a theta role from the verb *hit*. In (3b) there are only two theta roles to be assigned, but there are three noun phrases. This violates the theta criterion.

    Next, consider other sentences with a noun phrase:

(4) a. It was certain that Tom examined the patient.

    b. *It was certain Tom to examine the patient.

Sentence (4b) is ungrammatical. The noun phrase *Tom* cannot be assigned any Case, violating the Case filter since both the adjective *certain* and the nontense inflection (INFL) *to* are not Case-assigners.

    Finally, consider the following sentences:

멘토영어학 문제은행

(5) a. The dog was kissed.

    b. *It was kissed the dog.

Sentence (5a) is grammatically correct since the noun phrase *the dog* observes both the theta criterion and the Case filter. However, sentence (5b) is ungrammatical. The noun phrase *the dog* cannot be assigned any Case since it is in the object position of passive clause. A passivized verb loses the ability to assign the object Case to its complement. Case serves as a motivation for NP movement; the noun phrase *the dog* in (5b) moves to the subject position of the main clause to get a Case like in (5a). In the moved position it is assigned the subject Case by the tense inflection of the matrix clause.

---

⊣ B ⊢

(6) The book seemed to have been read by Tom.

---

**State whether sentence (6) in <B> is syntactically well-formed or ill-formed. Then, explain why, discussing whether the matrix subject can be assigned a theta role and Case with specifying its theta role assigner, case assigner, and the original position of the matrix subject, based on the description in <A>.**

_____

_____

_____

_____

_____

## 02 Read the passage <A> and the sentences in <B>, and follow the directions.

[4 points]

---

┤ A ├

Consider the following examples:

(1) Frank kicked a tiger.
(2) *Frank disappeared a tiger.

The contrast between (1) and (2) can be accounted for by Case Filter: Every overt Noun Phrase (NP) must be assigned (abstract) case. Case is assigned to every NP by case assigners, either inherently or structurally.

(3) Nominative case is assigned by [+ Tense]:
   *Mary* finish**ed** the assignment.

(4) Accusative case is assigned by a Transitive Verb or a Preposition:
   John **kill**ed *a dog*.
   The child stood **near** *the fence*.

(5) Genitive case is assigned by the frame [____ 's]:
   *John's* father

(6) Inherent case is assigned to the direct object of the ditransitive verb structure:
   Mary **gave** me *a book*.

Notice that the case assignment is concerned with Noun Phrases only. (1) is grammatical because the subject NP is nominative case-assigned by [+ past tense] of the verb *kicked*, and the object NP is accusative case-assigned by the transitive verb *kicked*. However, (2) is ungrammatical because the NP *a tiger* cannot be accusative case-assigned by the intransitive verb 'disappeared', violating the case filter.

---

---

┤ B ├

(a) John believed sincerely that Mary is smart.

(b) Constantly reading novels makes me feel alive.

(c) The river ran dry.

(d) John is envious Mary.

(e) It is vital that we act to stop the destruction the rainforests.

---

**In <B>, identify TWO ungrammatical sentences, and explain why, discussing a caseless NP and a case assigner, based on the description in <A>.**

_____

_____

_____

_____

_____

# UNIT 05

# Binding Theory

Answer Key p.12

**01** Read the passage &lt;A&gt; and the sentences in &lt;B&gt;, and follow the directions.

[4 points]

---
| A |
---

The evidence in support of positing a null PRO subject in clauses comes from the syntax of reflexive anaphors. Reflexives generally require a local antecedent (the reflexive being italicised and its antecedent bold-printed):

(1) a. They want [**John** to help *himself*].

    b. ***They** want [John to help *themselves*].

(1a) is grammatical because it satisfies this locality requirement: the antecedent of the reflexive *himself* is the noun *John*, and *John* is contained within the same (bracketed) *help*-clause as *himself*. By contrast, (1b) is ungrammatical because the reflexive *themselves* does not have a local antecedent (i.e. it does not have an antecedent within the same (bracketed) clause containing it); its antecedent is the pronoun *they*, and *they* is contained within the *want*-clause, not within the [bracketed] *help*-clause. Consider now how we account for the grammaticality of the following:

(2) John wants [PRO to prove himself].

Given the requirement for reflexives to have a local antecedent, it follows that the reflexive *himself* must have an antecedent within its own [bracketed] clause. This requirement is satisfied in (2) if we assume that the bracketed complement clause has a PRO subject, and that PRO is the antecedent of *himself*. Since PRO in turn is controlled by *John* (i.e. *John* is the antecedent of PRO), this means that *himself* is coreferential to (i.e. refers to the same individual as) *John*. Now consider other examples:

(3) a. We would like [PRO to stay].

  b. It's difficult [PRO to learn a foreign language].

Subjectless infinitive complements like *to stay* in (3a) have a null PRO subject; PRO has an explicit controller, which is the subject of the matrix clause. However, this is not always the case. In structures like (3b), PRO lacks an explicit controller. In such cases, PRO can either refer to some individual outside the sentence or can have arbitrary reference.

---

**⊣ B ⊢**

(a) Jack believed himself to be immortal.

(b) Jack believed himself was immortal.

(c) John seems to me to have perjured himself.

(d) It's important to prepare myself properly for the exam.

(e) It's important not to take oneself too seriously.

*Note: Reflexives should agree with their potential antecedents in number, gender, and person.*

---

**Identify ALL and ONLY ungrammatical sentence(s) in <B>, and explain why, ONLY based on the description in <A>.**

_____

_____

_____

_____

_____

**02** Read the passage <A> and the sentences in <B>, and follow the directions.

[4 points]

---

┤ A ├

Let us consider the binding principles:

(1) Principle A: An anaphor (reflexives or reciprocal) must be bound (c-commanded) by its antecedent within its smallest binding domain (clause or noun phrase).

(2) Principle B: An pronominal must not be bound (c-commanded) by its antecedent within its smallest binding domain (clause or noun phrase).

(3) C-command: $\alpha$ c-commands $\beta$ if the first branching node dominating $\alpha$ dominates $\beta$, and if neither $\alpha$ nor $\beta$ dominates the other.

Consider the following examples:

(4) a. *Mary said that herself discoed with John.

    b. *Mary said that John's mother loved himself.

    c. Mary said that John discoed with himself.

    d. Mary said that John's mother loved herself.

    e. John said that Mary discoed with him.

The binding principles above can explain the (un)grammaticality of the sentences in (4). Sentences (4a) and (4b) violate the binding principle A. (4a) is ungrammatical because the anaphor *herself* is not bound by its antecedent *Mary* within its smallest binding domain *that herself discoed with John*. (4b) is also ungrammatical because the anaphor *himself* cannot be c-commanded by its antecedent *John* although the anaphor and its antecedent are in the same binding domain. On the other hand, sentences (4c)—(4e) observe the binding principles.

---

---
**B**

(a) Frank promised Sally to feed himself.

(b) Frank persuaded Sally to behave himself.

(c) Frank persuaded Sally to behave herself.

(d) Frank ordered Sally to gather evidence about himself.

(e) Frank ordered Sally to gather evidence about herself.

(f) Frank ordered Sally to gather evidence about him.

---

**Identify TWO ungrammatical sentences in \<B\>, and explain why, stating the antecedent and the binding domain, based on the description in \<A\>.**

_____

_____

_____

_____

_____

**03** Read the passage <A> and the sentences in <B>, and follow the directions.

[4 points]

---

┤ A ├

Consider the case of the NP *herself* in the following sentence:

(1) Heidi bopped *herself* on the head with a zucchini.
(2) Art said that *he* played basketball.

In (1), this kind of NP, one that obligatorily gets its meaning from another NP in the sentence, is called an anaphor. There is yet another kind of NP. These are NPs that can optionally get their meaning from another NP in the sentence, but may also optionally get it from somewhere else (including context or previous sentences in the discourse). These NPs are called pronouns, as shown in (2). In this sentence, the word *he* can optionally refer to *Art* or it can refer to someone else.

We can postulate the following Binding Principle to explain (un)grammaticality of the sentences:

(3) Binding Principle A (revised): An anaphor must be bound in its binding domain.
(4) Binding Principle B: A pronoun must be free in its binding domain.
(5) Binds: A binds B if and only if A c-commands B and A and B are coindexed.
(6) Binding domain: The clause or NP containing the NP (anaphor or pronoun)

Consider the following examples:

(7) a. *[Heidi$_i$'s mother]$_j$ bopped herself$_i$ on the head with a zucchini.
    b. *Heidi$_i$ bopped her$_i$ on the head with the zucchini.

In (7a) the anaphor *herself* is not bound by the potential antecedent *Heidi* in its binding domain; it violates Binding Principle A. In (7b) the pronoun *her* is not free in its binding domain. It is bound by the potential antecedent *Heidi* in its binding domain; it violates Binding Principle B.

---

---
**┤ B ├**

(a) The girl who likes John bopped himself.

(b) Mary believes a description of herself.

(c) Bill believes Mary's description of herself.

(d) Bill's brother believes that John kicked him.

(e) Bill's mother-in-law admires himself.

---

Identify TWO ungrammatical sentences in <B>, and explain why, specifying the potential antecedent, based on the description in <A>.

_____

_____

_____

_____

_____

# Control Theory

Answer Key p.14

**01** Read the passage and fill in each blank with ONE word from the passage. Write your answers in the correct order. [2 points]

Let's observe that some parts of control are sensitive to syntactic structure. Consider what can control PRO in (1):

(1) [Jean$_i$'s father]$_j$ is reluctant PRO$_{j/*i}$ to leave.

If you draw the tree for (1), you'll see that while the whole DP *Jean's father* c-commands PRO, *Jean* by itself does not. The fact that *Jean* cannot control PRO strongly suggests that there is a c-command requirement on obligatory control. This said, the structure of the sentence doesn't seem to be the only thing that comes into play with control. Compare now a subject control sentence to an object control one:

(2) a. Robert$_i$ is reluctant [PRO$_i$ to behave].
     *subject control*
    b. Susan$_j$ ordered Robert$_i$ [PRO$_{i/*j}$ to behave].
     *object control*

In both these sentences PRO must be controlled by *Robert*. PRO in (2b) cannot refer to *Susan*. This would seem to suggest that the closest DP that c-commands PRO must control it. In (2a), *Robert* is the only possible controller, so it controls PRO. In (2b), there are two possible controllers: *Susan* and *Robert*. But only *Robert*, which is structurally closer to PRO, can control it. This hypothesis works well in most cases, but the following example shows it must be wrong:

(3) Jean$_i$ promised Susan$_j$ [PRO$_{i/*j}$ to behave].
*subject control*

In this sentence it is *Jean* doing the behaving, not *Susan*. PRO must be controlled by the subject *Jean*, even though *Susan* is structurally closer. So structure doesn't seem to be the only thing determining which DP does the controlling.

  The sentences in (4) all use the verb *beg*, which is traditionally viewed as an object control verb.

(4) a. Louis begged Kate PRO to leave her job.
    b. Louis begged Kate PRO to be allowed PRO to shave himself.

Considering the position of the controller, sentence (4a) shows ____①____ control; Sentence (4b) shows ____②____ control. Examples like these might be used to argue that control is not entirely syntactic or thematic, but may also rely on our knowledge of the way the world works. This kind of knowledge, often referred to as pragmatic knowledge, lies outside the syntactic system we're developing.

# Theta Theory

Answer Key p.14

**01** **Read the passage and fill in each blank with ONE word from the passage. Write your answers in the correct order.** [2 points]

Semantic roles were introduced as a way of classifying the arguments of predicators into a closed set of participant types. The italicized phrase below in each case carries a certain semantic role.

- Agent: A participant which the meaning of the verb specifies as doing or causing something, possibly intentionally. (e.g. *John* ate his noodle quietly.)
- Experiencer: A participant who is characterized as aware of something. (e.g. *The students* felt comfortable in the class.)
- Theme: A participant which is characterized as changing its position, or as being in a position. (e.g. John gave *a book* to the students.)
- Benefactive: The entity that benefits from the action or event denoted by the predicator. (e.g. John bought a lot of books for *his sons*.)
- Source: The one from which motion proceeds. (e.g. *John* promised Bill to leave tomorrow morning.)
- Goal: The one to which motion proceeds. (e.g. John told the rumor to *his friend*.)
- Location: The thematic role associated with the NP expressing the location in a sentence with a verb of location. (e.g. John put his books *in the attic*.)
- Instrument: The medium by which the action or event denoted by the predicator is carried out. (e.g. John wiped the window with *a towel*.)

Consider the following examples:

(1) John deprived *his sons* of game cards.
(2) *Mary* received an award from the department.
(3) *The government* kept all the money.
(4) a. *John* runs into the house.
　　b. *Mary* looked at the sky.

Based on the above list, the NP *his sons* in (1) can be a/an _____①_____, in (2) *Mary* carries a goal, and in (3) the NP *The government* can be a location. However, there are also cases where we might not be able to pin down the exact semantic role. The subject *John* in (4a) is both an agent and a theme: it is an agent since it initiates and sustains the movement but also a theme since it is the object that moves. Also, the subject *Mary* in (4b) can either be a/an _____②_____ or an agent depending on her intention—one can just look at the sky with no purpose at all.

_____

_____

**02** Read the passage and fill in each blank with ONE word from the passage. Write your answers in the correct order. [2 points]

Some linguists have attempted to devise a universal typology of the semantic roles played by arguments in relation to their predicates. In the table in (1) below are listed a number of terms used to describe some of these roles (the convention being that terms denoting semantic roles are CAPITALISED), and for each role an informal gloss is given, together with an illustrative example in which the italicized expression has the semantic role specified:

(1) List of roles played by arguments with respect to their predicates

| Role | Gloss |
|---|---|
| THEME | Entity undergoing the effect of some action<br>The FBI arrested *Larry Luckless* |
| AGENT | Entity instigating some action<br>*Debbie* killed Harry |
| EXPERIENCER | Entity experiencing some psychological state<br>*I* like syntax |
| LOCATIVE | Place in which something is situated or takes place<br>He hid it *under the bed* |
| GOAL | Entity representing the destination of some other entity<br>John went *home* |
| SOURCE | Entity from which something moves<br>He returned *from Paris* |
| INSTRUMENT | Means used to perform some action<br>He hit it *with a hammer* |

We can illustrate how the terminology in (1) can be used to describe the semantic roles played by arguments in terms of the following examples:

(2) *The audience* enjoyed *the play.*
(3) *The suspect* received *a caution.*
(4) *They* stayed *in a hotel.*

Using this terminology, we can say that in (2) *the audience* is the ____①____ argument of the predicate *enjoyed*, and that *the play* is the THEME argument of *enjoyed*. In (3) *the suspect* is the ____②____ argument of the predicate *received*, and *a caution* is the THEME argument of *received*. In (4) *they* is the THEME argument of the predicate *stayed*, and *in a hotel* is the LOCATIVE argument of *stayed*.

# Constituency

Answer Key p.15

**01** Read the passage and fill in each blank with TWO words from the passage. Write your answers in the correct order. [2 points]

> The main goal of syntax is building a grammar that can generate an infinite set of well-formed, grammatical English sentences.
>
> (1) a. A man kicked the ball.
>
>      b. The cat chased the long string.
>
> Given only the lexical categories that we have identified so far, we can set up a grammar rule for sentence (S) like the following:
>
> (2) S → Det (A) N V Det (A) N
>
> The rule tells us what S can consist of: it must contain the items mentioned, except that those which are in parentheses are optional. So this rule characterizes any sentence which consists of a Det, N, V, Det, and N, in that order, possibly with an A in front of either N.
>
>    Notice that even this simple grammar rule can easily extend to generate an infinite number of English sentences by allowing iteration of the A:
>
> (3) S → Det $A^*$ N V Det $A^*$ N

This iteration operator '*' is called the 'Kleene Star Operator', and is a notation meaning 'zero to infinitely many' occurrences. The operator allows us to repeat any number of As, thereby generating sentences like (4).

(4) a. The tall man kicked the ball.
   b. The tall, handsome man kicked the ball.
   c. The tall, kind, handsome man kicked the ball.

A grammar using only lexical categories can be specified to generate an infinite number of well-formed English sentences, but it nevertheless misses a great deal of basic properties that we can observe. For example, this simple grammar cannot capture the agreement facts seen in examples like the following:

(5) a. The mother of the boy and the girl is arriving soon.
   b. The mother of the boy and the girl are arriving soon.

Why do the verbs in these two sentences have different agreement patterns? Our intuitions tell us that the answer lies in two different possibilities for grouping the words. The different groupings indicate who is arriving: in (5a), _____①_____, while in (5b) it is both _____①_____ and _____②_____. The grouping of words into larger phrasal units which we call constituents provides the first step in understanding the agreement facts in (5).

_____

_____

**02** **Read the passages, and follow the directions.** [4 points]

---| A |---

Linguists have argued that one way of finding out whether a particular sequence of words behaves like a unit is by trying to move it to another position in the sentence. If we can move a particular string of words in a sentence from one position to another, then it behaves as a constituent.

Cleft sentences are special constructions in English which enable language users to highlight a particular string of words in a sentence.

(1) a. It was [your big brother] who built this house.

　　b. It was [for Mary] that John bought the flowers (not for Susan).

(2) a. *It was [your big] who built this house brother.

　　b. *It was [a book] [to Mary] that John gave.

In Cleft sentences, the material that occurs in the focused position must be a complete constituent, and only one constituent may appear in this position at a time.

Now let us look at another example. One way of emphasising the sequence *your elder sister* in (3a) is to prepose it.

(3) a. I can't stand [your elder sister].

　　b. [Your elder sister], I can't stand (though your brother's OK).

But only the whole NP (Noun Phrase) [your elder sister] can be preposed for emphasis, not just part of the phrase as shown in (4):

(4) a. *Your elder, I can't stand sister.

　　b. *Elder sister, I can't stand your.

　　c. *Sister, I can't stand your elder.

　　d. *Your, I can't stand elder sister.

| B |

Constituents are strings of one or more words that syntactically and semantically behave as a unit. Consider the following constituent tests:

(5) a. Which house does your friend live in?

   b. In which house does your friend live?

(6) a. It is that book that she lost with blue cover.

   b. It is that book with blue cover that she lost.

(7) a. It is that book that she left with her best friend.

   b. It is that book with her best friend that she left.

**Identify TWO ungrammatical sentences in <B>, and explain why, based on the description in <A>.**

_____

_____

_____

_____

_____

**03** Read the passage and fill in each blank with ONE word from the passage. (Use the SAME answer for both blanks.) [2 points]

In building up any phrase, there is one obligatory element in each phrase. That is, each phrase has one essential element as represented in the diagrams in (1):

(1)

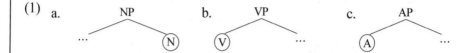

a.   NP       b.   VP       c.   AP

The circled element here is the essential, obligatory element within the given phrase. We call this essential element the head of the phrase. The head of each phrase thus determines its 'projection' into a larger phrasal constituent. The head of an NP is thus N, the head of a VP is V, and the head of an AP is A.

The notion of headedness plays an important role in the grammar. For example, the verb *put*, functioning as the head of a VP, dictates what it must combine with two complements, NP and PP. Consider other examples:

(2) a. The defendant denied the accusation.

b. *The defendant denied.

(3) a. The teacher handed the student a book.

b. *The teacher handed the student.

The verb *denied* here requires an NP object whereas *handed* requires two NP complements, in this use. The properties of the head verb itself determine what kind of elements it will combine with. The elements which a head verb should combine with are called complements.

The properties of the _____ become properties of the whole phrase. Why are the examples in (4b) and (5b) ungrammatical?

(4) a. They [want to leave the meeting].

    b. *They [eager to leave the meeting].

(5) a. The senators [know that the president is telling a lie].

    b. *The senators [certain that the president is telling a lie].

The examples in (4b) and (5b) are unacceptable because of the absence of the required _____. The unacceptable examples lack a finite (tensed) VP as the bracketed part, but we know that English sentences require a finite VP as their immediate constituent, as informally represented as in (6):

(6) English Declarative Sentence Rule:

    Each declarative sentence must contain a finite VP.

**04** Read the passage <A> and the sentences in <B>, and follow the directions.

[4 points]

---

| A |

In a large majority of the coordinate structures, the coordinates belong to the same category as in (1).

(1) a. John wrote <u>to Mary</u> and <u>to Fred</u>.    [PP + PP]

   b. John wrote <u>a letter</u> and <u>a postcard</u>.    [NP + NP]

But coordinates do not have to be of the same category. Other examples are given in (2):

(2) a. I'll be back [<u>next week</u> or <u>at the end of the month</u>].   [NP + PP]

   b. John is [<u>a banker</u> and <u>extremely rich</u>].    [NP + AP]

What makes the coordinations in (2) acceptable despite the differences of category is that each coordinate could occur alone with the same function.

(3) a. I'll be back <u>next week</u>.

   b. I'll be back <u>at the end of the month</u>.

(4) a. John is <u>a banker</u>.

   b. John is <u>extremely rich</u>.

In each pair here the underlined element in (b) has the same function as that in (a): time adjunct in (3), complement of the verb in (4).

   Now consider the following example:

(6) *We're leaving [<u>Rome</u> and <u>next week</u>].   [NP + NP]

Here the coordinates belong to the same category, but don't satisfy the requirement of functional likeness. In (6) the NP *Rome* is a complement, but the NP *next week* is an adjunct; the functions would be different. Therefore, the different functions cannot be conjoined.

---
**B**
---

(a) You can bring these and those books.

(b) He acted selfishly and with no thought for the consequences.

(c) I ran to the park and for health reasons.

(d) He won't reveal the nature of the threat or where it came from.

(e) He is a very shy and rather inarticulate man.

(f) The discussion of the riots and in the bar was full and frank.

---

Identify TWO ungrammatical sentences in <B>, and explain why, discussing each coordinate, based on the description in <A>.

_____

_____

_____

_____

_____

**05** Read the passage <A> and the sentences in <B>, and follow the directions.

[4 points]

---
| A |
---

Constituency tests involve so-called Cleft (*It*-Cleft) and Pseudocleft (*Wh*-Cleft) sentences, examples of which are given below:

| | |
|---|---|
| (1) Frank washed his shirts yesterday. | *'Regular' sentence* |
| (2) It was *Frank* who washed his shirts yesterday. | *Cleft* |
| (3) It was *his shirts* that Frank washed yesterday. | *Cleft* |
| (4) It was *yesterday* that Frank washed his shirts. | *Cleft* |
| (5) What Frank washed yesterday was *his shirts*. | *Pseudocleft* |
| (6) What Frank did yesterday was *wash his shirts*. | *Pseudocleft* |
| (7) What Frank did was *wash his shirts yesterday*. | *Pseudocleft* |

Clefts and Pseudoclefts are special constructions in English which enable language users to highlight a particular string of words in a sentence. Clefts and Pseudoclefts are easily recognisable because they have a typical structure. They always start with the same word: *it* in the case of the Cleft construction and *what* (and a few other *wh*-items) in the case of the Pseudocleft. Both Clefts and Pseudoclefts always contain a form of the copular verb *be* (is/was/were). The position following this copular verb is called the focus position (italicised in the examples above). The elements that occur here receive special prominence. Different elements are able to occupy the focus position in Clefts and Pseudoclefts, and for this reason a sentence can have more than one Cleft or Pseudocleft version, as the examples in (2)—(7).

For current purposes the following principle is important: Only constituents can occur in the focus position of a Cleft or Pseudocleft. In addition, we can explain the restrictions on *it*-cleft and *wh*-cleft sentences. VP and AP cannot be in the focus position of a *it*-cleft sentence, and TP cannot be in the focus position of a *wh*-cleft sentence, as shown in (8).

(8) a. *It is *go home* that I will.
    b. *It was *happy* that I made her.
    c. *What they believe is *him to be right*.

---
| B |
---

(a) What Arni wanted was for Karim to be quiet.

(b) What he promised was to have it today.

(c) What John considered was them to be conscientious.

(d) What Bill does is sell cars.

(e) It is not to make life easier for us that they are changing the rules.

(f) It is very pretty that she is.

**Identify TWO ungrammatical sentences in <B>, and explain why, based on the description in <A>.**

---

---

---

---

**06** Read the passage <A> and the sentences in <B>, and follow the directions. [4 points]

───────────────┤ A ├───────────────

Coordination involves the linking of two or more strings by a coordinating conjunction, typically *and, or* or *but*, e.g [*very clever*] *and* [*extremely eager*], [*in the box*] *or* [*on the floor*], [*that Mary likes poems*] *and* [*that John likes novels*], etc. AP can conjoin with another AP, PP with another PP, TP with another TP, and CP with another CP. The claim now is the following: only identical categories can be coordinated, but the different categories cannot be coordinated.

Let's see if coordination facts can confirm the constituent structure of Verb Phrases. Consider the following sentence:

(1) Frank washed his shirts yesterday.

For (1) we posited a structure like (2):

(2)

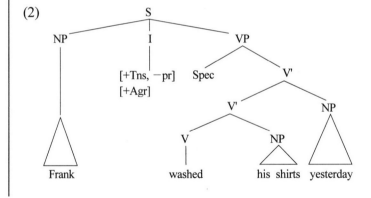

The constituents inside the VP of (2) are the (empty) Specifier position, the higher V-bar, the lower V-bar, the main verb and the Direct Object NP, as well as the Adjunct NP. The constituent status of all of these is confirmed by the fact that they can be coordinated with other similar units:

(3) Frank *washed* and *ironed* his shirts yesterday.      (coordinated main verbs)

(4) Frank *washed his shirts* and *polished his shoes* yesterday. (coordinated lower V-bars)

(5) Frank washed his shirts *yesterday* and *last week*.      (coordinated adjunct NPs)

(6) Frank *washed his shirts yesterday* and *polished his shoes last week*.

                                                  (coordinated higher V-bars)

---

**B**

(a) I wonder whether John likes fish and Mary meat.

(b) I wonder whether John likes fish and whether Mary likes meat.

(c) Anna loudly announced the election victory and cheerfully gave an interview to the press.

(d) They reported that John made a mistake and him to be in great pain.

(e) I would prefer there to be fried squid at the reception and for John to stay.

---

**Identify TWO ungrammatical sentences in <B>, and explain why, discussing the grammatical category of each coordinate, based on the description in <A>.**

---

 

---

 

---

 

---

 

---

 

---

**01** Read the passage <A> and the sentences in <B>, and follow the directions. [4 points]

---

| A |

A direct object (DO) is canonically an NP, undergoing the process denoted by the verb:

(1) a. His girlfriend bought this computer.
   b. That silly fool broke the teapot.

However, this is not a solid generalization. The objects in (2a) and (2b) are not really affected by the action. In (2a) *the dog* is experiencing something, and in (2b) *thunder* is somehow causing some feeling in the dog:

(2) a. Thunder frightens [the dog].
   b. The dog fears [thunder].

The data show us that we cannot identify the object based on semantic roles. A much more firm criterion is the syntactic construction of passivization, in which a notional direct object appears as Subject. The sentence in (3a) can be turned into the passive sentence in (3b):

(3) a. The child broke the teapot by accident.
   b. The teapot was broken by the child by accident.

What we can notice here is that the object *the teapot* in (3a) is promoted to the subject in the passive sentence as in (3b). The test comes from the fact that non-object NPs cannot be promoted to the subject as in (4b):

(4) a. This item belongs to the student.
   b. *The student is belonged to by this item.

The objects that undergo passivization are direct objects, distinct from indirect objects. An indirect object (IO) is one which precedes a direct object (DO). A caution is in order—when a DO follows an IO, the DO cannot be passivized as shown in (5b); however, in examples like (5a), passive has the property of making the IO into the subject as in (5c):

(5) a. John gave [the boys] [the CDs].

    b. *The CDs were given the boys by John.

    c. The boys were given the CDs (by John).

---

**⊣ B ⊢**

(a) A good friend is remained to me by him.

(b) This computer was bought for him by his girlfriend.

(c) A review copy of the book was sent to her by the publisher.

(d) A review copy of the book was sent her by the publisher.

(e) The shop is closed at five o'clock.

---

Identify TWO ungrammatical sentences in <B>, and explain why, EXACTLY based on the description in <A>.

_____

_____

_____

_____

_____

**02** Read the passage <A> and the sentences in <B>, and follow the directions. [4 points]

---| A |---

The PS rules allow us to represent the difference between phrasal verb (verb and particle) constructions and prepositional verb (verb and preposition) constructions. Consider a representative pair of contrasting examples:

(1) a. John suddenly got off the bus.
    b. John suddenly put off the customers.

By altering the position of *off*, we can determine that *off* in (1a) is a preposition whereas *off* in (1b) is a particle (Part):

(2) a. *John suddenly got the bus off.
    b. John suddenly put the customers off.

This in turn means that *off* in (1a) is a preposition, forming a PP with the following NP, but in (2a) the NP *the bus* precedes the preposition *off*, whereas *off* in (1b) is a particle that forms no constituent with the following NP *the customers*. This in turn means that the grammar needs to introduce the following VP rule:

(3) VP → V (Part) (NP) (Part) PP

Equipped with this rule, we then can easily represent the differences of these grammatical sentences in tree structures:

(4)

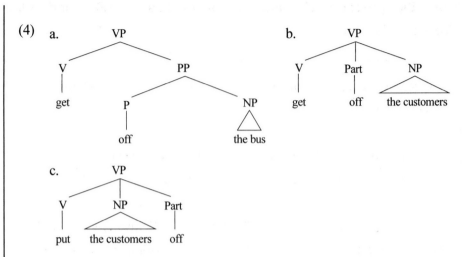

a. VP — V (get), PP — P (off), NP (the bus)

b. VP — V (get), Part (off), NP (the customers)

c. VP — V (put), NP (the customers), Part (off)

As represented here, the particle does not form a constituent with the following or preceding NP whereas the preposition does form a constituent with it.

---

| B |

(a) My uncle went the door <u>out</u>.

(b) My uncle threw the door <u>out</u>.

(c) It was Mary's nose that Steve looked <u>up</u>.

(d) It was <u>up</u> Mary's nose that Steve looked.

(e) It was Mary's number that Steve looked <u>up</u>.

(f) It was <u>up</u> Mary's number that Steve looked.

---

**Identify TWO ungrammatical sentences in <B>, and explain why, specifying the type of verb constructions and the underlined part, EXACTLY based on the description in <A>.**

_____

_____

_____

_____

_____

**03** Read the passage <A> and the sentences in <B>, and follow the directions. [4 points]

---

| A |

There are some verbs which select a sequence of an NP followed by a CP as complements:

(1) a. We told Tom that he should consult an accountant.

b. Mary convinced me that the argument was sound.

In addition to the *that*-type of CP, there is an infinitive type of CP, headed by the complementizer *for*. Some verbs select this nonfinite CP as the complement:

(2) a. Tom intends for Sam to review that book.

b. John would prefer for the children to finish the oatmeal.

The data show that verbs like *intend* and *prefer* select an infinitival CP clause.
Just like the complementizer *that, for* selects an infinitival S as its complement. The evidence that the complementizer *for* requires an infinitival S can be found from coordination data:

(3) a. For John to either [make up such a story] or [repeat it] is outrageous. (coordination of base VPs)

b. For John either [to make up such a story] or [to repeat it] is outrageous. (coordination of infinitive VPs)

c. For [John to tell Bill such a lie] and [Bill to believe it] is outrageous. (coordination of infinitive Ss)

Given that only like categories (constituents with the same label) can be coordinated, we can see that base VPs, infinitival VPs, and infinitival Ss are all constituents.
One thing to note here is that the verbs which select a CP complement can also take an infinitival VP complement:

(4) a. John intends to review the book.

b. John would prefer to finish the oatmeal.

However, this does not mean that all verbs behave alike: not all verbs can take variable complement types such as an infinitival VP or S. For example, the verb *try* selects only an infinitival VP, but it cannot select an infinitival CP as the complement as attested by the data:

(5) a. Tom tried to ask a question.
b. *Tom tried for Bill to ask a question.

---

| B |

(a) Jim wanted to leave London.
(b) Tom tends for Mary to avoid confrontations.
(c) I hate to disappoint you.
(d) Joe hoped for Beth to find a solution.
(e) She refused to take the money.
(f) I will plan for you to be back in time.

**Identify TWO ungrammatical sentences in <B>, and explain why, ONLY based on the description in <A>.**

_____

_____

_____

_____

_____

**04** Read the passage <A> and the sentences in <B>, and follow the directions. [4 points]

--- | A | ---

Let's look at two example sentences:

(1) a. John wants Mary to see a doctor.
   b. John persuaded Mary to see a doctor.

Semantically, in (1a) John wants an entire state of affairs, namely Mary's seeing a doctor. In (1b) John persuades a person to do something; he does not persuade an entire proposition. If we question the nonfinite clauses, our questions and answers take different forms for the two sentences:

(2) a. What did John want? For Mary to see a doctor.
      not *Who did John want? Mary.
   b. Who did John persuade (to see a doctor)? Mary.
      not *What did John persuade? For Mary to see a doctor.

If we passivize the embedded clause in the cases of *want* and *persuade*, we see a difference:

(3) a. Cian wants Sybil to write a best-selling novel.
   b. Cian wants a best-selling novel to be written by Sybil.
(4) a. John persuaded Mary to see a doctor.
   b. John persuaded a doctor to be seen by Mary.

In the *want* case, there is synonymy between the active and passive versions. In the *persuade* case, however, there isn't synonymy.

If we passivize the matrix clause, we also see a difference. In (5a) the verb *want* cannot allow for passivizing the matrix clause:

(5) a. *Megan was wanted by Barbara to feed the dog.
   b. Megan was persuaded by Barbara to feed the dog.

In pseudo cleft sentences, the two verbs, *want* and *believe*, behave differently. The verb *want* in (6a) takes a CP complement, and CP can be in the focus position of a pseudo cleft sentence. However, the verb *believe* in (6b) takes a TP complement; TP cannot be in the focus position of a pseudo cleft sentence:

(6) a. What Arni wanted was for Karim to be quiet.
  b. *What Arni believed was Karim to be quiet.

---

**┤ B ├**

(a) Megan was expected by Barbara to feed the dog.
(b) What I don't know is why they decided to do it today.
(c) For Megan to feed the dog was expected by Barbara.
(d) All parents were liked to visit the school.
(e) What he promised was to have it ready today.
(f) What Terry proved was Ashley to be an idiot.

---

**Identify TWO ungrammatical sentences in <B>, and explain why, based on the description in <A>.**

_____

_____

_____

_____

_____

**05** Read the passage <A> and the sentences in <B>, and follow the directions. [4 points]

---

┤ A ├

Verbs differ in terms of the number and type of phrases they can take as complements and/or adjuncts. Transitive verbs such as *find, hit, chase,* and so on take a direct object complement, whereas intransitive verbs like *arrive* or *sleep* do not. Ditransitive verbs such as *give* or *throw* take two objects, as in *John threw Mary a ball.* In addition, most verbs take a subject. The various NPs that occur with a verb are its arguments. Thus intransitive verbs have one argument: the subject; transitive verbs have two arguments: the subject and direct object; ditransitive verbs have three arguments: the subject, direct object, and indirect object. The argument structure of a verb is part of its meaning and is included in its lexical entry.

The verb not only determines the number of arguments in a sentence, but it also limits the semantic properties of both its subject and its objects. For example, *find* and *sleep* require animate subjects. The well-known *colorless green ideas sleep furiously* is semantically anomalous because *ideas* (colorless or not) are not animate. Components of a verb's meaning can also be relevant to the choice of arguments it can take. For example, the verbs in (1) and (3) can take two objects —they're ditransitive—while those in (2) and (4) cannot.

(1) John threw/tossed the boy the ball.
(2) *John pushed/pulled the boy the ball.
(3) Mary faxed/e-mailed Helen the news.
(4) *Mary murmured/mumbled Helen the news.

---

The ditransitive verbs have "transfer direct object to indirect object" in their meaning. In (1) the ball is transferred to the boy. In (3) the news is transferred, or leastwise transmitted, to Helen. The ditransitive verbs *give, write, send,* and *throw* all have this property. However, in (2) and (4), the monotransitive or intransitive verbs cannot take two objects; these verbs do not have such property as in (1) and (3). Even when the transference is not overt, it may be inferred. In *John baked Mary a cake*, there is an implied transfer of the cake from John to Mary. Subtle aspects of meaning are mirrored in the argument structure of the verbs, and indeed, this connection between form and meaning may help children acquire the syntactic and semantic rules of their language.

─┤ B ├─

(a) Tom played the boy a trick.
(b) Tom flung the boy the ball.
(c) John hauled the boy the ball.
(d) Sally radioed Helen the news.
(e) Sally phoned Helen the news.
(f) Mary shrieked Helen the news.

Identify TWO ungrammatical sentences in <B>, and explain why, based on the description in <A>.

_____

_____

_____

_____

_____

**06** Read the passage <A> and the sentences in <B>, and follow the directions. [4 points]

────────────────┤ A ├────────────────

There are verbs selecting not just a phrase but a whole clause as a complement, either finite or nonfinite. For example, consider the complements of *think* or *believe*:

(1) a. I think (that) the press has a check-and-balance function.

b. They believe (that) Charles Darwin's theory of evolution is just a scientific theory.

The complementizer (C) *that* here is optional, implying that this kind of verb selects for a finite complement clause of some type. These verbs select a CP complement.

We can also find somewhat similar verbs like *demand* and *require*:

(2) a. John demanded [that she stop phoning him].

b. The rules require [that the executives be polite].

Unlike *think* or *believe*, these verbs which introduce a subjunctive clause typically only take a CP as their complement: the finite verb itself is actually in the base form. The verb *require* selects a base CP complement.

There are also verbs which select a sequence of an NP followed by a CP as complements.

(3) a. We told Tom that he should consult an accountant.

b. Mary convinced me that the argument was sound.

In addition to the *that*-type of CP, there is an infinitive type of CP, headed by the complementizer *for*. Some verbs select this nonfinite CP as the complement. The data below show that verbs like *intend* and *prefer* select an infinitival CP clause:

(4) a. Tom intends for Sam to review that book.

　　b. John would prefer for the children to finish the oatmeal.

Just like the complementizer *that*, *for* selects an infinitival S as its complement. The evidence that the complementizer *for* requires an infinitival S can be found from coordination data:

(5) For [John to tell Bill such a lie] and [Bill to believe it] is outrageous. (coordination of infinitival Ss)

─────────────────┤ B ├─────────────────

(a) She pinched that he feels pain.

(b) We hope the availability of a new vaccine as soon as possible.

(c) Joe warned the class that the exam would be difficult.

(d) Cohen proved the independence of the continuum hypothesis.

**Identify TWO ungrammatical sentences in <B>, and explain why, based on the description in <A>.**

_____

_____

_____

_____

_____

**07** Read the passage <A> and the sentences in <B>, and follow the directions. [4 points]

---
**A**
---

Consider the following examples:

(1) Barnett *seemed* to understand the formula.
(2) Barnett *tried* to understand the formula.

The surface strings in (1) and (2) are identical. The sole surface difference is the choice of the matrix verb, *seem* vs. *try*. In the Raising construction in (1), the subject *Barnett* is semantically linked only to the embedded verb *understand*, while in (2) it is semantically linked to both the matrix verb *try* and the embedded verb. For this reason, the subject in (2) is said to "control" the reference of the subject of the embedded clause and the construction has come to be referred to as "Subject Control."

Parallel data are found with transitive matrix verbs where the locus of these differences is the immediate postverbal NP.

(3) Barnett believed the doctor to have examined Tilman.
(4) Barnett persuaded the doctor to examine Tilman.

Again, the surface strings are identical, but there are fundamental differences in the characteristics of the NPs immediately following the matrix verbs. In (3), *the doctor* is semantically linked only with the embedded verb *examine*, while in (4) *the doctor* is semantically linked to both the matrix verb *persuade* and the embedded verb. The construction in (3) is referred to as Raising-to-Object and that in (4) as Object Control.

When the matrix clause is passivized, these two constructions are different.

(5) The flood was believed to have destroyed the town.
(6) *The flood was persuaded to destroy the town.

The contrast indicates that the subject *the flood* in (5) is not selected by the verb *believe*, while that in (6) must selected by the verb *persuade*; thus, this sentence is semantically ill-formed. In *persuade*-type, the matrix passive is not always possible because of thematic relation between the matrix verb and the subject of the matrix passive.

---

**B**

(a) There proved to be toxins in the soap.

(b) There threatens to be a famine in Bulgaria.

(c) Mice are claimed to be afraid of cats.

(d) The avalanche was told to hit the town.

(e) The painting was declared to be a forgery.

(f) The key was asked to open the door.

---

**Identify TWO ungrammatical sentences in <B>, and explain why, ONLY based on the description in <A>.**

_____

_____

_____

_____

_____

# Syntactic Structures

Answer Key p.22

**01** **Read the passage and fill in each blank with ONE word from the passage. Write your answers in the correct order.** [2 points]

> We need to investigate the abstract content of PS rules, in order to develop a theoretical view of them. For example, it seems to be the case that each PS rule must have a 'head'.
>
> In order to understand more about the structures that rules describe, we need two more notions, 'intermediate categories' and 'specifiers'. We motivate the idea of the intermediate category, and then specifier is a counterpart of it. Consider the examples in (1):
>
> (1) a. Every photo of Max and sketch by his students appeared in the magazine.
>
> b. No photo of Max and sketch by his students appeared in the magazine.
>
> What are the structures of these two sentences? Do the phrases *every photo of Max* and *sketch by his students* form NPs? It is not difficult to see *sketch by his students* is not a full NP by itself, for if it was, it should be able to appear as subject by itself:
>
> (2) *Sketch by his students appeared in the magazine.
>
> In terms of the semantic units, we can assign the following structures to the above sentences, in which *every* and *no* operate over the meaning of the rest of the phrase:
>
> (3) a. [Every [[photo of Max] and [sketch by his students]]] appeared in the magazine.
>
> b. [No [[photo of Max] and [sketch by his students]]] appeared in the magazine.

The expression *photo of Max* and *sketch by his students* are phrasal elements but not full NPs—so what are they? We call these are '_____①_____ phrases', notationally represented as N-bar or N'. The phrase N' is thus intuitively bigger than a noun, but smaller than a full NP, in the sense that it still requires a determiner from the class *the, every, no, some,* and the like.

Now consider the following examples:

(4) a. [the enemy's] [$_{N'}$ destruction of the city]

    b. [The enemy] [$_{VP}$ destroyed the city].

The phrase *the enemy's* in (4a) and the subject *the enemy* in (4b) are semantically similar in the sense that they complete the specification of the event denoted by the predicate. These phrases are treated as the _____②_____ of N' and of VP, respectively.

**02** Read the passage and fill in each blank with ONE word from the passage. Write your answers in the correct order. [2 points]

The largest unit of syntactic analysis is the sentence. Sentences typically consist of an NP (often called 'the subject') and a VP that are linked together by an abstract category dubbed 'T' (for 'tense'). As illustrated in figure 1, T serves as the head of the sentence, taking the VP as its complement and the subject NP as its specifier. What we think of as a sentence or a sentential phrase, then, is really a TP.

Figure 1

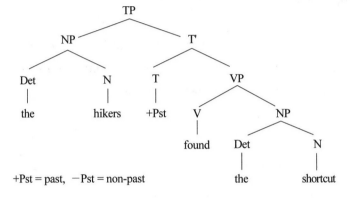

+Pst = past, −Pst = non-past

The tense feature in T must be compatible with the form of the verb. So a sentence like the one above, whose head contains the feature +Pst, must contain a verb marked for the past tense (hence, *found* rather than *find*).

Although somewhat abstract, this analysis has the advantage of giving sentences the same internal structure as other phrases (with a specifier, a head, and a complement), making them consistent with the X' Schema. Moreover, because T, like all heads, is obligatory, we also account for the fact that all sentences have _____①_____ (i.e., they are all past or non-past).

The TP structure also provides us with a natural place to locate modal auxiliaries such as *can, may, will,* and *must,* most of which are inherently _____②_____, as shown by their incompatibility with time adverbs such as *yesterday*: *\*He can/will/must work yesterday.* The modals *could* and *would* can be either past or non-past: *He could swim when he was three/He could swim tomorrow.* Because modals are themselves markers of tense, we will assume that it is not necessary to have the feature ±Pst in the T position when they are used.

## 03 Read the passage and fill in the blank with TWO words from the passage.

[2 points]

Verb Raising (Move V to the T position) can apply in English, but only to *have* and *be*. To begin, consider the sentences in (1), which contain two auxiliaries—modal and non-modal.

(1) a. The students should have finished the project.
  b. The children could be playing in the yard.

Modal auxiliaries occur under T, but what about non-modal auxiliaries? They are considered to be a special type of V that takes a VP complement.
  As expected, only the modal auxiliary can undergo Inversion in these structures.

(2) a. The modal auxiliary verb moves to the C position (grammatical):
    [CP Should [TP the students _t_ have finished the project]]?
  b. The non-modal auxiliary moves to the C position (ungrammatical):
    *[CP Have [TP the students should _t_ finished the project]]?

  Crucially, however, a non-modal auxiliary can undergo Inversion when there is no _____ in the sentence as shown in (3).

(3) [CP Have [TP the students _t_ finished the project]]?
  (from: The students have finished the project.)

Since Inversion involves movement from T to C, *Have* in (3) must have moved to the T position, and from there to the C position, as depicted in (4).

(4)

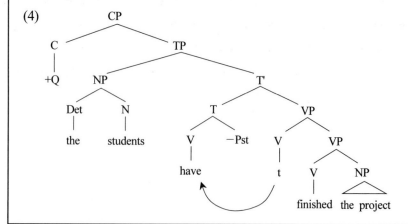

# Additional Tests

Answer Key p.23

**01** Read the passage and fill in the blank with ONE word from the passage.

[2 points]

> The following is a short rule for English subject-verb agreement.
>
> (1) In English, the main verb agrees with the _____ element of the subject.
>
> This rule can pinpoint what is wrong with the following two examples:
>
> (2) a. *The recent strike by pilots have cost the country a great deal of money from tourism and so on.
>
>  b. *The average age at which people begin to need eyeglasses vary considerably.
>
> In (2a), the main verb should be *has* but not *have* to observe the basic agreement rule in (1). Meanwhile, in (2b), the main verb *vary* needs to agree with the singular noun *age*. It would not do to simply talk about 'the noun' in the subject in the examples in (2), as there is more than one. We need to be able to talk about the one which gives its character to the phrase, and this is the head. If the head is singular, so is the whole phrase, and similarly for plural.
>
> Now let us look at some slightly different cases. Can you explain why the following examples are unacceptable?

(3) a. *Despite of his limited educational opportunities, Abraham Lincoln became one of the greatest intellectuals in the world.

   b. *A pastor was executed, notwithstanding on many applications in favor of him.

To understand these examples, we first need to recognize that the words *despite* and *notwithstanding* are prepositions, and further that canonical English prepositions combine only with noun phrases. In (3), these prepositions combine with the prepositional phrases again (headed by *of* and *on* respectively), violating the rule.

**02** Read the passage <A> and the sentences in <B>, and follow the directions. [4 points]

---

┤ A ├

A clausal subject is not limited to a finite *that*-headed CP, but there are other clausal types:

(1) a. [That John sold the ostrich] surprised Bill.
     (*that*-clause CP subject)
   b. [(For John) to train his horse] would be desirable.
     (infinitival CP or VP subject)
   c. [Which otter you should adopt first] is unclear.
     (*wh*-question CP subject)

Like verbs, certain adjectives can also select CPs as their complements. For example, *confident* selects a finite CP, whereas *content* selects an infinitival CP:

(2) a. Tom is confident [that the elephants respect him].
   b. We are content [for the cleaners to return the drapes next week].

Nouns can also select an infinitival CP or VP complement, for example, *eagerness*:

(3) a. (John's) eagerness [for Harry to win the election]
   b. (John's) eagerness [to win the election]

One pattern that we can observe is that when a verb selects a finite CP complement as in (4), if there is a corresponding noun, it also selects a finite CP in (5):

(4) a. Bill alleged that Fred signed the check.
   b. We believe that the directors were present.
(5) a. the allegation that Fred signed the check
   b. the belief that the directors were present

---

This shows us that the derivational process which derives a noun from a verb preserves the value of that verb.

A caution here is that not all nouns can of course select a finite CP complement. Some nouns cannot combine with a finite CP complement:

(6) a. *his attention that the earth is round

   b. *his article that the earth is flat

---

**B**

(a) Tom seems eager for her brother to catch a cold.

(b) Tom seems eager to catch a cold.

(c) It is true that he is a genius.

(d) It is easy that we please him.

(e) That the king or queen be present is a requirement on all Royal weddings.

(f) It is true for him to be a genius.

---

**Identify TWO ungrammatical sentences in <B>, and explain why, specifying the type of complements, ONLY based on the description in <A>.**

_____

_____

_____

_____

_____

**03** Read the passage <A> and the sentences in <B>, and follow the directions. [4 points]

---

┤ A ├

Consider the following constraints and an example of how each one serves to block transformational movement in a derivation.

*Unit Movement Constraint* states that no string of elements that do not form a constituent can be moved together in a single application of a movement rule.

(1) a. Did he climb [PP up the ladder]?
  b. *Where* did he climb [PP ___]?
(2) a. Did he [V fold up] [NP the ladder]?
  b. **Where* did he [V fold ___] [NP ___]?

*Up the ladder* is a constituent (i.e., a PP) in (1a), and thus can be questioned and subsequently moved, as illustrated in (1b). However, *up the ladder* is not a constituent in (2a), and thus cannot be questioned and moved, as in (2b).

*Subjacency Constraint* prohibits an element from being moved across more than one S or NP boundary in a single application of a movement rule.

(3) a. The fact that [S[NP an article *about Trump*] was just published] was unexpected.
  b. The fact that [S[NP an article _____] was just published *about Trump*] was unexpected.
  c. **The fact that [S[NP an article _____] was just published] was unexpected *about Trump*.

*About Trump* is a PP contained in the NP *an article about Trump*, as illustrated in (3a). Thus, *about Trump* can be moved via Extraposition to the end of the interior clause as in (3b), since it crosses only one NP boundary. However, it cannot be moved to the end of the exterior clause as in (3c), since it would have to cross both an NP and an S boundary in a single application of a movement rule.

*Tensed S Constraint* prohibits an element from being moved outside of a tensed clause.

(4) a. *All hell* is expected [s ___ to break loose].

    b. *\*All hell* is expected [s ___ might break loose].

*All hell* is the subject of an untensed (infinitive) verb (*to break*) in (4a) and thus can be moved outside of that clause. However, *all hell* is the subject of a tensed verb (*might break*) in (4b) and thus cannot be so moved.

---

┤ B ├

(a) Who did he think she saw?

(b) Ed seems will be incompetent.

(c) The car into the garage was put by Muffy.

(d) Which book do you think that John read?

(e) Tom was reported to be in great pain.

**Identify TWO ungrammatical sentences in <B>, and explain why, specifying the relevant constraint, ONLY based on the description in <A>.**

_____

_____

_____

_____

_____

**04** Read the passage <A> and the sentences in <B>, and follow the directions. [4 points]

─────────── ┤ A ├ ───────────

There are certain semantic arguments in support of positing a rule of WH-MOVEMENT. One such argument relates to the interpretation of Reflexives (i.e. *self*-forms). Non-subject reflexives generally require a sometime clausemate antecedent. In the light of this generalisation, consider the apparent problem posed by *wh*-questions such as the following:

(1) WHICH WITNESS did you say you thought
   [ — perjured *himself*]?

Clearly, the italicised Reflexive *himself* must be construed with the capitalised *wh*-NP *which witness* in (1); but this is in apparent violation of our sometime clausemate condition on Reflexives, because *which witness* is not contained in the same (bracketed) S as *himself* at S-structure: more precisely, *which witness* is positioned at the front of the *say* Clause, whereas *himself* is contained in the *perjured*-clause. How can we deal with this apparent counterexample to our sometime clausemate condition on Reflexives? One simple answer would be to posit that the *wh*-NP *which witness* in (1) originates at D-structure in the position marked by —, as the Subject of the bracketed Complement Clause. If this is so, then the capitalised *wh*-phrase and the italicised Reflexive would be clausemates at D-structure, so satisfying our sometime clausemate condition as shown in (2):

(2) You did say you thought
   [WHICH WITNESS perjured *himself*]?

But how is it that the D-structure result in the S-structure like (1)? The answer is that I-MOVEMENT applies to move the Auxiliary *did* in front of the main S, and WH-MOVEMENT applies to move the capitalised *wh*-NP *which witness* in front of the preposed Auxiliary *did*.

Naturally, any such solution would commit us to the twin assumptions of (i) an abstract level of underlying structure, and (ii) a rule of WH-MOVEMENT mapping this abstract underlying structure into the associated superficial syntactic structure.

**Identify whether sentence (3) below is ambiguous or not, and explain why, stating the two different D-structures like the sentence in (2), based on the description in <A>.**

---
| B |
---

(3) To whom did you say that Mary was talking?

## 05 Read the passages and follow the directions. [4 points]

┤ A ├

In addition to *wh*-relatives like the example in (1a) below and bare relatives like the corresponding (1b) example, we also find relative clauses introduced by *that* as in (1c):

(1) a. It's hard to find people [*who* you can trust].

　　b. It's hard to find people [you can trust].

　　c. It's hard to find people [*that* you can trust].

What's the status of *that* in (1c)? One answer is that the word *that* is a relative pronoun which behaves in much the same way as other relative pronouns like *who* and *which*. However, an alternative analysis which we will adopt here is to take *that* to be a relative clause complementiser (= C). The C analysis accounts for several properties of relative *that*. Firstly, it is homophonous with the complementiser *that* found in declarative clauses like that bracketed in (2):

(2) I said [*that* you were right].

Secondly, unlike a typical *wh*-pronoun, it can only occur in finite relative clauses like that bracketed in (1c) above, not in infinitival relative clauses like that bracketed in (3b) below:

(3) a. The director is looking for locations

　　　[*in which* to film a documentary about the FBA].

　　b. *The director is looking for locations

　　　[*that* to film a documentary about the FBA in].

Thirdly, unlike a typical *wh*-pronoun such as *who* (which has the formal-style accusative form *whom* and the genitive form *whose*), the relative pronoun *that* is invariable and has no variant case-forms—e.g. it lacks the genitive form *that's* in standard varieties of English, as shown in (4):

(4) a. Lord Lancelot Humpalot is someone
    [*whose* ego is even bigger than his libido]
  b. *Lord Lancelot Humpalot is someone
    [*that's* ego is even bigger than his libido]

Observations such as these suggest that relative *that* is a complementiser rather than a relative pronoun, and hence that it occupies the head C position in the relative clause CP which it introduces.

─────────────┤ B ├─────────────

In (5) below, the two, *which* and *that*, might function as the Complement of a Preposition *for*.

(5) a. There are still diseases *for which* there is no cure.
  b. There are still diseases *for that* there is no cure.

**In <B>, identify the grammaticality of each sentence in (5), and explain why, considering the property of a pronoun and a complementiser, based on the description in <A>.**

_____

_____

_____

_____

_____

## 06 Read the passages and follow the directions. [4 points]

┤ A ├

Consider sentence (1) and decide whether the sequence *a stream that had dried up* is a constituent or not.

(1) Sam sunbathed beside a stream that had dried up.

(2)

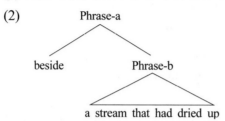

Does the sequence *beside a stream* form a constituent in sentence (1)? The answer is 'No': *beside a stream* is not a constituent in (1). *Beside* forms a phrase, not with *a stream*, but with the sequence *a stream that had dried up*. If we wanted to say that *beside a stream* formed a phrase in (1), we would be forced to represent the complete phrase *beside a stream that had dried up* as in (3):

(3)

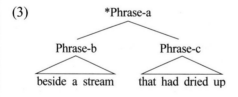

But (3) is wrong: it fails to represent *a stream that had dried up* as a phrase. The moral is that an element can belong directly only to one phrase at a time. Look at (2). The sequence *a stream that had dried up* is represented as a constituent because the elements (words, in this case) can all be traced back to a single node that does not dominate any other element, namely, PHRASE-b. The sequence *beside a*, on the other hand, is not represented as a constituent because the only node that dominates both of those words (namely, PHRASE-a) dominates other elements as well (namely, *stream, that, had, dried,* and *up*). Similarly, in the incorrect phrase marker (3), *a stream that had dried up* is not represented as a constituent because there is no node that dominates all and only those words. The only node that dominates all of them is PHRASE-a, but PHRASE-a doesn't dominate only those words, it also dominates *beside*.

---

┤ B ├

We've looked the examples in which a sequence of words functioning as a constituent in one sentence does not function as a constituent in another. Now consider the following example which is known as a structurally ambiguous sentence:

(4) Heseltine asked how old Sam was.

---

**First, state the two interpretations of sentence (4) in <B>, providing the two different questions that could have been asked by Heseltine. Note that you must start each sentence with the word "How". Second, state that which word goes with which word to form what phrase in each interpretation.**

---
___
___
___
___
___

**07** Read the passage, and fill in the blank ① with the ONE most appropriate word and the blank ② with ONE word from the passage. Write your answers in the correct order. [2 points]

The bracketed sequences in (1) below might all be argued to be Small Clause Complements of the immediately preceding Verb:

(1) a. I believe [*the President* incapable of deception].
   b. I consider [*John* extremely intelligent].
   c. Could you let [*the cat* into the house]?

Note that the italicised NP in such cases can be replaced by an appropriate Subject Expression:

(2) a. I believe [*it* inevitable that war will break out].
   b. I consider [*it* time to leave].
   c. Why did you let [*the cat* out of the bag]?

This strongly suggests that the bracketed Complements in (1) are Subject + Predicate structures, and hence Clauses of some sort.

So far, we have implicitly assumed that Small Clauses occur only as the Complements of Verbs. However, Absolute Prepositional Phrases (typically introduced by *with/without*) such as those italicised below involve a bracketed Small Clause complement of the canonical [NP XP] form:

(3) a. I don't want you preparing food with [*your hands dirty*].
   b. With [*the kitchen a mess*], how can I possibly cook anything?

Some support for the Small Clause analysis comes from the fact that Subject Expressions can typically occur immediately after the Preposition in the absolute construction:

(4) a. With [the cat out of the bag], there's not much point in trying to hide the truth anymore.

b. What with [it raining all day long], I didn't get a chance to hang the washing out.

Such facts suggest that the NP immediately following the Preposition *with* is not the ____①____ of the Preposition, but rather the ____②____ of a Small Clause Complement.

**08** Read the passage <A> and the sentences in <B>, and follow the directions. [4 points]

┤ A ├

By traditional tests of auxiliarihood, perfect *have* is an auxiliary, and causative *have* is a main verb. Evidence in support of this claim comes from facts about cliticisation. The form *have* can cliticise onto an immediately adjacent pronoun ending in a vowel/diphthong.

(1) a. They've seen a ghost. (= perfect *have*)

b. *They've their car serviced regularly. (= causative *have*)

How can we account for this contrast? If we assume that perfect *have* in (1a) is a finite (present tense) auxiliary which occupies the head T position of TP, but that causative *have* in (1b) is a main verb occupying the head V position of a VP complement of a null T, then prior to cliticisation the two clauses will have the respective simplified structures indicated by the partial labeled bracketings in (1a-b) below (where *Tns* is an abstract Tense affix):

(2) a. [$_{TP}$ They [$_T$ *have* + *Tns*] [$_{VP}$ [$_V$ seen] a ghost]].

b. [$_{TP}$ They [$_T$ *Tns*] [$_{VP}$ [$_V$ *have*] their car serviced regularly]].

Since cliticisation of *have* onto a pronoun is blocked by the presence of an intervening (overt or null) constituent, it should be obvious why *have* can cliticise onto *they* in (2a) but not in (2b): after all, there is no intervening constituent separating the pronoun *they* from *have* in (2a), but *they* is separated from the verb *have* in (2b) by an intervening T constituent containing a Tense affix (Tns), so blocking contraction.

Since *to* infinitive clauses are also TPs (with *to* serving as a nonfinite tense particle) we can generalise still further and say that all finite and infinitival clauses are TPs. This in turn has implications for how we analyse bare (i.e. *to*-less) infinitive complement clauses. The null T analysis is lent plausibility by the fact that some bare infinitive clauses have *to* infinitive counterparts in present-day English:

(3) a. I've never known [Tom (to) criticise anyone].

b. Tom has never been known [*to* criticise anyone].

The infinitive particle in the bracketed TPs in (3) must be overtly spelled out as *to* when the relevant TP is used as the complement of a passive participle like *known* in (3b), but can have a null spellout when the relevant TP is the complement of an active transitive verb like the perfect participle *known* in (3a). A null spellout for the infinitive particle is optional in structures like (3a) but obligatory in other structures.

---
**B**

(a) I can't let you have my password.
(b) I can't let you've my password.
(c) A reporter saw Senator Sleaze leave Benny's Bunny Bar.
(d) Senator Sleaze was seen to leave Benny's Bunny Bar.

---

**Identify ONE ungrammatical sentence in <B>, and explain why, ONLY based on the description in <A>.**

_____

_____

_____

_____

_____

**09** **Read the passage and fill in each blank with ONE word from the passage. Write your answers in the correct order.** [2 points]

There are NPs which follow a verb but which do not behave as direct objects (DOs) or indirect objects (IOs). Consider the following sentences:

(1) a. This is *my ultimate goal.*
    b. Michelle became *an architect.*
(2) a. They elected Graham *chairman.*
    b. I consider Andrew *the best writer.*

The italicized elements here are traditionally called 'predicative complements' in the sense that they function as the predicate of the subject or the object. However, even though they are NPs, they do not passivize:

(3) a. *Chairman was elected Graham.
    b. *The best writer was considered Andrew.

The difference between objects and predicative complements can also be seen in the following contrast:

(4) a. John made Kim *a great doll.*
    b. John made Kim *a great doctor.*

Even though the italicized expressions here are both NPs, they function differently. The NP *a great doll* in (4a) is the direct object, as in *John made a great doll for Kim,* whereas the NP *a great doctor* in (4b) cannot be an object: it serves as the predicate of the object *Kim.* If we think of part of the meaning informally, only in the second example would we say that the final NP describes the NP *Kim.*

(5) a. (4a): Kim ≠ a great doll

    b. (4b): Kim = a great doctor


In addition, phrases other than NPs can serve as predicative complements:


(6) a. The situation became *terrible*.

    b. This map is *what he wants*.

    c. The message was *that you should come on time*.

(7) a. I made Kim *angry*.

    b. I regard Andrew *as the best writer*.

    c. They spoil their kids *rotten*.


The italicized complements function to predicate a property of the _____①_____ in (6) and of the _____②_____ in (7).

**10** Read the passage <A> and the sentences in <B>, and follow the directions. [4 points]

┤ A ├

The following sentence is incomprehensible. Note that the letter *'t'* stands for 'trace':

(1) *[$_{CP1}$ Who$_k$ did [$_{TP}$ you wonder [$_{CP2}$ what$_i$ [$_{TP}$ $_{tk}$ kissed $_{ti}$ ]]]]?

*Wh*-phrases move to the specifier of a CP, so let's hypothesize that there is a further restriction: *movement* must always target the nearest potential position. This is a locality condition: the Minimal Link Condition (MLC).

(2) Minimal Link Condition (MLC): Move to the closest potential landing site.

In (1) there are two CPs, but both the *wh*-phrases start in the embedded clause. This means that for both *wh*-phrases the embedded CP2 is the closest potential landing site. If we start by moving *what* to CP2, this move meets the Minimal Link Condition because the movement has targeted the closest potential landing site. And then the other *wh*-phrase *who* moves to CP1, but the closest potential position CP2 is already filled by *what*. This would be a violation of the MLC because this movement skips the first potential position CP2. Notice that it doesn't matter what order we apply the operations in. If we move *who* first, stopping off in the specifier of CP2 (thus meeting the MLC), then that specifier is occupied by the trace, so there is no place for *what* to move to.

Now consider the following sentence:

(3) [$_{CP1}$ Who$_i$ do you think [$_{CP2}$ $_{ti}$ [$_{TP}$ $_{ti}$ kissed the gorilla]]]?

At first glance, this seems to be a violation of the MLC, since the *wh*-phrase ends up in the specifier of a CP1 that is higher up in the tree. CP1 is not the closest potential landing site. We can say that *wh*-movement that crosses clause boundaries does so in two hops: first to the specifier of the lower CP2, then on to the higher CP1. The MLC requires that all movement be local. In order to maintain this locality, the movement happens in two hops. This phenomenon is called *successive cyclic movement*.

---

**| B |**

(a) How do you think Tom killed the dog?

(b) How do you think John bought what?

(c) Who might they wonder he said the fact to?

(d) Who might they wonder what he said to?

**Identify ONE ungrammatical sentence in <B> and explain why, discussing whether it violates the Minimal Link Condition (MLC) or not, ONLY based on the description in <A>.**

_____

_____

_____

_____

_____

**11** **Read the passage and fill in each blank with ONE word from the passage. Write your answers in the correct order.** [2 points]

Prototypical adjectives have comparative and superlative forms and take degree modifiers such as *very, too* ("excessively") and *pretty*. Adjectives of this kind are said to be gradable. They denote scalar properties that can apply in varying degrees. *Good, old, big* and so on denote properties of this kind—and one can ask about the degree to which the property applies with *how*: *How big is it?*, etc.

Not all adjectives are of this kind. There are also non-gradable adjectives, as in *an alphabetical list*. It makes no sense to ask how alphabetical a list is, or to say that one list is more alphabetical than another. *Alphabetical* thus denotes a non-scalar property. Other examples of non-gradable adjectives are seen in (1):

(1) the <u>chief</u> difficulty       <u>federal</u> taxes

    <u>glandular</u> fever        my <u>left</u> arm

    a <u>medical</u> problem     <u>phonetic</u> symbols

    <u>pubic</u> hair          their <u>tenth</u> attempt

Some adjectives can be used in either way: like the distinction between count and non-count in nouns, the gradable vs. non-gradable distinction applies to uses rather than lexemes as such. Compare:

(2) a. in the <u>public</u> interest

    b. the <u>British</u> government

    c. The motorway is now <u>open</u>.

(3) a. a very <u>public</u> quarrel

    b. a very <u>British</u> response

    c. He was more <u>open</u> with us than the boss.

Typically, as in these examples, the non-gradable sense is the basic one, with the gradable sense representing an extended use. Therefore, the adjectives in (2) are _____①_____ , and the adjectives in (3) are _____②_____ .

**12** Read the passage and fill in each blank with ONE word from the passage. Write your answers in the correct order. [2 points]

Adverbs do not normally occur as dependents of nouns: in related adjective-adverb pairs it is the adjective that appears in this function. No such restriction applies to prepositions. Compare:

(1) a. She criticised them <u>with tact</u>.
 b. She criticised them <u>tactfully</u>.
(2) a. [A manager <u>with tact</u>] is needed.
 b. *[A manager <u>tactfully</u>] is needed.

The underlined expressions in (1) modify the _____①_____, and we see that both PP and Adverb are admissible. In (2), however, they modify the noun *manager* and here the PP is admissible but the adverb is not; instead we need an adjective in (2b): *a tactful manager*.

Adverbs cannot normally function as complement to the verb *be*: here we again have adjectives, in their predicative use. Compare:

(3) a. The key is <u>under the mat</u>.
 b. The meeting is <u>on Tuesday</u>.
(4) a. *Lucy was <u>enthusiastically</u> today.
 b. *Rain is <u>again</u>.

The examples in (3), with a PP functioning as complement of *be*, are impeccable, but the ones in (4), with an adverb in this function, are ungrammatical.

However, it has often been suggested that the traditional adverb category has something of the character of a classificatory wastebasket. Now consider the following examples:

(5) a. She went <u>aboard</u> the liner.

    b. He sat <u>outside</u> her bedroom.

(6) a. She went <u>aboard</u>.

    b. He sat <u>outside</u>.

The words *aboard, outside* are traditionally analysed as prepositions when they have an NP complement but as adverbs when they have no complement. The best way to remove this inconsistency is to amend the definition of prepositions so that they are no longer required to have an NP complement. *Aboard, outside* and similar words will then be _____②_____ both when they have NP complements and when they occur alone. This revision simultaneously gets rid of the complication of a dual classification for these words.

## 13 Read the passage and fill in each blank with TWO words from the passage. Write your answers in the correct order. [2 points]

The two functions a predicative complement (PC) and a direct object (DO) are distinguished syntactically in a number of ways.

Both DO and PC can have the form of an ordinary NP, but only PC can also have the form of an adjective phrase (AdjP):

(1) a. He seemed *a very nice guy*.

    b. He seemed *very nice*.

(2) a. He met a very nice guy.

    b. *He met *very nice*.

In (1) with *seem, a very nice guy* is a predicative complement and hence can be replaced by the AdjP *very nice*. In (2) with *meet*, no such replacement is possible because *a very nice guy* is a direct object.

A bare role NP is a singular NP that is 'bare' in the sense of lacking the determiner which would elsewhere be required, and that denotes some kind of role, office, or position. A predicative complement can have the form of a bare role NP, but an object (O) can't:

(3) a. She became *the treasurer*.

    b. She knew *the treasurer*.

(4) a. She became treasurer.

    b. *She knew *treasurer*.

(3a) and (3b) examples are fine because an ordinary NP like *the treasurer* can be either a PC or an O. In (4), *treasurer* is a bare role NP, so it is permitted with *become*, which takes a PC, but not with *know*, which takes an object.

There is another test for these two functions. A typical object in an active clause corresponds to the subject of the passive clause that has the same meaning. A PC shows no such relationship. Consider the following examples:

(5) a. They arrested *a member of the party*.

  b. She remained *a member of the party*.

In (5a) *a member of the party* is a/an _____①_____ , but in (5b), *a member of the party* is a/an _____②_____ .

_____

_____

**14** Read the passage and fill in each blank with ONE word from the passage. Write your answers in the correct order. [2 points]

In their predicative use, adjectives (AdjPs) generally function as complement, not adjunct, in clause structure. Predicative complements occur in complex-intransitive and complex-transitive clauses:

(1) The suggestion is ridiculous.
    COMPLEX-INTRANSITIVE CLAUSE
(2) I consider the suggestion ridiculous.
    COMPLEX-TRANSITIVE CLAUSE

The adjective is related to a predicand (*the suggestion*), which is subject in the complex-intransitive construction, and object in the complex-transitive construction.

In addition to being a complement, licensed by the head, a predicative adjective phrase can be a/an ____①____. Compare, for example:

(3) a. Max was <u>unwilling to accept these terms</u>.
    b. <u>Unwilling to accept these terms</u>, Max resigned.

In (3a) the underlined AdjP is a complement licensed by the verb (*be*), but in (3b) it is a/an ____①____, —it is, more specifically, a supplement, detached by intonation or punctuation from the rest of the clause. It is nevertheless still ____②____, in that it is related to a predicand. We understand in (3b), no less than in (3a), that the unwillingness to accept these terms applies to *Max*.

In addition, there are two relatively minor functions in which adjectives are found. Postpositive adjectives function in NP structure as post-head internal modifier. There are three cases to consider:

(4) a. everything <u>useful</u>           somebody <u>rich</u>

    b. children <u>keen on sport</u>     a report <u>full of errors</u>

    c. the only modification <u>possible</u>   the ones <u>asleep</u>

The examples in (4a) have fused determiner-heads, making it impossible for the adjectives to occur in the usual pre-head position—compare *everything useful* with *every useful thing*. The modifiers in (4b) would be inadmissible in pre-head position because the adjective has its own post-head dependents; the postpositive construction provides a way of getting around the fact that such AdjPs cannot be used as attributive modifiers. A limited number of adjectives can occur postpositively without their own dependents and with a non-fused head noun, as in (4c): *possible* can also be attributive whereas *asleep* cannot.

Certain forms of AdjP occur right at the beginning of the NP, before the indefinite article *a*:

(5) a. [<u>How long</u> a delay] will there be?

    b. He'd chosen [<u>too dark</u> a colour].

(6) a. It seemed [<u>such</u> a bargain].

    b. [<u>What</u> a fool] I was.

**15** Read the passage <A> and the sentences in <B>, and follow the directions. [4 points]

---

| A |

There are some constraints on what categories you can move out of. Compare the following two sentences:

(1) a. What$_i$ did Bill claim [$_{CP}$ that he read $\underline{t_i}$ in the syntax book]?

    b. *What$_i$ did Bill make [$_{NP}$ the claim [$_{CP}$ that he read $\underline{t_i}$ in the syntax book]]?

*Note: the letter 't' stands for 'trace.'*

In (1a), *wh*-movement out of a complement clause is grammatical, but in (1b), movement out of a CP that is dominated by an NP is ungrammatical. This phenomenon has come to be known as the *complex NP island* phenomenon. NPs are islands. You cannot move out of an island, but you can move around within it.

    The second constraint is a *wh*-island. It is possible to the specifier of the main CP as in (2a). However, in (2b), look at what happens when you try to do both (move one *wh*-phrase to the embedded specifier, and the other to the main CP specifier). This sentence is ungrammatical. Movement of both, *what* and *how*, results in terrible ungrammaticality. Once you move a *wh*-phrase into the specifier of a CP, then that CP becomes an island for further extraction.

(2) a. [$_{CP}$ How$_k$ do [$_{TP}$ you think [John bought the sweater $\underline{t_k}$ ]]]?

    b. *[$_{CP}$ How$_k$ do [$_{TP}$ you wonder [$_{CP}$ what$_i$ [$_{TP}$ John bought $\underline{t_i}$ $\underline{t_k}$ ]]]]?

    The third constraint is a *subject condition*. Consider (3a); it has a CP in its subject position. When you try to *wh*-move the *wh*-equivalent to *several rioters* (*who* in (3b)), the sentence becomes ungrammatical. No constituent can be moved out of a sentential subject.

(3) a. [$_{TP}$ [$_{CP}$ That the police would arrest several rioters] was a certainty].

    b. *Who$_i$ was [$_{TP}$ [$_{CP}$ that the police would arrest $\underline{t_i}$ ] $t_{was}$ a certainty]?

---

**⊣ B ⊢**

(a) Whom would for Mary to kiss be strange?

(b) I wonder what John bought with the $20 bill.

(c) I wonder what John bought how.

(d) Who did you think kissed Mary?

(e) Who did you wonder what kissed?

(f) I asked what John kissed.

---

Identify TWO ungrammatical sentences in <B>, and explain why, stating what constraint each sentence violates, based on the description in <A>.

_____

_____

_____

_____

_____

**16** Read the passage and fill in each blank with ONE word from the passage. Write your answers in the correct order. [2 points]

---

The crucial distinction between adverbs and adjectives is a matter of function. Adjectives modify nouns whereas adverbs modify other categories. But there is another functional difference that is no less important. Most adjectives can function as predicative complement as well as noun modifier, but adverbs do not normally occur in this function. Again the difference is most easily seen by taking adjective-adverb pairs related by -ly:

(1) a. an *impressive* performance
   MODIFIER
   b. Her performance was *impressive*.
   PREDICATIVE COMPLEMENT
(2) a. She performed *impressively*.
   MODIFIER
   b. *Her performance was *impressively*.
   PREDICATIVE COMPLEMENT

*Impressive* and *impressively* can both function as modifier (here of noun and verb respectively), but only the adjective can be used predicatively. The same applies to those adverbs that are not derived from adjectives—they cannot be used as predicative complements:

(3) a. She *almost* succeeded.
   b. *Her success was *almost*.

We do find some overlap between the adjective and adverb categories—items that belong to both by virtue of occurring in both sets of functions. Compare:

(4) a. their *early* departure

    b. They departed *early*.

(5) a. that *very* day

    b. It's *very* good.

(6) a. I didn't play *well*.

    b. I don't feel *well*.

With some items, such as *early*, the meaning is the same, while in others it is different. The adjective *very*, for example, means something like "particular": it emphasises the identity of the day (that one, not any other). The adverb *very*, on the other hand, means approximately "extremely". Now compare the examples in (6): In (6a) the word *well* is used as the _____①_____ category, and in (6b) the word *well* is used as the _____②_____ category.

**17** Read the passage and fill in each blank with ONE word from the passage. Write your answers in the correct order. [2 points]

The reliable criterion for determining a word's category involves its distribution —the type of elements, especially functional categories, with which it can co-occur. For example, nouns can typically appear with a determiner, verbs with an auxiliary, and adjectives with a degree word in the patterns illustrated in (1).

(1)

| Category | Distributional property | Examples |
|---|---|---|
| Noun | occurrence with a determiner | *a car, the wheat* |
| Verb | occurrence with an auxiliary | *has gone, will stay* |
| Adjective | occurrence with a degree word | *very rich, too big* |

In contrast, a noun cannot occur with an auxiliary, and a verb cannot occur with a determiner or degree word.

(2) a. a noun with an auxiliary:        *will destruction*
    b. a verb with a determiner:      *the destroy*
    c. a verb with a degree word:     *very arrive*

Distributional tests for category membership are simple and highly reliable. They can be used with confidence when it is necessary to categorize unfamiliar words. Thanks to distributional and inflectional clues, it's often possible to identify a word's category without knowing its meaning. In (3), the poem "Jabberwocky," by Lewis Carroll, illustrates this point in a particularly brilliant way—it's interpretable precisely because readers are able to figure out that *gyre* is a/an _____①_____ (note the auxiliary verb to its left), that *borogoves* is a/an _____②_____ , and so on.

(3) 'Twas brillig, and the slithy toves
 Did <u>gyre</u> and gimble in the wabe;
 All mimsy were the <u>borogoves,</u>
 And the mome raths outgrabe.

 'Beware the Jabberwock, my son!
 The jaws that bite, the claws that catch!
 Beware the Jubjub bird, and shun
 The frumious Bandersnatch!"

**18** Read the passage and fill in each blank with ONE word from the passage. Use the SAME answer for both blanks. [2 points]

The head is the obligatory nucleus around which a phrase is built. For now, we will focus on four categories that can function as the head of a phrase—nouns (N), verbs (V), adjectives (A), and prepositions (P).

The type of specifier that appears in a particular phrase depends on the category of the _____. Determiners serve as the specifiers of Ns, while degree words serve as the specifiers of As and (some) Ps. A special class of preverbal adverbs, which we will call 'qualifiers', can function as the specifiers of Vs.

| TABLE 1. Some Specifiers | | |
|---|---|---|
| *Head* | *Specifier* | *Examples* |
| N | Determiner (Det) | |
| | *the, a, some,* | *a picture, the map,* |
| | *this, those...* | *those people, some guests* |
| V | Preverbal adverb (Adv) | |
| | *never, perhaps, often,* | *never quit, perhaps go,* |
| | *always, almost...* | *often failed, almost forgot* |
| A or P | Degree word (Deg) | |
| | *very, quite, more,* | *very smart, quite rich,* |
| | *almost...* | *almost in* |
| | | *Note: Almost* can be either an adverb or a degree word. |

Specifiers have no single semantic function or grammatical category. Structurally, though, they are alike in that they occur at the edge of a phrase. As illustrated in table 1 above, the specifier position in English is at a phrase's left margin (the beginning). Semantically, specifiers help to make the meaning of the _____ more precise. Hence, in *the books*, the determiner *the* indicates that the speaker has in mind specific books, and in *never overeat*, the qualifier *never* indicates non-occurrence of the event.

memo

# 02

PART Grammar

**01** Read the passage <A> and the sentences in <B>, and follow the directions. [4 points]

───┤ A ├───

The existential construction is characteristically used to introduce addressee-new entities into the discourse, and for this reason the displaced subject NP is usually indefinite. In many cases, the presence of an indefinite NP makes the existential pragmatically obligatory in that the corresponding non-existential is infelicitous as shown in (1):

(1) a. There is a serious flaw in your own argument.
    b. #A serious flaw is in your own argument.

Conversely, replacing an indefinite NP in an existential with a corresponding definite often results in infelicity as in (2):

(2) a. There is a more serious flaw, however, in your own argument.
    b. #There is the more serious flaw, however, in your own argument.

We will examine these two constraints in turn, and then consider very briefly a constraint on the occurrence as displaced subject of NPs containing certain quantifiers. With indefinite NPs, there is in general a preference for the existential. In many cases the non-existential is infelicitous. Compare (3) and (4), where the non-existentials are felicitous in (3) but not in (4):

(3) a. A furniture van was in the drive.

    b. There was a furniture van in the drive.

(4) a. #Sincerity was in her voice.

    b. There was sincerity in her voice.

When the indefinite NP denotes a physical entity, as in (3), both constructions are felicitous, but when it denotes an abstract entity, as in (4), the existential is required; the non-existential is infelicitous.

---

┤ B ├

(a) A hole is in my jacket.

(b) Two copies of Sue's thesis are on my desk.

(c) A peace delegation was in the region.

(d) An accident was in the studio.

(e) There's plenty of room on the top shelf.

(f) There was peace in the region.

**Identify TWO infelicitous sentences in <B>, and explain why, based on the description in <A>.**

_____

_____

_____

_____

_____

**02** Read the passage <A> and the sentences in <B>, and follow the directions. [4 points]

---

| A |

There are some constructions involving subject-auxiliary inversion.

I. Closed interrogatives: The subject occurs after an auxiliary verb instead of in its default preverbal position.

(1) a. *She speaks* French.　　　　　DEFAULT ORDER

　　 b. *Does she* speak French?　　　SUBJECT-AUXILIARY INVERSION

II. Open interrogatives: Here inversion accompanies the placement in prenuclear position of a non-subject interrogative phrase.

(2) a. *Who told* you that?　　　　　SUBJECT + VERB ORDER

　　 b. *What did she* tell you?　　　 SUBJECT-AUXILIARY INVERSION

III. Exclamatives: Here inversion is optional after a non-subject exclamative phrase in prenuclear position.

(3) a. What a fool I have been!

　　 b. What a fool have I been!

IV. Initial negative constituents: Inversion occurs with a negative non-subject element in prenuclear position. In (4a) we have the default subject + verb order when the negative is within the VP; inversion applies when it precedes the subject, as in (4b).

(4) a. He found *not one of them* useful.

　　 b. *Not one of them did he* find useful.

---

V. Initial *only*: *Only* is not a marker of negation. *He has only seen her once* (unlike *He hasn't seen her once*) is a positive clause. But it has a close connection with negation, for such an example entails that he has not seen her more than once. And this connection with negation is reflected in the fact that as far as inversion is concerned it behaves just like a negative.

(5) a. She had complained *only once*.
   b. *Only once had she* complained.

VI. Initial *so/such*: These behave like *only*, though they do not have any similar connection with negation.

(6) a. He would make *such* a fuss that we'd all agree.
   b. *Such* a fuss would he make that we'd all agree.

---
| B |

(a) He pointed out that not once she had complained.
(b) Not long afterwards, he moved to Bonn.
(c) Only a few days later, he moved to Bonn.
(d) Only two of them he found useful.
(e) Nowhere does he mention my book.

---

**Identify TWO ungrammatical sentences in \<B\>, and correct the sentences, based on the description in \<A\>.**

_____

_____

_____

_____

_____

**03** Read the passage <A> and the sentences in <B>, and follow the directions. [4 points]

─┤ A ├─

Negative and positive clauses differ in several respects in their syntactic distribution, i.e. in the way they combine with other elements in larger constructions. Consider the following examples:

(1) a. He didn't read the report, *not even* the summary.
    b. *He read the report, *not even* the summary.
(2) a. He didn't read the report, and *nor* did his son.
    b. He read the report, and *so* did his son.
(3) a. He didn't read it, *did he*?
    b. He read it, *didn't he*?

Negative clauses allow a continuation with *not even*, but positive clauses do not, as shown in (1). The connective adjunct *nor* (or *neither*) follows a negative clause, whereas the corresponding adjunct following a positive clause is *so*, as in (2). The third difference concerns the form of the confirmation 'tag' that can be appended, with (3a) taking a positive tag (*did he?*) and (3b) taking a negative one (*didn't he?*).

Clausal negation is negation that yields a negative clause, whereas subclausal negation does not make the whole clause negative. This distinction is seen very clearly when we apply the tests to such a pair of examples:

(4) a. We were friends *at no time*, and *neither* were our brothers.
    b. We were friends *in no time*, and *so* were our brothers.
(5) a. We were friends *at no time*, *were we*?
    b. We were friends *in no time*, *weren't we*?

**B**

(a) They were rather unfriendly, not even towards me.

(b) She works for nothing, does she?

(c) Not for the first time, she found his behaviour offensive, and so indeed did I.

(d) She's interested in nothing, is she?

(e) They scarcely seem to care, do they?

(f) I hardly have any friends, and neither do you.

Identify TWO ungrammatical sentences in <B>, and explain why, specifying the type of clauses (positive or negative), based on the description in <A>.

_____

_____

_____

_____

_____

**04** Read the passage <A> and the sentences in <B>, and follow the directions. [4 points]

---
┤ A ├
---

While *be* passives are the most common type of passive in English, passive sentences may also be formed with the verb *get*. They occur in the same range of forms as *be* passives, as the examples in (1) suggest.

(1) a. John *got arrested*.
   b. John *is getting arrested*.
   c. John *has gotten arrested*.

*Get* passives cannot occur with verbs that describe cognition. Compare (2a) with (2b).

(2) a. His solution to the problem *was known* by everyone.
   b. *His solution to the problem *got known* by everyone.

On the other hand, as with *be* passives, sentences that look like *get* passives may actually be active sentences. Sentence (3a) looks like a short *get* passive, but it is in fact an active sentence in which the past participle form *complicated* is an adjective. Here the verb *get* expresses the idea of becoming or of coming into a state or condition. Sentence (3a) may, for instance, be paraphrased as in (3b).

(3) a. His explanation is *getting complicated*.
   b. His explanation is *becoming complicated*.

Sentences in which *get* means "become" do not have active counterparts; that is, they cannot be changed into active sentences while maintaining the same meaning. Thus, (4a) does not mean the same thing as (4b).

(4) a. He got stuck in the elevator.
   b. Someone stuck him in the elevator.

In addition, there are some expressions such as *gradually, increasingly, less (and less),* and *more (and more).* These are adverbs modifying the participial adjective as in (5b). Insertion of these expressions is not possible with a passive sentence as in (6b).

(5) a. Education is getting specialized.

    b. Education is getting more and more specialized.

(6) a. We're getting paid.

    b. *We're getting more and more paid.

---

**⊣ B ⊢**

(a) His solution to the problem was understood by everyone.

(b) His solution to the problem got comprehended by everyone.

(c) Calm down! You're getting all worked up about a very trivial matter.

(d) He got increasingly frustrated by all the petty politics in his department, so he resigned.

(e) He got more reprimanded for not following company policy.

---

**Identify TWO ungrammatical sentences in <B>, and explain why, based on the description in <A>.**

_____

_____

_____

_____

_____

**05** Read the passage <A> and the sentences in <B>, and follow the directions. [4 points]

---

| A |

Stative verbs describe states or situations rather than actions. States are continuous and unchanging and can be emotional, physical, or cognitive.

(1) He *owns* a large blue car.

Activity verbs express actions that go on for a potentially indefinite period of time. The actions are constant (e.g., *run, swim, walk*) or involve an inherent change (e.g., *decline, develop, grow*).

(2) This plant is really *growing* fast.

Achievement verbs describe an action that occurs instantaneously—either *punctually* (e.g., *bounce, hit, kick*) or as *a change of state* (e.g., *find*). Change of state actions involve a preliminary activity that is terminated by the achievement verb.

(3) He *bounced* the ball several times.

Accomplishment verbs have a termination that is logical in terms of their action, as is the case, for example, with *build* (*a house*) or *paint* (*a picture*).

(4) She made a model of the house.

Lexical aspectual verbs (*stop, start, cease, resume,* etc.) pertain to the temporal structure of the eventuality described by its complement. Achievement expressions *finding the key* in (5b) do not occur as complement to the lexical aspectual verb *stop*, whereas process (activities and accomplishments) expressions do as in (5a).

(5) a. He stopped snoring/reading it. [processes]
   b. *He stopped finding the key. [achievements]

---

*In* phrases are acceptable in situations in which natural endpoints exist (accomplishments and achievements). By contrast, *for* phrases are acceptable in situations in which such endpoints do not exist (states and activities).

(6) a. Ron peeled the carrot *in three minutes* (*\*for three minutes*).
  b. Karen talked to Martha *for thirty minutes* (*\*in thirty minutes*).

---

**B**

(a) He began to work.
(b) He began to reach the summit.
(c) He began to write a letter.
(d) He was dying for an hour.
(e) It took him an hour to die.
(f) It took him an hour to walk a mile.

Identify **TWO** ungrammatical sentences in <B>, and explain why, specifying the type of verbs, based on the description in <A>.

_____

_____

_____

_____

_____

**06** Read the passage <A> and the sentences in <B>, and follow the directions. [4 points]

---| A |---

The default type of internal complement is an object (O). Whereas all canonical clauses contain a subject (S), they may or may not contain an O, depending on the nature of the verb.

(1) a. I *fainted*.                 [intransitive]

    b. They *destroyed* all the evidence. [transitive]

The category of transitivity applies to both clauses and verbs: *I fainted* is an intransitive clause because it contains no object, and *faint* is an intransitive verb because it has no object as dependent. More precisely, transitivity applies to uses of verbs, for although *faint* is always intransitive many verbs can occur either with or without an object. For example, *open* is intransitive in *The door opened* and transitive in *She opened the door*.

The transitive class of verbs and clauses can be divided into monotransitive and ditransitive subclasses according as there is just one object (a direct object) or two (indirect + direct):

(2) a. She *wrote* a novel.       [monotransitive]

    b. She *told* him the truth.      [ditransitive]

One further subtype of internal complement is the predicative complement (PC), illustrated by *quite competent* in:

(3) a. Ed *seemed* quite competent.      [complex-intransitive]

    b. She *considered* Ed quite competent. [complex-transitive]

The most important property of complements in clause structure is that they require the presence of an appropriate verb that licenses them. Compare:

(4) a. I don't *eat* any meat.

    b. *I *overate* meat.

(5) a. She *thought* him unreliable.

    b. *She *said* him unreliable.

In (4), the verb *eat* licenses an object *any meat*, but *overate* does not. Similarly, in (5), *think* licenses O + PC, but *say* does not. Different patterns of complementation are found with different subcategories (classes) of verb: 'intransitive', 'monotransitive', etc., are names of verb subcategories in this sense: *overeat* can't occur in (4b) because it doesn't belong to the class of verbs that license O, namely monotransitive verbs; it belongs to intransitive verbs. The verb *say* can't occur in (5b) because it does not belong to the class of verbs that license O + PC complementation, namely complex transitive verbs.

---

┤ B ├

(a) Ed seemed a decent guy.

(b) She alluded the letter.

(c) She read.

(d) She perused.

(e) He doesn't know whether or not she likes him.

(f) I'm inviting him, whether or not she likes him.

---

**Identify ALL and ONLY ungrammatical sentence(s) in <B>, and explain why, specifying the class of the verbs, based on the description in <A>.**

_____

_____

_____

_____

_____

**07** Read the passage <A> and the sentences in <B>, and follow the directions. [4 points]

---

┤ A ├

Verbal features, like features on nouns, may have syntactic consequences. For example, verbs can either describe events or states. The eventive/stative difference is mirrored in the syntax. Eventive sentences still sound natural when passivized, when expressed progressively, when used as imperatives, and with most manner adverbs as shown in (1):

(1) Eventives: Mary was kissed by John. / John is kissing Mary.

　　　　　　Kiss Mary! / John deliberately kissed Mary.

However, stative sentences sound unnatural when passivized, when expressed progressively, when used as imperatives, and with most manner adverbs as shown in (2). (The preceding "?" indicates the strangeness.):

(2) Statives: ?Mary is known by John. / ?John is knowing Mary.

　　　　　　?Know Mary! / ?John deliberately knows Mary.

Negation is a particularly interesting component of the meaning of some verbs. Expressions such as *ever, anymore,* and many more are ungrammatical in certain simple affirmative sentences, but grammatical in corresponding negative ones.

(3) a. *Mary will ever smile. (cf. Mary will not ever smile.)

　　b. *I can visit you anymore. (cf. I cannot visit you anymore.)

Such expressions are called negative polarity items because they require a negative element such as "not" elsewhere in the sentence. Consider these data:

---

(4) a. *John thinks that he'll ever fly a plane again.

    b. John refuses to ever fly a plane again.

This suggests that verbs such as *refuse*, but not *think* have "negative" as a component of their meaning. *Refuse* may be analyzed as 'intend not to.' The negative feature in the verb needs the negative polarity item *ever* to occur grammatically without the overt presence of *not*.

---

┤ B ├

(a) It's not worth a red cent.

(b) John despairs that he'll ever fly a plane again.

(c) John doubts that he'll sometimes fly a plane again.

(d) John deliberately likes oysters.

(e) John deliberately ate oysters.

(f) I don't like her much.

**Identify ONE ungrammatical sentence and ONE unnatural sentence respectively in <B>, and explain why, based on the description in <A>.**

_____

_____

_____

_____

_____

**08** **Read the passage and follow the directions.** [4 points]

─────────────── ┤ A ├ ───────────────

Tag questions consist of a tag, which is a short question form, attached to a stem, which is a statement. Opposite polarity tag questions are shown in (1) and (2). Notice that the subject in the tag corresponds to the subject in the stem. The subject in the tag must be a pronoun and agree in number and gender with the subject in the stem. The tag has the opposite value from the stem: if the stem is positive, then the tag is negative, as in (1); if the stem is negative, the tag is positive, as in (2):

(1) a. Betty can come.                    *Stem*

    b. Betty can come, *can't she*?        *Tag Question*

(2) a. They haven't finished it.            *Stem*

    b. They haven't finished it, *have they*? *Tag Question*

It is also possible to use a tag to form an imperative statement. Then, the imperative tag structure may have one of the following functions: a polite request, a suggestion, an urgency, a reminder, an admonition, or a feedback, etc.

(3) Turn out the light, will you?

(4) Get me a glass of water, would you?

Now consider each modal and its tag:

(5) You *had better* see a doctor at once, _____?

(6) We *ought to* go now, oughtn't/shouldn't we?

(7) You *used to* write to her, didn't you?

---

┤ B ├

(a) It follows that we won't have to pay any more, will we?

(b) The police had few real facts about the case, did they?

(c) Few of them liked it, did they?

(d) The others were taken by her, didn't she?

(e) The others she took, didn't they?

(f) I don't think it's legal, is it?

---

First, in <A>, fill in the blank with the appropriate TAG. Second, in <B>, identify TWO ungrammatical sentences on the basis of opposite polarity tag questions, and correct the sentences by revising the tag (Note that write the full sentence in your answer), based on the description in <A>.

---

 

---

 

---

 

---

 

---

 

---

**09** Read the passage <A> and the sentences in <B>, and follow the directions. [4 points]

---

┤ A ├

A number of words or larger expressions are sensitive to polarity in that they favour negative over positive contexts or vice versa. Words such as *any longer*, which normally occur only in negative statements but are themselves not negative, are called negative polarity items. On the other hand, words such as *somewhat* normally occur only in positive statements and are therefore referred to as positive polarity items. Compare:

(1) a. She doesn't live here *any longer*.

    b. *She lives here *any longer*.

(2) a. He was feeling *somewhat* sad.

    b. *He wasn't feeling *somewhat* sad.

We say, then, that *any longer* is negatively oriented, but *somewhat* is positively oriented.

It is not, however, simply a matter of negative vs positive contexts: *any longer*, for example, is found in interrogatives and the complement of conditional *if*. Consider the following examples:

(3) a. Will you be needing me *any longer?*

    b. If you stay *any longer* you will miss your bus.

These clauses have it in common with negatives that they are not being used to make a positive assertion: we use the term non-affirmative to cover these (and certain other) clauses. *Any longer* thus occurs in non-affirmative contexts, and we can also say that *any longer* is a non-affirmative item, using this as an alternative to negatively-oriented polarity-sensitive item.

---

━━━━━━━━━━━━━━━━━━━ B ━━━━━━━━━━━━━━━━━━━

(a) She's taking a stick with her in case she has any trouble on the way.

(b) If you ever touch me again, I'll scream.

(c) She works as hard as she ever did.

(d) Students who have any complaints should raise their hands.

(e) Her mother's not coming, too.

(f) I hardly have some friends, and neither do you.

Identify TWO ungrammatical sentences in <B>, and correct the sentences by revising the polarity item (Note that write the full sentence in your answer), based on the description in <A>.

_____

_____

_____

_____

_____

**10** Read the passage <A> and the sentences in <B>, and follow the directions. [4 points]

---

| A |

Determiners are words that precede head nouns in a noun phrase. There are different types of determiners, including the following: articles, cardinal numbers, ordinal numbers, multipliers, fractions, demonstrative determiners, possessive determiners, nouns as possessive determiners, quantifiers, partitives, etc.

Determiners fall into three groups that describe their relative order of appearance before head nouns: predeterminers, central determiners, and postdeterminers. This order represents a general tendency that applies to a sequence of prenominal modifiers. Note that different types of quantifiers can occupy different positions and are categorized accordingly. For example, *all* is a predeterminer, *every* is a central determiner, and *many* is a postdeterminer. The other determiner types (multipliers, articles, partitives, etc.) each occupy just one category. A head noun can be directly preceded by a member of any category, but if determiners from different categories are used, switching the order—predeterminer, central determiner, postdeterminer—results in ungrammaticality, as (1d) and (1h) demonstrate.

(1) a. Both sisters wanted to go.
  b. The sisters wanted to go.
  c. Both the sisters wanted to go.
  d. *The both sisters wanted to go.
  e. Those children are coming.
  f. Two children are coming.
  g. Those two children are coming.
  h. *Two those children are coming.

Moreover, determiners belonging to the same category generally cannot be combined with each other, as in (2).

(2) *the this book

Postdeterminers fall into two classes: (a) ordinals and (b) quantifiers and cardinals. When they can co-occur, items from (a) usually precede items from (b), as shown in (3).

(3) a. the first two poems
    b. John's last five attempts

---

┤ B ├

(a) my last few possessions
(b) her other many accomplishments
(c) one-third of her last salary check.
(d) his both sisters
(e) all twice the number

Identify TWO ungrammatical phrases, and explain why, specifying the category of each determiner (i.e., predeterminer, central determiner, postdeterminer), based on the description in <A>.

_____

_____

_____

_____

_____

**11** Read the passage <A> and the sentences in <B>, and follow the directions. [4 points]

---

**⊣ A ⊢**

Modality is centrally concerned with the speaker's attitude towards the factuality or actualisation of the situation expressed by the rest of the clause. We begin here with the distinction between *epistemic* and *deontic* modality, and then introduce a third category of *dynamic* modality. Three main kinds of modal meaning are distinguished in (1)—(3):

(1) a. You *must* come in immediately.

 b. You *can* have one more turn.

(2) a. It *must* have been a mistake.

 b. You *may* be right.

(3) a. Liz *can* drive better than you.

 b. I asked Ed to go but he *won't*.

In (1) *deontic modality* typically has to do with such notions as obligation and permission, or—in combination with negation—prohibition (cf. *You can't have any more*). In (2) *epistemic modality* qualifies the speaker's commitment to the truth of the modalised proposition. While *It was a mistake* represents an unqualified assertion, *It must have been a mistake* suggests that I am drawing a conclusion from evidence rather than asserting something of whose truth I have direct knowledge. And *You may be right* merely acknowledges the possibility that "You are right" is true. In (3) *dynamic modality* generally concerns the properties and dispositions of persons, etc., referred to in the clause, especially by the subject. Thus in (3) we are concerned with Liz's driving ability and Ed's willingness to go.

All three kinds of modality are commonly expressed by other means than by modal auxiliaries : lexical verbs (*You don't <u>need</u> to tell me*), adjectives (*You are <u>likely</u> to be fined*), adverbs (*<u>Perhaps</u> you are right*), nouns (*You have my <u>permission</u> to leave early*).

---

---

| B |

(a) She can stay as long as she likes.

(b) She can easily beat everyone else in the club.

(c) She can speak French.

---

First, identify ONE ambiguous sentence in <B>, and provide its two possible interpretations by ONLY stating its two different categories (i.e., the kinds of modality). Second, state the kinds of modality for the other two sentences in <B>, respectively, based on the description in <A>.

_____

_____

_____

_____

_____

**12** Read the passage <A> and the sentences in <B>, and follow the directions. [4 points]

---

| A |

A predicative complement (PC) commonly has the form of an NP, and in that case it contrasts directly with an object (O).

(1) a. Stacy *was* a good speaker.          *predicative complement*
    b. Stacy *found* a good speaker.        *object*
(2) a. Lee *became* a friend of mine.       *predicative complement*
    b. Lee *insulted* a friend of mine.     *object*

There is a sharp semantic distinction in elementary examples of this kind. The object NPs refer to participants in the situation: in each of (1b) and (2b) there are two people involved. The predicative NPs, however, do not refer to participants like this. There is only a single person involved in the (a) examples, the one referred to by the subject NP. The predicative complement NP denotes a property that is ascribed to this person.

PCs are most clearly illustrated by examples like (1a). The verb *be* here has basically no semantic content. The most important thing that *be* does in this example is to carry the preterite tense inflection that indicates reference to past time. The meaning of the clause is really just that Stacy spoke in an entertaining manner. So although *a good speaker* is syntactically an NP complement, it is semantically comparable to a predicate like *spoke well*. This is the basis for the term 'predicative complement': the complement typically represents what is predicated of the subject-referent in a way that is similar to that in which a whole predicate does.

A few verbs can take either a PC or an O, but with obvious differences in meaning as shown in (3) and (4):

(3) a. This *proved* a great asset.
    b. This *proved* my point.
(4) a. He *sounded* a decent guy.
    b. He *sounded* the gong.

Again, the objects denote participants but the predicative complements don't.

---

**B**

(a) Honestly, I felt a fool standing there alone on the platform.

(b) Suddenly, I felt a fool pushing in front of me on the platform.

---

Identify whether the NP *a fool* is a predicative complement or an object in each sentence in <B>, and explain why, discussing participants, based on the description in <A>.

---

**13** Read the passage <A> and the sentences in <B>, and follow the directions. [4 points]

---
⊣ A ⊢
---

Phrases linked by the coordinator *and* may express combinatory or segregatory meaning. The distinction is clearest with noun phrases. When the coordination is segregatory, we can paraphrase it by clause coordination as shown in (1).

(1) a. *John and Mary* know the answer.

b. = John knows the answer, and Mary knows the answer.

When it is combinatory we cannot do so, because the conjoins function in combination with respect to the rest of the clause, as in (2).

(2) a. *John and Mary* make a pleasant couple.

b. ≠ *John makes a pleasant couple, and Mary makes a pleasant couple.

Many conjoint noun phrases are in fact ambiguous between the two interpretations:

(3) *John and Mary* won a prize.

This may mean that they each won a prize or that the prize was awarded to them jointly.

Certain markers explicitly indicate that the coordination is segregatory. The adverb *respectively* indicates which constituents go with which in the two parallel sets of conjoint phrases. Sentence (4a) has only the segregatory meaning:

(4) a. *Thomas Arnold and his son Matthew* were *respectively* the greatest educator and the greatest critic of the Victorian age.

b. = Thomas Arnold was the greatest educator of the Victorian age, and his son Matthew was the greatest critic of the Victorian age.

Further examples of combinatory meaning are shown in (5).

(5) a. *Peter and Bob* separated (from each other).

b. *Mary and Paul* are just good friends.

c. *Paula and her brother* look alike.

d. *Law and order* is a primary concern of the new administration.

---

**⊢ B ⊢**

(a) Jill and Ben visited their uncles.

(b) Both John and Mary have won a prize.

(c) old and new furniture

(d) old and valuable books

---

Identify TWO unambiguous sentences or phrases in <B>, and stating the type of coordination (i.e., the combinatory or segregatory meaning), based on the description in <A>.

_____

_____

_____

_____

_____

**14** Read the passage <A> and the sentences in <B>, and follow the directions. [4 points]

---
| A |
---

Positive and negative clauses differ in the way they combine with other expressions in the structure of larger units. Here are the three major differences.

First, after a negative clause we can add a constituent introduced by *not even*, and it makes sense. This is not possible with positive clauses:

(1) a. *I have read your book, *not even* the introduction.
POSITIVE CLAUSE
 b. I haven't read your book, *not even* the introduction.
NEGATIVE CLAUSE

The addition in (1b) is interpreted as "*I haven't even read the introduction*". The *not* isn't obligatory (cf. *I haven't read your book, even the introduction*) but the crucial point is that it can occur in the negative clause (1b) but is impossible in the positive as in (1a).

Second, when we add a related clause of the same polarity, the positive pair may be linked by *so*, the negative pair by *neither* or *nor*:

(2) a. I have read your book, and *so* have my students.
POSITIVE CLAUSE
 b. I haven't read your book, and *neither* have my students.
NEGATIVE CLAUSE

Switching the connectives leads to ungrammaticality: *I have read your book and neither have my students; *I haven't read your book and so have my students.

A common device for seeking confirmation of what one says is to add a truncated interrogative clause known as a tag (*reversed polarity tags*). It generally consists of just an auxiliary verb + personal pronoun subject, and its polarity is the reverse of that of the clause to which it is attached:

(3) a. They have read my book, *haven't they*?
POSITIVE CLAUSE + NEGATIVE TAG
 b. They haven't read my book, have they?
NEGATIVE CLAUSE + POSITIVE TAG

In (3a) the negative tag *haven't they?* attaches to the positive clause, while in (3b) the positive tag *have they?* attaches to the negative clause.

---

**| B |**

(a) He was unkind, and so was Sue.

(b) He wasn't kind, and neither was Sue.

(c) He was unkind, not even to me.

(d) He wasn't kind, not even to me.

(e) Few of them realised it was a hoax, didn't they?

(f) There's scarcely any food left, is there?

---

**Identify TWO ungrammatical sentences in <B>, and explain why, based on the description in <A>.**

_____

_____

_____

_____

_____

**15** Read the passage <A> and the sentences in <B>, and follow the directions. [4 points]

---| A |---

Several form criteria distinguish nonrestrictive relative clauses from their restrictive counterparts.

Nonrestrictive relative clauses have commas around them, as in (1a). Restrictive relative clauses must not be separated by commas, as shown in (1b).

(1) a. My sister, *who lives in Seoul*, is a chemist.
  b. My sister *who lives in Seoul* is a chemist.

Nonrestrictive relative clauses may modify an entire sentence, that is, a preceding independent clause, and must be set off from the main clause by a comma, as in (2a). Restrictive relative like (2b) cannot modify an entire sentence, and may only modify noun phrases.

(2) a. Professor Fish gave everyone an A, *which was just fine with Alice.*
  b. *Professor Fish gave everyone an A *which was just fine with Alice.*

Nonrestrictive relative clauses may not modify *any, every,* or *no* + noun or indefinite pronouns such as *anyone, everyone,* or *no one*, as shown by (3a); restrictive relatives may, as shown in (3b).

(3) a. *Any man, *who goes back on his word*, is no friend of mine.
  b. Any man *who goes back on his word* is no friend of mine.

Nonrestrictive relative clauses cannot be stacked. Stacking results in ungrammatical sentences like (4a). Restrictive relatives can be stacked, as in (4b).

(4) a. *They gave job to Rob, *who is very qualified, who starts next month.*
  b. I really like that car *that you have that your wife is always zipping around town in.*

---
**B**
---

(a) Bill, who is a lawyer, was not impressed by Professor Fish's arguments.

(b) Triangles, which have three sides, are fascinating.

(c) Susan is afraid of dogs which doesn't surprise me at all.

(d) The 2022 winners for Literature, whose books have sold well, who everyone likes, are all from Oxford.

(e) The books which John has consulted are out of date.

(f) The tornado which struck the town destroyed several homes.

First, identify TWO ungrammatical sentences in <B>, and explain why, based on the description in <A>.

_____

_____

_____

_____

_____

**16** Read the passage <A> and the sentences in <B>, and follow the directions. [4 points]

---
┤ A ├
---

There are some syntactic circumstances that can make preposition stranding almost or completely impossible.

(1) a. *This is the safe [which the key to was stolen].　　STRANDED

　　b. This is the safe [to which the key was stolen].　　FRONTED

(2) a. *I have a lecture ending at two [which I'll be free all day after].　STRANDED

　　b. I have a lecture ending at two [after which I'll be free all day].　FRONTED

(3) a. *What way am I annoying you in?　　STRANDED

　　b. In what way am I annoying you?　　FRONTED

In (1a) the stranded preposition occurs within a subject NP (the subject of *was stolen*). That is fairly clearly ungrammatical. In (2) the PP is in adjunct rather than complement function, specifically an adjunct of time. There is a tendency for the stranding construction to be avoided in adjuncts generally. With adjuncts of place it is not so strong, so you may hear sentences like *?That's the town [which I first met her in]*; but the tendency is quite strong for many other adjuncts, like adjuncts of time or duration. In (3) this is more than just a tendency with some fixed adjunct expressions: the manner adjunct *in what way*, as in (3b), can never be split up by stranding.

There are also syntactic circumstances that make the nonstranded version, with preposition fronting, almost or completely impossible.

(4) a. That depends on [who I give it to].　　STRANDED

　　b. *That depends on [to whom I give it].　　FRONTED

(5) a. What did you hit me for?　　STRANDED

　　b. *For what did you hit me?　　FRONTED

(6) a. Which metals does it consist of?　　STRANDED

　　b. ?Of which metals does it consist?　　FRONTED

In (4) the bracketed clause containing the preposition is a subordinate interrogative clause functioning as complement to a preposition (*on*); here stranding is obligatory. In (5) we have the idiom *what for* meaning "why", where *for* is never fronted. The verb *consist* in (6) is one of those that license a PP complement with a specified preposition, and there is a fairly strong preference for the stranding construction with such verbs. The (3b) version isn't grammatically forbidden, but it sounds very stiff and formal.

---

┤ B ├

(a) What circumstances would you do a thing like that under?

(b) We can't agree on for which grant we should apply.

(c) That wasn't the one which we were looking out for.

(d) This is the sort of English which I will not put up with.

(e) What are you asking for?

**Identify TWO ungrammatical sentences in <B>, and explain why, based on the description in <A>.**

_____

_____

_____

_____

_____

**17** Read the passage &lt;A&gt; and the sentences in &lt;B&gt;, and follow the directions. [4 points]

---

**A**

Declarative content clauses mostly function as complement of a verb, noun, adjective, or preposition. The range of complement functions is illustrated in (1):

(1) a. <u>That they refused</u> didn't surprise us.        SUBJECT
    b. It didn't surprise us <u>that they refused</u>.        EXTRAPOSED SUBJECT
    c. I realise <u>that you feel insulted</u>.        INTERNAL COMP OF VERB
    d. You can't ignore the fact <u>that he was drunk</u>.        COMP OF NOUN
    e. I'm glad <u>that you could come</u>.        COMP OF ADJECTIVE
    f. You can go provided <u>that you are careful</u>.        COMP OF PREPOSITION

In (1a), the content clause is subject. It is licensed by *surprise*. In (1b), we see a much more frequent kind of case than (1a), but synonymous with it: the subordinate clause is extraposed. In (1c), the content clause is internal complement to the verb *realise* of a clause. In the next two, the content clause is complement to the noun *fact* in (1d) and the adjective *glad* in (1e). Finally, in (1f), the content clause is complement of a preposition.

Like declaratives, interrogative content clauses usually function as complements, as illustrated in (2):

(2) a. <u>What caused the delay</u> remains unclear.        SUBJECT
    b. It remains unclear <u>what caused the delay</u>.        EXTRAPOSED SUBJECT
    c. I've discovered <u>where they keep the key</u>.        INTERNAL COMP OF VERB
    d. The question <u>whether it's legal</u> was ignored.        COMP OF NOUN
    e. I'm uncertain <u>what we can do about it</u>.        COMP OF ADJECTIVE
    f. That depends on <u>how much time we have</u>.        COMP OF PREPOSITION

The range of functions is almost like that illustrated for declaratives in (1). One difference from declaratives, however, is that prepositions are often optional; for example, we could add *of* after *question* in (2d), and we could omit *on* in (2f). There is only partial overlap between the items that license declaratives and those that license interrogatives. For example, some verbs accept both declaratives and interrogatives, and others accept only declaratives or only interrogatives.

┤ B ├

(a) I know she's right.

(b) I know what he did.

(c) I insist that she's right.

(d) I insist what he did.

(e) I inquire that he's ill.

(f) I inquired what he did.

In <B>, identify TWO ungrammatical sentences, and explain why, based on the description in <A>.

_____

_____

_____

_____

_____

**18** Read the passage <A> and the sentences in <B>, and follow the directions. [4 points]

---
┤ A ├
---

Adverbs that modify verbs can occur in several positions in a sentence but never between a verb and its object, as the comparison in (1) show.

(1) a. He *often* takes the metro.
  b. *He takes *often* the metro.

The possible positions that an adverb that modifies a verb can occupy are the following: sentence initial, before a main verb (including between an auxiliary or modal and a main verb), between the main verb and a following element such as a PP, and sentence final.

Fewer types of adverbs are acceptable in sentence-initial position. Prominent among them are time adverbs, as in (2a), and certain frequency adverbs, as in (2b). But others, such as *always*, cannot appear in initial position, as shown by (2c).

(2) a. *Earlier* he told us a different story.
  b. *Sometimes* she comes in over an hour late.
  c. **Always* she speaks English to her mother.

Adverbs of a given type may differ considerably in the positions in which they can occur. For example, although many degree adverbs occur in sentence-final position, others, such as *almost*, cannot occur sentence finally, as shown in (3a). This variation is especially evident with frequency adverbs. *sometimes* can occur in sentence finally and sentence initially. In contrast, *always* cannot appear in initial position, as shown by (2c), except in imperative sentences, as in (3b), and sounds odd in sentence-final position, as in (3c).

(3) a. *He fainted *almost*.
  b. *Always* remember to call your mother once a week.
  c. ?She speaks English to her mother *always*.

Particularly worth mentioning in this context are negative frequency adverbs. When a negative frequency adverb appears sentence initially, the rule of subject-aux inversion must be applied, as shown in (4).

(4) a. *Never have I* seen anything as brilliant as that.
    b. *\*Never I have* seen anything as brilliant as that.

---

┤ B ├

(a) She caught up nearly.
(b) She enjoyed the party tremendously.
(c) The price of stocks rose enormously in the late 1990s.
(d) Not long ago there was a rainstorm.
(e) Seldom John forgets to do his taxes on time.
(f) Hardly had he arrived when she started complaining.

---

**Identify TWO ungrammatical sentences in <B>, and explain why, stating the type of adverbs, based on the description in <A>.**

_____

_____

_____

_____

_____

**19** **Read the passage <A> and follow the directions.** [4 points]

| A |

In general, there is little difficulty in distinguishing verbs from prepositions. Verbs usually function as predicator in clause structure, and in finite or infinitival clauses they are easily recognizable as verbs by this function. There is, for example, no doubt about the status of *follow* as a verb in (1):

(1) a. We always *follow* the manual.

   b. I advise you to *follow* the manual.

There are, however, a number of prepositions which have the same shape as the gerund-participle or past participle forms of verbs. These are cases where historical change led to a word taking on the properties of a preposition in addition to its original verbal properties, so that it now belongs to both categories. Two examples, with the relevant word underlined, are given in (2) and (3):

(2) a. Following the meeting, there will be a reception.

   b. Liz did remarkably well, given her inexperience.

(3) a. Following the manual, we tried to figure out how to assemble the unit.

   b. Liz was given only three months to live.

Predicative adjectives have to be related to a predicand, and verbs in predicator function have to be related to a subject, either overt or understood. In (3a) *following* is predicator in a gerund-participial clause functioning as adjunct; this clause itself has no overt subject, but an understood subject is retrievable from the subject of the main clause: the sentence implies that *WE* were following the manual. Example (3b) is a passive clause, and *Liz* is the subject—compare the active version *They gave Liz only three months to live*.

However, in (2), there is no such predicational relationship to a subject. The underlined words derive historically from verbs, but they have developed meanings distinct from the verbal ones, and in this use these words belong to the preposition category. *Following* means "after", and *given X* means roughly "if we take X into account".

**Identify whether each underlined word in <B> below is a preposition or a verb, and explain why, based on the description in <A>.**

---
**B**

(4) <u>Owing</u> so much to the bank, farmers can't afford any luxuries.

(5) <u>Owing</u> to the drought, many farms are going bankrupt.

---

_____

_____

_____

_____

_____

**20** **Read the passage <A> and follow the directions.** [4 points]

┤ A ├

Although most adjectives can be used both attributively and predicatively, there are nevertheless many that are restricted to one or other of these two uses:

(1) a. a *huge* hole
   b. *utter* nonsense
   c. *the *asleep* children
(2) a. The hole was *huge*.
   b. *That nonsense was *utter*.
   c. The children were *asleep*.

*Huge* illustrates the default case, where the adjective appears both attributively and predicatively. *Utter* is an exceptional case: an attributive-only adjective, which can't be used predicatively, as shown in (2b). *Asleep* is the opposite kind of exception; it can occur predicatively but not attributively: it is a never-attributive adjective.

NPs containing a sample of other adjectives that are attributive-only are given in (3):

(3) the *sole* survivor        the *eventual* winner      her *former* husband
   our *future* prospects      the *main* problem          a *mere* child
   the *only* drawback         their *own* fault           the *principal* advantage

Here are some further examples of predicative uses of never-attributive adjectives:

(4) a. The house was *ablaze*.
   b. Something was *amiss*.
   c. It is *liable* to flood.
   d. I was utterly *bereft*.

---

**B**

(a) Corruption was rife.

(b) The heir is lawful.

(c) It was devoid of interest.

(d) the content baby

(e) a veritable jungle

(f) the putative father

---

Identify TWO ungrammatical sentences or phrases in <B>, and explain why, specifying the type of adjectives, based on the description in <A>.

_____

_____

_____

_____

_____

**21** **Read the passage and follow the directions.** [4 points]

---

**A**

Two information-structuring principles help determine the choice of pattern in sentences with an indirect object. According to the given-new contract, information that has been mentioned in the previous context and is therefore given, or old, generally comes before new information in a sentence. In sentences with an indirect object, if the indirect object is given information, the dative movement pattern is preferred; otherwise it is inappropriate.

(1) Susan: You know, I can't figure out what to get John for his birthday. Any ideas?

    Ann: <u>Give him a CD</u>. You know how much he likes music.

If the direct object is given information, the prepositional pattern is preferred.

(2) I have two pistols here, a Colt .45 and a German Luger. Here are the rules of the duel. I'm going to <u>give the Colt to Fred and the Luger to Alex</u>. They will then walk in opposite directions for 20 paces, turn, and wait for my command to fire.

According to the end weight principle, a long, complex ("heavy") noun phrase can be moved to the end of the sentence to increase comprehension and avoid ambiguity as in (3b). However, in (3a), in the prepositional pattern, the heavy direct object NP in the middle of the sentence is inappropriate.

(3) a. ?Abby gave <u>foot-long frankfurters that had been roasted over an open hickory fire</u> to the kids.

    b. Abby gave the kids <u>foot-long frankfurters that had been roasted over an open hickory fire</u>.

---

---

**B**

(a) When Alice arrived at the auditorium, she saw that hall was packed. But she wasn't worried about finding somewhere to sit because she was sure that John had saved a seat for her.

(b) A: There were two more items on the table, a package and a letter. Do you remember who you sent them to?

   B: We sent the package to a Mr. Green and the letter to a Mrs. Harrison.

(c) John reported to the police the theft of his new sky-blue BMW convertible with the heated leather seats and the yellow fog lights.

(d) The mediator recommended an alternative solution for eliminating the barriers to a negotiated settlement of the dispute to the strikers.

---

In <B>, identify TWO inappropriate discourses or sentences due to the information-structuring principles, and explain why, based on the description in <A>.

_____

_____

_____

_____

_____

**22** Read the passage <A> and the sentences in <B>, and follow the directions. [4 points]

---

| A |

A fair number of words or larger expressions are polarity-sensitive in the sense that they occur readily in clauses of one polarity but not of the other.

(1) a. I have *some* objections to make.

    b. *I don't have *some* objections to make.

(2) a. *I have *any* objections to make.

    b. I don't have *any* objections to make.

*Some* is by no means wholly excluded from negative clauses; it has positive orientation. Conversely *any* has negative orientation; it occurs freely in negatives but is excluded from positives. What excludes *any* from (2a) is not just that the clause is positive; it is also declarative. If we look instead at an interrogative clause, we find it is freely admitted:

(3) a. Have you *any* objections to make?

    b. Who has *any* objections to make?

We refer to items like *any*, therefore, as non-affirmatives. The verb *affirm* contrasts with question and hence suggests declarative; the adjective *affirmative* is a synonym of positive. In general, then, the restriction on non-affirmative items is that they cannot occur in clauses that are both declarative and positive.

It is not only negatives and interrogatives that allow non-affirmative items to appear. They are also found in a number of other constructions, as illustrated in (4). Sentence (4) has a semantic affinity with negation. Because of the *too* in (4), we understand that she did NOT say anything.

(4) She was too taken aback to say *anything*.

In addition, the versions with nonverbal negation can often be paraphrased using verbal negation, as illustrated in (5).

| (5) Nonverbal Negation | Verbal Negation |
|---|---|
| a. We found *no* mistakes. | We *didn't* find *any* mistakes. |
| b. There is *no one* here. | There *isn't anyone* here. |

---

┤ B ├

(i) a. She ran faster than she had ever run before.

b. We slipped away without anyone noticing.

c. He denies I ever told him.

d. We were unaware of some hostility.

(ii) a. We knew neither of them.

b. He never apologises.

---

In <B>, first, identify ONE ungrammatical sentence in (i), and explain why. Second, in (ii), for each sentence with nonverbal negation, provide an equivalent sentence with verbal negation, based on the description in <A>.

_____

_____

_____

_____

_____

**23** Read the passage <A> and the sentences in <B>, and follow the directions. [4 points]

---
 ⊢ A ⊢
---

There is, in fact, a "middle voice," intermediate between active and passive voices. The middle voice allows the subject of a sentence to be nonagentive, as in the passive voice, but the morphology of the verb to be in the active voice.

(1) a. Her high C shattered the glass. (active voice)
   b. The glass was shattered by her high C. (passive voice)
   c. The glass shattered. (middle voice)

English uses special verbs to express spontaneous occurrences. Such verbs, which allow the object of a transitive clause to be a subject of an intransitive clause without changing voice, are called *ergative*, or *change-of-state verbs*. Ergative verbs, such as *shatter*, can appear in all three voices and thus take either agents or undergoers of the action (sometimes called patients or themes) as subjects. The idea of an ergative verb is new for ESL/EFL students.

(2) The window broke.

The students argue that windows can't break themselves, and thus they feel obliged to use the passive or express an agent, as shown in (3).

(3) a. The window was broken.
   b. Someone broke the window.

While such sentences are not wrong, of course, the active voice sentence with a nonagentive subject is perfectly permissible in English with ergative verbs. The difference between the two options is that the passive sentence suggests the existence of an agent, even if the agent is not explicit. The verb used ergatively does not permit an agent; thus, it cannot be used with a by-phrase. The following are situations in which ergative sentences are needed: (a) when the focus is on the change of state, and the agent is irrelevant; (b) when it is natural to expect change to occur (i.e., physical, social, or psychological "laws" seem to be involved); (c) when there are so many possible causes for a change of state that it would be misleading to imply a single agent, and so on.

---

┤ B ├

(a) The expression on her face suddenly changed from sadness to rage.

(b) The name of the company was changed to avoid confusion with another company.

(c) The weather suddenly changed.

(d) The ice on the pond was melted earlier than usual.

(e) It is ridiculous that most women in developing countries suffered from extreme poverty.

(f) The window broke by the gang.

---

In <B>, identify TWO inappropriate sentences, and explain why, based on the description in <A>.

_____

_____

_____

_____

_____

**24** **Read the passage and follow the directions.** [4 points]

---
| A |
---

There are many verbs that take a PP complement. They are called *prepositional verbs*, and occur in a range of constructions, as illustrated in (1):

(1) a. He asked for water.

    b. We came across some errors.

(2) He'll treat me to lunch.

(3) That counts as satisfactory.

(4) They rated it as a success.

The examples in (1) are all intransitive. The example in (2) is transitive—the PP complement follows an NP object. In (3)—(4) the complement of the preposition is predicative.

Some verb + preposition combinations are *fossilised*, in the sense that they don't permit any variation in their relative positions. Now consider the following examples:

(5) NON-FOSSILISED

    a. I asked for some information.

    b. the information [which I asked for]

    c. the information [for which I asked]

(6) FOSSILISED

    a. I came across some letters.

    b. the letters [which I came across]

    c. *the letters [across which I came]

In the stranded preposition construction, *which* occupies front position in the clause, and the preposition occurs after the verb, separated from its complement, as shown in (5b) and (6b). In the fronted preposition construction, the preposition is fronted along with its complement *which*, as in (5c) and (6c). Both variants are permitted with *ask for*, but only the first is permitted with *come across*: (6c) is not grammatical. The reason is that fossilisation doesn't allow any departure from the fixed order of verb + preposition.

---

**┤ B ├**

(i) a. He accused her of a crime.

    b. the crime which he accused her of

    c. the crime of which he accused her

(ii) a. I let him off some work.

    b. the work which I let him off

    c. the work off which I let him

---

In <B>, identify ONE ungrammatical phrase, and then explain why, ONLY based on the description in <A>.

_____

_____

_____

_____

_____

**25** **Read the passage and follow the directions.** [4 points]

─────────────────────────────┤ A ├─────────────────────────────

In the light of the syntactic distribution, the prepositional phrases readily modify nouns or function as predicative complement to verbs like *be*; the adverb phrases are used for modifying verbs, adjectives, and other adverbs.

Prepositions take a range of complement types comparable to that of verbs:

| | |
|---|---|
| (1) a. I was talking [to <u>a friend</u>]. | Object NP Complement |
|     b. I regard her [as <u>a friend</u>]. | Predicative Complement |
|     c. I stayed [until <u>after lunch</u>]. | PP Complement |
|     d. I hadn't met her [till <u>recently</u>]. | ADVP Complement |
|     e. We agreed [on <u>how to proceed</u>]. | Clause Complement |

As with verbs, we need to make a distinction between objects and predicative complements: *the friend* examples in (1a) and (1b) contrast in the same way as those in (2):

| | |
|---|---|
| (2) a. I was visiting [a friend]. | Object NP Complement |
|     b. I consider her [a friend]. | Predicative Complement |

The crucial syntactic difference is that a predicative can have the form of an AdjP (*I regard her as very bright*, where *as* is the preposition) or a bare role NP (*They elected her as treasurer*).

There are a handful of PreP + AdvP combinations, which could be seen as prepositions taking adverb phrases as complements. But there are very few: in addition to the one in (1d), we find *before long, for later, until recently,* and a very few others. They are basically fixed phrases (for example, we get *before long* but not *\*after long*).

Now consider the following sentence:

(3) She arrived <u>two weeks ago</u>.

What is the categorial status of *ago*? Is it an adverb or a preposition? The order here reflects the historical origin of *ago*: it derives from the form *agone*, containing the past participle of *go*. Originally *two weeks ago* meant something like "two weeks gone", i.e., located at a point in time that is now two weeks gone by into the past.

---

**⊢ B ⊢**

(i) a. I took him for <u>dead</u>.

　　b. It won't last for <u>long</u>.

(ii) a. That was <u>two weeks ago</u>.

　　b. I recall his behaviour <u>two weeks ago</u>.

---

In <B>, first, in (i) identify each underlined part with specifying a range of complement types as shown in (1). Second, in (ii) identify whether the phrase *two weeks ago* is the prepositional phrase or the adverb phrase, and explain why, discussing the characteristic of the syntactic distribution, ONLY based on the description in <A>.

_____

_____

_____

_____

_____

# 03

PART **Phonetics &
Phonology**

Answer Key p.45

**01** Read the passage and fill in the blank ① with the ONE most appropriate word and the blank ② with ONE word from the passage. Write your answers in the correct order. [2 points]

The abstract underlying units are known as phonemes while the predictable surface elements are known as allophones. Speakers of most accents of English habitually utter both aspirated and unaspirated voiceless stops. The following English data exhibit both of these.

(1) Aspirated and unaspirated voiceless stops in English

| | | | |
|---|---|---|---|
| (a) ['pʰuːɫ] | 'pool' | (b) [ə'pʰɪə] | 'appear' |
| (c) ['spɜːt] | 'spurt' | (d) [də'spaɪt] | 'despite' |
| (e) ['tʰɒp] | 'top' | (f) [ə'tʰæk] | 'attack' |
| (g) ['stɒp] | 'stop' | (h) [də'stɹɔɪ] | 'destroy' |
| (i) ['kʰɪlɪŋ] | 'killing' | (j) [ə'kʰɹuː] | 'accrue' |
| (k) ['skoʊɫd] | 'scold' | (l) [dɪ'skʌvə] | 'discover' |

English speakers systematically produce aspiration on voiceless stops at the beginning of a _____①_____ syllable as in *killing* and *accrue*, but not on voiced stops. However, voiceless stops are unaspirated when preceded by a voiceless alveolar fricative, as in *spurt*. That is, in these data, wherever the unaspirated voiceless stops appear, the aspirated ones do not, and vice versa; the distribution of unaspirated and aspirated stops is mutually exclusive.

Furthermore, if we take the stops [t] and [tʰ] in the English data, it is clear that they are phonetically similar: both are stops, both are voiceless, both are alveolar. And yet, for most speakers of English, the alveolar stops in *still* and *till* sound the same, despite the fact that the former is unaspirated and the latter aspirated. That is, the two types of stops are interpreted as belonging to a single mental category. The English speaker interprets the six phonetic segments [p], [pʰ], [t], [tʰ], [k] and [kʰ] in terms of only three _____②_____: /p/, /t/ and /k/.

**02** **Read the passage and follow the directions.** [4 points]

---| A |---

Nearly all English nouns have a plural form: *cat/cats, dog/dogs, fox/foxes*. Take a look at the pronunciation of the plurals of the following nouns in (1):

(1) a. cab      cad      bag      love      lathe

    b. cap      cat      back      cuff      faith

    c. bus      dish      buzz      garage      match

    d. child      ox      mouse      criterion      sheep

The final sound of the plural nouns in (1a) is a [z]—a voiced alveolar fricative. For (1b) the plural ending is an [s]—a voiceless alveolar fricative. And for (1c) it's [əz]. These are the examples of a morpheme with different pronunciations. Note that there is a regularity in (1a), (1b), and (1c) that does not exist in (1d).

Apparently, the distribution of plural allomorphs in English is conditioned by the final segment of the singular form. We can make the chart by considering just the final segment as in (2).

(2) **Allomorph**         **Environment**

     [z]             After [b], [d], [g], [v], [ð]

     [s]             After [p], [t], [k], [f], [θ]

     [əz]           After [s], [ʃ], [z], [ʒ], [ʧ]

We now want to understand why the English plural follows this pattern. Questions of this type is answered by inspecting the phonetic properties of the conditioning segments. Such an inspection reveals that the segments that trigger the [əz] plural share the same property. Considering the rest of the segments, the voiceless segments take the [s] plural, and the voiced segments take the [z] plural.

A concise way to express the rules is to assume that the basic or underlying form of the plural morpheme is /z/, with the meaning "plural." This is the "default" pronunciation. The rules tell us when the default does not apply:

Rule 1. Insert a [ə] before the plural morpheme /z/ when _____.

Rule 2. Change the plural morpheme /z/ to a voiceless [s] when a regular noun ends with a voiceless sound.

If the rules are applied in reverse order, an incorrect phonetic form of the plural would be derived.

⊣ B ⊢

series    stomach    mirage    epoch    moose    bush    species

Based on <A>, first, identify TWO words in <B> whose plural endings are the same as (1c) in <A>. Second, complete the rule 1 in <A> by filling in the blank with the condition.

_____

_____

_____

_____

_____

**03** **Read the passage and follow the directions.** [4 points]

> For many speakers of American English, words such as *letter, atom, header,* and *ladder* are pronounced as [lɛɾɚ], [æɾəm], [hɛɾɚ], [læɾɚ], respectively. This process, which is known as flapping, converts an alveolar stop to a voiced flap.
>
> The most conductive environment for this process is intervocalic, when the second syllable is not stressed. Thus, while *attic* [ǽɾɪk] has a flap, *attack* [əthǽk] does not. This pattern is also revealed in morphologically related but prosodically different word pairs. Thus, while alveolar stops in the left column below undergo this process, they do not do so in the morphologically related words in the right column.
>
> (1) atom [æɾəm]          atomic [ətɑmɪk]
>
>     metal [mɛɾəl]          metallic [mətælɪk]
>
>     Italy [ɪɾəli]          Italian [ɪtæljən]
>
>     autumn [ɔɾəm]          autumnal [ətʌmnəl]
>
>     rhetoric [ɹɛɾəɹɪk]          rhetorical [ɹətɔɹəkəl]
>
>     notable [noɾəbl]          notation [noteʃən]
>
>     addict [æɾɪkt]          addiction [ədɪkʃən]
>
> Thus, the generalization could be assumed as in (2).
>
> (2) Alveolar stops /t/ and /d/ become an alveolar flap [ɾ] when they occur between two vowels; the first of which is stressed and the second of which is unstressed.
>
> This condition also includes the secondary stress; thus, we don't have flapping in words in which /t/ targets are in syllables with secondary stress, as shown in (3).
>
> (3) sanitary [sǽnətɛ̀ɹɪ]    sabotage [sǽbətɑ̀ʒ]    latex [létɛ̀ks]

Although in a great majority of cases of flapping the first vowel is stressed, this is not a necessary condition. Now consider the following examples:

(4) nationality [næʃənæləɾi]
    calamity [kəlæməɾi]
    sorority [səɾɔɾɛ́ɾi]

In (4) flapping occurs between two _____ vowels.

First, fill in the blank with ONE word from the passage. Second, based on the passage, state the only condition related to stress where alveolar stops cannot be flapped.

_____

_____

_____

_____

_____

**04** Read the passage and fill in each blank with ONE word from the passage. Write your answers in the correct order. [2 points]

A phonetic feature is distinctive when the + value of that feature in certain words contrasts with the − value of that feature in other words. At least one feature value difference must distinguish each phoneme from all the other phonemes in a language.

Because the phonemes /b/, /d/, and /g/ contrast in English by virtue of the place of articulation features—*labial, alveolar,* and *velar*—these place features are also distinctive in English. The distinctive features of the voiced stops in English are shown in the following:

|          | b | m | d | n | g | ŋ |
|----------|---|---|---|---|---|---|
| **Voiced**   | + | + | + | + | + | + |
| **Labial**   | + | + | − | − | − | − |
| **Alveolar** | − | − | + | + | − | − |
| **Velar**    | − | − | − | − | + | + |
| **Nasal**    | − | + | − | + | − | + |

Each phoneme in this chart differs from all the other phonemes by at least one distinctive feature.

Vowels, too, have distinctive features. For example, the feature [±back] distinguishes the vowel in *look* [lʊk] ([+back]) from the vowel in *lick* [lɪk] ([−back]) and is therefore distinctive in English. Similarly, [±tense] distinguishes [i] from [ɪ] (*beat* versus *bit*) and is also a distinctive feature of the English vowel system.

Some features may be distinctive for one class of sounds but nondistinctive for another. For example, nasality is a _____①_____ feature of English consonants. There is no way to predict when an /m/ or an /n/ can occur in an English word. On the other hand, the nasality feature value of the vowels in *bean, mean, comb,* and *sing* is predictable because they occur before nasal consonants. The feature nasal is _____②_____ for vowels.

**05** Read the passages and follow the directions. [4 points]

┤ A ├

Syllable weight is a major factor in determining the position of stress in a word: essentially, no stressed syllable in English may be light. This means that no lexical word, or full word, of English can consist of a short vowel alone, with or without an onset, since such words, including nouns, verbs and adjectives, must be able to bear stress: thus, we have *be*, *say*, but not *[bɪ], *[sɛ]. On the other hand, function words like the indefinite article *a*, or the pronunciation [tə] for the preposition *to*, which are part of the grammatical structure of sentences and are characteristically unstressed, can be light. In cases where these do attract stress, they have special pronunciations [e] and [tu], where the vowel is long, the nucleus branches, and the syllable is therefore heavy.

There is one set of cases where a conflict arises between syllable weight on the one hand, and the guidelines for the placement of syllable boundaries on the other. In most cases, these two aspects of syllable structure work together.

(1) potato     report     about

Each in (1) has a consonant which could form either the coda of the first syllable, or the onset of the second. Onset Maximalism would force the second analysis, placing the first [t] of *potato*, the [p] of *report* and the [b] of *about* in onset position in the second syllable of each word; this is supported by the evidence of aspiration in the first two cases. The first syllable of each word is therefore light; and since all three of these initial syllables are unstressed, this is unproblematic.

(2) penny     follow     camera

Similarly, in words in (2), Onset Maximalism would argue for the syllabifications *pe.nny*, *fo.llow*, and *ca.me.ra*. However, in these cases, the initial syllable is stressed, in direct contradiction of the pervasive English rule which states that no stressed syllable may be light. In these cases, rather than overruling Onset Maximalism completely, the problematic medial consonant can be regarded as ambisyllabic, or belonging simultaneously in the coda of the first syllable and the onset of the second. It therefore contributes to the weight of the initial, stressed syllable, but its phonetic realisation will typically reflect the fact that it is also in the onset of the second syllable.

Now, take a look at the following words in (3).

| (3) danger | unstable | anxious | discipline |
|---|---|---|---|
| beyond | narrow | bottling | legal |

---

| B |

### Onset Maximalism
Where there is a choice, always assign as many consonants as possible to the onset, and as few as possible to the coda. However, remember that every word must also consist of a sequence of well-formed syllables.

**Based on the passages, first, identify TWO words whose consonant can be regarded as ambisyllabic in (3). Second, explain why each word is ambisyllabic, mentioning the positions of the problematic consonant in the syllable structure respectively, as described in the passage <A>.**

_____

_____

_____

_____

_____

**06** **Read the passage and follow the directions.** [4 points]

Consider the voiceless alveolar stop /t/ along with the following examples in (1).

(1) tick [tʰɪk]
    stick [stɪk]
    blitz [blɪts]
    bitter [bɪɾər]

In *tick* we normally find an aspirated [tʰ], whereas in *stick* and *blitz* we find an unaspirated [t], and in *bitter* we find the flap [ɾ]. We account for this knowledge of how *t* is pronounced: the aspirated voiceless stop [tʰ] occurs initially in a stressed syllable, the unaspirated [t] occurs directly before or after /s/, and the flap [ɾ] occurs between a stressed vowel and an unstressed vowel.

The range of places within a word which a given sound may occur in is called its distribution. In the English data we have looked at, the distribution of [tʰ], [t], and [ɾ] is mutually exclusive: where you get one kind of sound, you never get the other. This is called complementary distribution.

In the English data, it is clear that swapping these [tʰ], [t], and [ɾ] sounds around will not change word meaning. If we pronounce *bitter* with a [tʰ], it will not change the word; it will simply sound unnatural. They are interpreted as belonging to a single mental category. We will refer to such a category as a phoneme. Realizations of a phoneme which are entirely predictable from context are called its allophones. We therefore say that [tʰ], [t], and [ɾ] are allophones of the /t/ phoneme in most accents of English.

Compare the English data with the following data in (2). A learner of English as a second language has the following pronunciations:

(2) a. that [dat]      dog [dɒg]      bead [bɛd]      Daddy [dædɪ]

      leather [lɛðɚ]      leader [liðɚ]      either [iðɚ]      loathe [lod]

   b. sing [ʃɪŋ]      sat [sat]      loss [lɒs]      ship [ʃɪp]

      fish [fɪʃ]      miss [mɪʃ]      push [pus]      usher [ʌsɚ]

Since we know the speaker in this case is a learner of English, we can hypothesise that in that language, [d] and [ð] are allophones of a single phoneme /d/, and likewise [ʃ] and [s] are allophones of a single phoneme /s/, with a distribution like the one our learner imposes on English.

**Based on the passage, write the rules accounting for where the allophones [ð] in (2a) and [ʃ] in (2b) occur, respectively.**

_____

_____

_____

_____

_____

**07** **Read the passage and follow the directions.** [4 points]

Elision can be described in terms of two categorisations, based on the kind and the position of the sound(s) omitted. The categorisation based on the kind of sound(s) omitted distinguishes between elision of consonants, elision of vowels, and elision of whole syllables.

Elision of consonants can often occur in order to simplify consonant clusters. The consonants elided are most typically plosives and _____①_____ as the words in (1) show.

(1)  old man     /old mæn/     → [ol mæn]

    acts        /ækts/        → [æks]

    clothes      /kloðz/       → [kloz]

    months      /mʌnΘs/      → [mʌns]

Elision of vowels can occur in unstressed syllables of polysyllabic words, most typically just before or after a/an _____②_____ syllable, and after one of the fortis plosives, /p, t, k/ as shown in (2). The gap left by the elided vowels is filled by aspiration. When elision is compensated for with aspiration, it always results in a reduction in the number of syllable.

(2)  potato      /pəteto/      → [pʰteto]

    today       /təde/       → [tʰde]

    tomato      /təmɑto/     → [tʰmɑto]

    canary      /kənɛəri/     → [kʰnɛərɪ]

When an elided vowel can be followed by /n, 1/ or /r/, however, the gap is sometimes filled by syllabic consonants which function as the nucleus of the syllable as in (3).

(3) tonight     /tənaɪt/     → [tn̩aɪt]
    police      /pəlis/      → [pl̩is]
    correct     /kərɛkt/     → [kr̩ɛkt]

Elision of whole syllables can occur when the syllables are unstressed, most typically just before or after a stressed syllable, especially when the elided syllable contains a consonant that is repeated in the following syllable as in (4).

(4) library         /laɪbrərɪ/       → [laɪbrɪ]
    particularly    /pətɪkjələlɪ/    → [pətɪkjəlɪ]
    probably        /prabəblɪ/       → [prablɪ]

Based on the passage, first, fill in the blank ① with the ONE most appropriate word and the blank ② with ONE word from the passage. Second, identify whether an elided vowel followed by /n, 1/ or /r/ in (3) results in a reduction in the number of syllables or not. Explain why.

_____

_____

_____

_____

_____

**08** **Read the passage and follow the directions.** [4 points]

> If a sound is articulated further forward in the mouth than the underlying phoneme, usually under the influence of the surrounding sounds, that sound is said to be fronted, or advanced. Conversely, if a sound is articulated further back in the mouth than the underlying phoneme, again usually under the influence of the surrounding sounds, that sound is said to be retracted, or, less commonly, backed. Since fronting and retraction are usually conditioned by the phonetic environment, a fronted or retracted allophone and its corresponding "normal" allophone are usually in complementary distribution.
>
> The alveolar stops and the alveolar nasal may be fronted, or, more specifically here, dentalised, through the influence of the place of articulation of a following consonant, particularly the dental fricatives, /Θ, ð/ as exemplified in (1).
>
> (1) eighth [eɪt̪Θ]      width [wɪd̪Θ]      tenth [tɛn̪Θ]
>
> It should be noted that these processes also operate across word boundaries.
>
> (2) not thin [nɑt̪ Θɪn]  had then [hæd̪ ðɛn]  when they [wɛn̪ ðe]
>
> Similarly, /t, d, n/ may be retracted through the influence of the place of articulation of a following consonant, namely the post-alveolar approximant, /ɹ/. The retraction process can be exemplified in the words in (3):
>
> (3) try [tɹaɪ]      dry [dɹaɪ]      unrest [ʌnɹɛst]

The velar stops /k, g/ are often fronted through the influence of a neighboring sound, indicated by a small cross [ˌ] as in (4):

(4) cap [k̟æp]     kept [k̟ɛpt]     kit [k̟ɪt]
    gap [g̟æp]     get [g̟ɛt]       geese [g̟is]

The velar stops may be retracted through the influence of a neighboring sound, and retraction can be indicated by an underbar, [_], as in (5):

(5) cord [k̠ɔɹd]   cart [k̠ɑɹt]   goose [g̠us]   go [g̠o]

**Based on the passage, state the environment where the velar stops /k, g/ are fronted as in (4) and retracted as in (5) respectively.**

**09** Read the passage and fill in the blank ① with ONE word from the passage and the blank ② with the ONE most appropriate word. Write your answers in the correct order. [2 points]

---

Consider the following English words, each of which is accompanied by its phonemic and phonetic representations.

(1) *words*        *phonemic*        *phonetic*
   *heat*          /hit/              [hit]
   *leaf*          /lif/              [lif]
   *cease*         /sis/              [sis]

(2) *words*        *phonemic*        *phonetic*
   *heed*          /hid/              [hi:d]
   *seize*         /siz/              [si:z]
   *keel*          /kil/              [k$^h$i:l]
   *leave*         /liv/              [li:v]

In these data, /i/ has two _____①_____, [i] and [i:] (a colon after a vowel indicates that it is lengthened). Consider, for example, *seize* [si:z] and *cease* [sis]. The former has a long vowel and the latter has a short vowel; the vowels in *heat*, *leaf,* and *cease* are short, the vowels in *heed, leave, seize,* and *keel* are long.

Our task is to determine under what conditions /i/ becomes [i:]. We might assume that some property of the surrounding conditions makes vowels become lengthened. /i/ becomes [i:] when it precedes a/an _____②_____ consonant. If we were to go beyond the data above and include examples containing allophones of the other vowels in English, we would see that all vowels become lengthened whether the same phenomenon occurs under the same conditions. Note that phonological rules apply to *classes* of segments (e.g., vowels) rather than to individual segments (e.g., /i/, /e/, /æ/, and so on).

---

**10** Read the passages and follow the directions. [4 points]

┤ A ├

The rhythm of English is *trochaic*: the basic rhythmic pattern consists of a stressed syllable followed by zero or more unstressed syllables. For instance, in the phrase *made in a factory* ['meɪdɪnə'fæktəɹi], there are two trochaic feet: ['meɪdɪnə] and ['fæktəɹi]. But what is the evidence for the metrical foot? And what evidence is there for the claim that all feet in English are trochaic?

The first evidence is Rhyming. Consider the words *witty* ['wɪti] and *city* ['sɪti]: they rhyme because they both have a trochaic metrical foot of the same sort. Considering the two words in terms of rhyming, they share the same metrical foot, ['ɪti]. Clearly, for two words to rhyme, onset consonants play no role in rhyming; two words rhyme only if they have identical rhyme constituents in the syllable. The reason why *entity* does not rhyme with either *witty* or *city* is that the metrical foot structure of *entity*, ['ɛntɪti], is different from that of *witty* and *city*, ['ɪti], in case of rhyming.

The second one is Expletive Insertion. Expletives such as *bloody* are frequently used in informal spoken English by many speakers. It consists of a bisyllabic trochaic metrical foot: ['blʌdi]. It can be inserted into the internal structure of words, as in *abso-bloody-lutely*, where *bloody* is inserted into the word *absolutely*. This word is an adverb derived from the adjective *absolute* ['æbsəlu:t]. There is, however, an emphatic pronunciation with final primary stress and a secondary stress on the antepenult: [ˌæbsə'lu:t]. It is in this emphatic form that the expletive can be inserted into, as in:

A : Do you like Amy Winehouse?
B : Abso-bloody-lutely!

It is not possible to reply *ab-bloody-solutely*, or *absolute-bloody-ly*. The words into which the expletives can be inserted will contain trochaic metrical feet. The trochaic metrical structure should remain when an expletive is inserted into the word. It respects the trochaic bisyllabic metrical foot structure of *absolute*, inserting another such foot in between those two.

Finally, many neologisms are based on the trochaic metrical foot. Here are some examples: *alcoholic, workaholic, shopaholic, sexaholic, chocaholic*. All of these neologisms are based on analogy with the metrical structure of the word *alcoholic* ([ˌælkəˈhɒlɪk]), which contains two _____ trochaic metrical feet: [ˌælkə] and [ˈhɒlɪk]. The reason why the forms *work, shop, sex* and *choc* have to be written with the letter <a> is that this letter represents a schwa vowel ([ə]) which is present in the first trochaic metrical foot of *alcoholic*, on which the analogy is based.

---
**B**

Now, consider the following examples in Received Pronunciation (RP).

(a) phone ya (phone you) [ˈfəʊnje]
(b) pneumonia [njuːˈməʊnje]

First, fill in the blank with ONE word from the passage. Second, based on the passage in <A>, identify whether the phrase (a) *phone ya (phone you)* rhymes with the word (b) *pneumonia* in <B>, and then state their metrical foot structures in case of Rhyming, just as described in <A>.

_____
_____
_____
_____
_____

## 11 Read the passage and follow the directions. [4 points]

Speakers and listeners are able to distinguish the separate words of an utterance despite the fact that much spoken language actually consists of a continuous sequence of words, with only a few pauses between them. But how is that possible? If we transcribed an utterance without the conventional spaces between the words, then how could we identify where one word ends, and the next word begins?

(1) /əhaʊs/ vs. /ənem/
    /naɪtʃɪft/ vs. /naɪtret/

It is certainly relatively easy to see, for example, that /əhaʊs/ consists of the words *a* and *house*, but what about /ənem/? Does it consist of *a* and *name*, or of *an* and *aim*? To give another example, /naɪtʃɪft/ is easily recognisable as *night* and *shift*, but what about /naɪtret/? Is it *night rate* or just one word, *nitrate*? These examples show that a phonemic, or phonological, transcription cannot always disambiguate potentially ambiguous utterances. There are, nevertheless, phonological and, in actual speech, also phonetic features that mark the beginning and the end of linguistic units; i.e. they signal the boundary between syllables, words, and clauses, enabling us to distinguish between *a name* and *an aim*, and between *night rate* and *nitrate*. Such boundary signals are collectively termed *juncture*.

What may be the most reliable boundary signals are the rule-governed phonetic processes that take place when phonemes occur at the beginning or end of linguistic units, such as the partial devoicing of some lenis consonants in word-initial position, and the full devoicing of these consonants in word-final position. In other words, maybe the most reliable clues as to how to distinguish the separate words of an utterance come from allophones in complementary distribution.

Juncture through allophones can be exemplified by the sequence in (2):

(2) /kɪpstɪkɪŋ/

It is the allophonic realisation of the phonemes preceding and following the word boundary which makes that word boundary perceptible, and helps us recognise the sequence as either *keep sticking* or *keeps ticking*. In *keep sticking*, the word-initial /s/ is articulated with its usual fortis intensity, and the following /t/ is unaspirated. In *keeps ticking*, on the other hand, the word-final /s/ is articulated with less intensity, and the word-initial /t/ is aspirated. Further examples of unaspirated or aspirated plosives signalling word boundaries are shown in (3):

(3) a. how strained vs. house trained

    b. I scream vs. ice cream

Now, consider the following transcription which is ambiguous:

(4) /ðætstʌf/

**Based on the passage, first, provide the TWO possible utterances of the transcription in (4). Second, explain the allophonic realisation of the phoneme /t/ following the word boundary (i.e., the underlined /t/) in each utterance, based on the description in the passage.**

_____

_____

_____

_____

_____

**12** **Read the passage and fill in the blank with a distinctive feature.** [2 points]

Many languages have rules that refer to [+ voiced] and [− voiced] sounds. For example, the aspiration rule in English applies to a class of sounds in word-initial position. We do not need to consider individual segments. The rule automatically applies to initial /p/, /t/, /k/, and /ʧ/.

Phonological rules often apply to natural classes of sounds. A natural class is a group of sounds described by a small number of distinctive features such as [− voiced] and _____, which describe /p/, /t/, /k/, and /ʧ/.

The relationships among phonological rules and natural classes illustrate why segments are to be regarded as bundles of features. If segments were not specified as feature matrices, the similarities among /p/, /t/, and /k/ or /m/, /n/, and /ŋ/ would be lost. It would be just as likely for a language to have a rule such as

Rule 1. Nasalize vowels before p, i, or z.

as to have a rule such as

Rule 2. Nasalize vowels before m, n, or ŋ.

Rule 1 has no phonetic explanation, whereas Rule 2 does: the lowering of the velum in anticipation of a following nasal consonant causes the vowel to be nasalized. In Rule 1, the environment is a motley collection of unrelated sounds that cannot be described with a few features. Rule 2 applies to the natural class of nasal consonants, namely sounds that are [+ nasal], [+ consonantal].

The various classes of sounds also define natural classes to which the phonological rules of all languages may refer. They also can be specified by + and − feature values. The presence of + / − indicates that the sound may or may not possess a feature depending on its context. For example, word-initial nasals are [− syllabic], but some word-final nasals can be [+ syllabic], as in *wagon* [wægn̩], where the diacritic below the [n̩] indicates its syllabicity.

## 13 Read the passage and follow the directions. [4 points]

┤ A ├

Allophones are the concrete entities of speech. The allophones of a particular phoneme typically have phonetic similarity, that is to say, they have both articulatory and acoustic features in common.

Taken to the finest level of analysis, no two realisations of a phoneme are ever totally identical. Even if we ask the same person to produce the same sound under carefully controlled conditions, there will still be very slight differences between one utterance and the next. In reality, most allophones can be placed in fairly well-defined categories, and it is usually possible to provide descriptive rules to predict their occurrence in a particular phonetic context.

Let's take the case of the English phoneme /l/. This has three clearly defined recurring allophones as in (1).

(1)

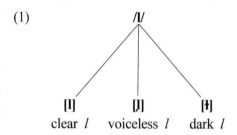

/l/

[l]   [l̥]   [ɫ]
clear *l*   voiceless *l*   dark *l*

It is possible to state, in broad terms, the chief phonetic contexts where the particular allophones of the phoneme /l/ are likely to occur.

Clear [l] occurs before vowels, e.g. *leap, yellow,* and before /j/, as in *value, million.* The tongue shape is slightly palatalised with a convex upper surface giving a close front vowel [i]-type resonance.

Dark [ɫ] occurs before _____ and pause. The articulation is slightly velarised, with a concave upper surface, giving a back-central vowel [ʊ]-type resonance, e.g. *still, help.*

Devoiced [l̥] occurs in initial clusters following the voiceless plosives /p k/ in stressed syllables, e.g. *plain, claim.*

The occurrence of allophones in this instance is therefore predictable. They can be considered as complements to each other. Such an allophonic patterning, which is very frequent in language, is termed complementary distribution.

---| B |---

Lesley told Paul to clean the children's playroom.

Based on the passage, first, fill in the blank with the ONE most appropriate word. Second, identify ALL and ONLY word(s) in <B> where /l/ is realised as clear [l]. Then, explain why clear [l] occurs in the word(s) that you choose, stating the phonetic context of clear [l], ONLY based on the passage in <A>. If clear [l] occurs in a word, you must state all the segments realised as clear [l].

**14** Read the passage and fill in the blank with the TWO most appropriate words. [2 points]

English contains a general phonological rule that determines the contexts in which vowels are nasalized. The following examples show this:

(1) bean [bĩn]    bead [bid]
    roam [rõm]    robe [rob]

Taking oral vowels as basic—that is, as the phonemes—we have a phonological rule that states:

(2) Vowels are nasalized before a nasal consonant.

This rule expresses your knowledge of English pronunciation: nasalized vowels occur only before nasal consonants and never elsewhere. The effect of this rule is seen in Table 1.

**Table 1**

| Words | | | Nonwords | | |
|---|---|---|---|---|---|
| be [bi] | bead [bid] | bean [bĩn] | *[bĩ] | *[bĩd] | *[bin] |
| lay [le] | lace [les] | lame [lẽm] | *[lẽ] | *[lẽs] | *[lem] |

As the table shows, oral vowels in English occur in final position and before non-nasal consonants; nasalized vowels occur only before nasal consonants. You may be unaware of this variation in your vowel production, but this is natural. Whether you speak or hear the vowel in *bean* with or without nasalization does not change the word's meaning.

Now consider the following examples:

(3) a. dental     [dɛ̃ntəl]
    b. denote     [dɪnot]

A word such as *dental* will be pronounced [dɛ̃ntəl]; however, the first vowel in *denote* will not be nasalized. We need to revise the vowel nasalization rule in (2) as follows:

(4) Vowels are nasalized before a nasal consonant within the _____.

## 15 Read the passage and follow the directions. [4 points]

Stress in the isolated word is termed *word stress*. But we can also analyse stress in connected speech, termed *sentence stress*, where both polysyllables (a word more than one syllable) and mono-syllables (single-syllable words) can carry strong stress while other words may be completely unstressed.

Many of the potential stresses of word stress are lost in connected speech (i.e. sentence stress). The general pattern is that words which are likely to lose stress completely are those which convey relatively little information. These are the words important for the structure of the sentence, i.e. the function words (articles, auxiliary verbs, verb *be*, prepositions, pronouns, conjunctions). Only two types of function words are regularly stressed: the demonstratives (e.g. *this, that, those*) and *wh*-interrogatives (e.g. *where, who, which, how*). Note, however, that when *wh*-words and *that* are used as relatives, they are unstressed. The content words (nouns, main verbs, adjectives, most adverbs), which carry a high information load, are normally stressed.

(1) I've **heard** that **Jack** and **Jane spent** their **ho**lidays in Ja**mai**ca.
　　F F　　C　　　F　　C　　F　　C　　C　　F　　　C　　　　F　　　C

*Note: C = content words, F = function words*

One stressed syllable will show the major pitch change, indicating the most important part of the speech. This major pitch-changing accent is called the *tonic accent*, and a syllable carrying the tonic accent is called the *tonic syllable*. If there is no context given, the most likely place for the tonic syllable is in the last content word. In (1), for example, the tonic syllable is the second syllable of the last content word, *Jamaica*.

Sentence stress is the basis of rhythm in English. Stressed syllables tend to occur at roughly equal intervals of time. This is because the unstressed syllables in between give the impression of being compressed if there are many and being expanded if there are few. Take a look at the following sentences in (2):

(2) a. Jimmy's bought a house near Glasgow.

   b. Alastair claimed he was selling the company.

Notice how the stressed syllables give the impression of coming at regular intervals. This effect is termed stress-timing, and it's characteristic of languages such as English, Dutch, German, Danish, Russian and many others.

   For the most part, the stresses fall on the content words, whereas the function words usually lack stressing. In terms of timing, the intervals between the strong beats of the stresses are roughly equal. Where you have a sequence of more than one weak syllable, the weak syllables are compressed, taking up much less time.

Based on the passage, first, identify whether the number of the stressed words in the sentences in (2) is the same or not. Then, explain why, including all the content words in (2a) and (2b) respectively. Second, state the tonic syllable of each sentence.

_____

_____

_____

_____

_____

## 16 Read the passage and follow the directions. [4 points]

┤ A ├

Phonetic conditioning is a term used to cover the way in which speech segments are influenced by adjacent (or near-adjacent) segments, causing phonemes to vary in their realisation according to the phonetic context.

Assimilation is the process where, as a result of phonetic conditioning, one phoneme is effectively replaced by a second under the influence of a third. Take the English word *broadcast*, which in careful pronunciation is /ˈbrɔdkæst/, but in connected speech may well become /ˈbrɔgkæst/. Here, one phoneme /d/ has been replaced by a second /g/ under the influence of a third /k/. This could be stated as a rule:

/d/ → /g/ before /k/

We can distinguish here the two forms of the word *broad*: (a) /brɔd/, (b) /brɔg/, where form (a) can be considered the ideal form, corresponding to the target that native speakers have in their minds. This is what is produced in the slowest and most careful styles of speech; it often bears a close resemblance to the spelling representation. Form (b), more typical of connected speech, is termed the assimilated form.

Assimilations involving a change in place of articulation are termed place assimilations. For instance, final alveolars in ideal forms are often replaced by bilabials (preceding /p b m/) or velars (preceding /k g/) or palato-alveolars (preceding /ʃ/).

(1) woodpecker /ˈwʊdpɛkɚ/ → /ˈwʊbpɛkɚ/
    night-cap /ˈnaɪtkæp/ → /ˈnaɪkkæp/
    horseshoe /ˈhɔɹsʃu/ → /ˈhɔɹʃʃu/

Assimilations may involve a reduction of the fortis/lenis contrast, a type which is termed energy assimilation. In stressed syllables, energy assimilations are less frequent in English than in most other languages, but they do occur in a few common words and phrases, e.g. newspaper /ˈnjuzpepə/ → /ˈnjuspepə/. Here, a lenis /z/ has been replaced by a fortis /s/ under the influence of a fortis /p/. In two verb forms, *have to* (meaning 'must') and *used to*, this type of assimilation is so common as to be effectively obligatory as in (2). In unstressed syllables, they occur regularly.

(2) I have to do it /aɪ ˈhæftə ˈdu ɪt/
    I used to do it /aɪ ˈjustə ˈdu ɪt/

Assimilations may involve a change in the manner of articulation, e.g. an ideal form containing a fricative may be replaced by a nasal or a lateral. This is termed manner assimilation. Nasal and lateral assimilations occur in English, mainly affecting initial /ð/ in unstressed words.

(3) join the army /ˈdʒɔɪn ði ˈɑɪmi/ → /ˈdʒɔɪn ni ˈɑɪmi/
    fail the test /fel ðə ˈtɛst/ → /fel lə ˈtɛst/

| ───────────────── | B | ───────────────── |
|---|---|---|
| (a) wet blanket | | (b) statement |
| (c) it was spectacular | | (d) till they meet again |
| (e) weed-killer | | (f) white pepper |

Based on the passage, identify ONE example of manner assimilation and ONE example of energy assimilation respectively in <B>. Then, state the assimilation process of each example, specifying the target words, ONLY based on the explanation in <A>.

_____

_____

_____

_____

_____

**17** Read the passage and fill in the blank ① with the ONE most appropriate word and the blank ② with ONE word from the passage. Write your answers in the correct order. [2 points]

---

Intonation is variation of pitch that is not used to distinguish words. Languages that are not tone languages, such as English or French, are called intonation languages. The pitch contour of an utterance may affect the meaning of the whole sentence, so that *John is here* spoken with falling pitch at the end is interpreted as a statement, but with rising pitch at the end, a question.

In English, intonation may reflect syntactic, semantic or pragmatic differences. A sentence that is ambiguous in writing may be unambiguous when spoken because of differences in the pitch contour. Written, the following sentence is unclear as to whether Tristram intended for Isolde to read and follow directions, or merely to follow him:

(1) Tristram left directions for Isolde to follow. ⇐ ambiguous

Spoken, if Tristram wanted Isolde to follow him, the sentence would be pronounced with a rise in pitch on the first syllable of *follow*, followed by a fall in pitch:

(2) Tristram left directions for Isolde to |*fo*llow.

In this pronunciation of the sentence, the primary stress is on the word *follow*. However, if the meaning is to read and follow a set of directions, the highest pitch comes on the ____①____ syllable of ____②____.

---

**18** **Read the passage and follow the directions.** [4 points]

If an intrinsically voiced sound is articulated with less voice than usual or with no voice at all, that sound is said to be partly or fully devoiced. We already know that some lenis consonants are partly devoiced in word-initial position because the vocal folds do not usually begin to vibrate at the onset of speaking. The time that elapses between the onset of speaking and the point at which the vocal folds begin to vibrate is called voice onset time (VOT). Because of the VOT, they are partly devoiced in words like *bill*, *joy*, and *van*.

Now, we want to focus on the three main processes whereby lenis consonants are being fully devoiced. Full devoicing can be indicated in the IPA by a small circle, [.], under the relevant symbol, as in the transcription [kæb̥] for the word *cab*.

The vibration of the vocal folds generally diminishes at the end of speaking, so that all lenis _____ are fully devoiced in word-final position as in (1).

(1) cab [kæb̥]    lid [lɪd̥]      bag [bæg̊]    judge [dʒʌdʒ̊],
    leave [liv̥]   breathe [brið̥]   freeze [friz̥]   rouge [ruʒ̊]

The lenis lateral /l/ and the two lenis approximants /r, w/ can be fully devoiced as in (2).

(2) try [tr̥aɪ]      please [pl̥iz]      quick [kw̥ɪk]

The lenis approximant /j/ can be fully devoiced as shown in (3). While the first two devoicing processes as in (1) and (2) do not significantly affect the intensity of the articulation (i.e. lenis consonants remain lenis), full devoicing here produces a sound that is not only voiceless, but also fortis, namely a fortis palatal fricative [ç].

(3) cube [kçub]      pew [pçu]      tune [tçun]

The opposite process, the voicing of an intrinsically voiceless sound, does not occur very often. If it occurs, it can be indicated by the diacritic [ˌ] under the relevant symbol. The fortis glottal fricative, /h/, to give only one example, may be somewhat voiced between voiced sounds, as in the word *anyhow*, which can then be transcribed as [ɛnɪɦaʊ].

**Based on the passage, fill in the blank with the ONE most appropriate word. Second, state the environment where the lenis lateral and the three lenis approximants in (2) and (3) are fully devoiced.**

**19** **Read the passage and follow the directions.** [4 points]

The phonetic transcription proper certainly shows too many fine details whereas a phonemic transcription often does not seem detailed enough. For that reason, it has become customary to use an intermediate type of transcription. This type of transcription is best regarded as a broad phonetic transcription. Although it is largely phonemic, we cannot use the word phonemic in the label because two of the symbols that are commonly used are not phonemes of English.

A good example to illustrate the intermediate status of a broad phonetic transcription is the representation of *i*- and *u*-sounds. It is relatively easy to distinguish the long /iː/ (as in *bee*) from the short [ɪ] (as in *fish*), and the long /uː/ (as in *goose*) from the short /ʊ/ (as in *pudding*). In some cases, however, the distinction is not so clear. In the words in (1), the *i*- and *u*-sounds seem to be intermediate between the respective long and short vowels.

(1) eas<u>y</u>     r<u>e</u>act     eval<u>u</u>ate     act<u>u</u>al

What symbols, then, do we use to transcribe these sounds? Neither /iː/ nor [ɪ], and neither /uː/ nor /ʊ/, seem to be wholly satisfactory here. In a broad phonetic transcription, therefore, the sounds in question are often represented by [i] or [u], using the basic symbols for the long vowels, but without a length mark. This compromise suggests that the two sounds have the quality of the respective long vowels, and the length of the respective short vowels. As indicated above, a transcription using [i] and [u] cannot be regarded as phonemic because the symbols represent sounds that are not phonemes of English.

The distinction between the long and the short *i*- and *u*-sounds is not so clear in "some" cases. More specifically, the intermediate [i] usually occurs in the following phonetic environments:

(2) a. eas<u>y</u>   hur<u>ry</u>

b. r<u>e</u>act   pr<u>e</u>occupied

c. appre<u>ci</u>ate   hilar<u>i</u>ous

d. h<u>e</u>   sh<u>e</u>   w<u>e</u>   m<u>e</u>   b<u>e</u>

The intermediate [u] is much less common, but if it occurs, it usually occurs in these phonetic environments:

(3) a. y<u>ou</u>   t<u>o</u>   int<u>o</u>   d<u>o</u>

b. thr<u>ough</u>   wh<u>o</u>

c. eval<u>u</u>ate   act<u>u</u>al

We then generalize the condition where the intermediate [i] in (2) and the intermediate [u] in (3) occur:

(4) The intermediate [i] and [u] occur in _____ syllables.

**Based on the passage, first, fill in the blank with the ONE most appropriate word. Second, state the ONE shared phonetic environment of [i] in (2b)―(2c) and [u] in (3c).**

_____

_____

_____

_____

_____

**20** Read the passage and fill in the blank with the TWO most appropriate words. [2 points]

---

Segment deletion rules are commonly found in many languages and are far more prevalent than segment insertion rules. One such rule occurs in casual or rapid speech. We often delete the unstressed vowels that are shown in bold type in words like the following:

(1) mys**te**ry  gen**e**ral  mem**o**ry  fun**e**ral  vig**o**rous  Barb**a**ra

These words in casual speech sound as if they were written as in (2):

(2) mystry  genral  memry  funral  vigrous  Barbra

The silent *g* that torments spellers in such words as *sign* and *design* is actually an indication of a deeper phonological process, in this case, one of segment deletion. Consider the following examples:

(3)      A                                          B
   sign [sãɪn]                         signature [sɪgnətʃər]
   design [dəzãɪn]                  designation [dɛzɪgneʃə̃n]
   paradigm [pʰærədãɪm]     paradigmatic [pʰærədɪgmærək]

In none of the words in column A is there a phonetic [g], but in each corresponding word in column B a [g] occurs. Our knowledge of English phonology accounts for these phonetic differences. The "[g]−no [g]" alternation is regular, and we apply it to words that we never have heard. Suppose someone says: "He was a salignant [səlɪgnə̃nt] man." Not knowing what the word means (which you couldn't, since we made it up), you might ask: "Why, did he salign [səlãɪn] somebody?" It is highly doubtful that a speaker of English would pronounce the verb form without the *-ant* as [səlɪgn], because the phonological rules of English would delete the /g/ when it occurred in this context. If we state the rule in terms of the syllable, this rule might be stated as:

(4) Delete a /g/ when it occurs before a/an _____ consonant.

---

## 21 Read the passage and follow the directions. [4 points]

Consider the adjectives in (1). All consist of at least a prefix morpheme and a root morpheme.

(1) impossible [ɪmpʰɑsɪbəɫ]        imbalanced [ɪmbælənst]
    infelicitous [ɪɱfəlɪsɪtəs]       intangible [ɪntʰændʒɪbəɫ]
    indirect [ɪndɹɛkt]             insane [ɪnsen]
    incorrect [ɪŋkəɹɛkt]           inglorious [ɪŋglɔɹɪəs]

These words all have the same prefix. That prefix is one of the morphemes of English. But what is the phonological form of that morpheme? English has three nasal phonemes: /m/, /n/ and /ŋ/, so the phonological form of this prefix might be [ɪm], [ɪn] or [ɪŋ]. Let us consider [ɪŋ]. We could say that the /ŋ/ phoneme is realized as [n] before /t/, /d/ and /s/, and as [m] before /p/ and /b/. This seems to make sense: we can say that, when the prefix is added to a root, the place of articulation of the nasal becomes identical to that of the first consonant in the root. Further evidence that nasals in English undergo place of articulation assimilation is not hard to come by. Consider the following data:

(2) unclear [ʌŋkʰliɚ]     ungodly [ʌŋgɑdlɪ]     unfair [ʌɱfɛɚ]
    unvalued [ʌɱvæljud]   untrue [ʌntʰɹu]       undone [ʌndʌn]
    unbearable [ʌmbɛəɹəbəɫ]  unbiased [ʌmbaɪəst]

While the [ɪŋ] solution is plausible, it faces a difficulty: we might equally say that the phonological form of the morpheme is [ɪn], or [ɪm], and that, in either case, the nasal assimilates to a following consonant. On the evidence presented thus far, there is no non-arbitrary way of choosing between the three alternatives: each is as plausible as the others. The following data, however, allow us to make a non-arbitrary choice:

(3) inactive [ɪnæktɪv]    inoperative [ɪnɑpəɹətɪv]

    ineffable [ɪnɛfəbəł]    inadvisable [ɪnədvaɪzəbəł]

    inaudible [ɪnɔdɪbəł]    inalienable [ɪneljənəbəł]

From these data, we can conclude that the phonology of the prefix takes the form [ɪn], and that the nasal does not change its place of articulation if the root-initial segment is a certain environment. Note that this is generally true of /n/ in English, as the following data, involving the prefix seen in (2), suggest:

(4) unaided [ʌnedəd]    unattractive [ʌnətʰɹæktɪv]

    uneventful [ʌnɪvɛntfəł]    unorthodox [ʌnɔɹθədɑks]

**Based on the passage, state the condition(s) where /n/ does not change its place of articulation in the words in (1)—(4).**

_____

_____

_____

_____

_____

## 22 Read the passages and follow the directions. [4 points]

┤ A ├

Morphemes are a kind of mental representation which have three properties: a syntactic category, a meaning and a phonological form. The phonological form of a morpheme is present in the speaker's mentally constituted grammar, and that this phonological form consists in either a single phonological segment or a sequence of such segments. But this is only part of the story: there is more to the phonological form of a morpheme than that. There is evidence that those segments are organized into phonological constituents, rather in the way that words are organized into syntactic constituents (such as phrases and sentences). One of those constituents is the syllable. The evidence for the existence of the syllable comes largely in the form of phonological generalizations which cannot be adequately expressed without reference to the notion 'syllable'. What evidence is there for this division between onset and rhyme? The device of alliteration depends on identity of onsets, independently of the content of the rhyme, as in *little* and *light*, *poor* and *packed*, and so on. This constitutes evidence for the onset/rhyme division, and thus evidence that the rhyme is a well-founded syllabic constituent.

The two main constituents within a syllable are the onset and the rhyme. In the word *bile*, for instance, the first segment, /b/, constitutes the onset of the syllable and the last two segments, /aɪ/ and /l/, taken together, constitute the rhyme. The onset is defined as any and all consonants occurring before the vowel.

The rhyme may be further subdivided into the constituents nucleus and coda. Thus, in the word *bile*, the diphthong /aɪ/ constitutes the nucleus, and the consonant /l/ constitutes the coda. We may represent the constituency of the single-syllable morpheme *bile* as follows, where Greek 'σ' (sigma) stands for 'syllable', 'O' stands for 'onset', 'R' stands for 'rhyme', 'N' stands for 'nucleus', and 'C' stands for 'coda'.

┤ B ├

Some of the evidence for the existence of the syllable as a phonological constituent comes from the fact that there are significant phonological generalizations which cannot be adequately expressed without appeal to syllable structure. One such generalization concerns the distribution of the vowels [ɒʊ] and [ʌʊ] in London English.

(1) roll [ɹɒʊl]     load [lʌʊd]     old [ɒʊld]

    cola [kʌʊlʌ]    stroll [stɹɒʊl]    tombola [tɒmbʌʊlʌ]

**Based on the passages, state the phonological environments where the phoneme /ʌʊ/ is realized as [ɒʊ] and [ʌʊ] respectively in (1).**

_____

_____

_____

_____

_____

**23** Read the passage and fill in each blank with ONE word from the passage. Change the word form(s) if necessary. Write your answers in the correct order. [2 points]

There is an important principle governing syllable division, namely Onset Maximalism (also known as Initial Maximalism), which is set out in (1).

(1) Onset Maximalism

Where there is a choice, always assign as many consonants as possible to the onset, and as few as possible to the coda. However, remember that every word must also consist of a sequence of well-formed syllables.

Consider the alternation between dark [ɫ] in *hill,* but clear [l] in *hilly.* Since *hill* has only a single syllable, and moreover has a vowel occupying the nuclear slot, the /l/ must necessarily be in the coda, and is therefore dark. However, in *hilly,* there are two syllables, and Onset Maximalism means /l/ must be in the onset of the second, where it automatically surfaces as clear. This kind of alternation, where the form that surfaces depends on its position in the syllable, is quite common in English and other languages. For instance, in non-rhotic accents of English, /r/ has two realisations, namely [ɹ] in onsets, and zero in codas: it surfaces in *red, bread, very,* but not in *car, park.* Again, as with the alternation between clear and dark variants of /l/, we find that the addition of suffixes can change the situation: so for instance, *star* has no final consonant for non-rhotic speakers, but there is a medial [ɹ] in *starry,* where the /r/ constitutes the onset of the second syllable. It also follows that syllable boundaries will not always coincide with _____①_____ boundaries: in *starry,* the two morphemes are *star,* the stem, and *-y,* the suffix, but the syllables are divided as *sta.rry* (note that a dot signals a syllable boundary). Although *car* has no final [ɹ], and the same is true of *car keys,* where the second word begins with a consonant, in *car engine* the second word begins with a vowel, and the /r/ can be allocated to the _____②_____ of that syllable, where it duly surfaces as [ɹ]. As far as native speakers' knowledge goes, there are two ways of analysing this. We could assume that speakers store *car* mentally as /kɑr/, and delete the /r/ before a consonant or pause. Alternatively, the entry in the mental lexicon or dictionary might be /kɑ/, with [ɹ] being inserted before vowels.

## 24 Read the passage and follow the directions. [4 points]

English has both suffixes (as in *sorted*, with the *-ed* suffix) and prefixes (as in *indirect*, with the prefix *in-*). Suffixes may be subdivided into inflectional and derivational suffixes. Among the English derivational suffixes, some have no effect on stress when added to a word, while others do affect the stress pattern. These two classes of suffix are referred to as the stress-neutral and stress-shifting suffixes, respectively.

Let us now turn to the stressing of prefixes. Most separable monosyllabic prefixes bear secondary stress. By 'separable', we mean that, if the prefix is removed, we are left with an existing English word, as in the verbs ˌre-ˈallocate, ˌre-ˈfabricate, ˌre-ˈrun, ˌreˈskill, ˌreˈspray.

(1) co- ('together')             ˌco-conˈspirator, ˌco-ˈedit

    de- ('get rid of/reverse')    ˌde-reguˈlation, ˌde-ˈlouse

    dis- (negative)              ˌdisaˈppear, ˌdisˈpleasure

    ex- ('former')               ˌex-adˈministrator, ˌex-ˈboss, ˌex-ˈserviceman

    in- (negative)               ˌincoˈrrect, ˌinˈactive

    mal- ('badly')               ˌmalaˈdjusted, ˌmaˈlodorous

    mis- ('wrongly')            ˌmis-aˈddressed, ˌmis-ˈspelled

    pre- ('before')              ˌpre-eˈxist, ˌpre-ˈpay

    pro- ('in favour of')        ˌpro-ˈhunting, ˌpro-ˈchoice, ˌpro-ˈlife

    re- ('again')                ˌre-aˈppear, ˌre-ˈfill (verb)

    sub- ('beneath')            ˌsub-aˈtomic, ˌsub-ˈhuman

    un- (negative)               ˌunaˈttractive, ˌunˈfair

It is striking that some of these can be used as independent words, as in 'I'm having dinner with my ex tonight' and 'Are you with the pros or the antis?'

Bisyllabic prefixes can form a trochaic foot, and so, in accordance with the Rhythmic Principle, will have the penultimate syllable of the prefix bearing secondary stress, as in ˌmegalithic, ˌmegacephalic, etc. While these all have secondary stress, there are some cases where there is primary stress on the bisyllabic prefix mega-, as in ˈmegabyte, ˈmegadeath, and ˈmegaphone. It is perhaps wise to consider these latter cases as compounds (words made from two or more words). Equally, while anti- can have secondary stress, there are clear cases where it has primary stress.

(2) anticatholic     antimatter     antibacterical
     antiabortion     anticlimactic     antihero

These too may be used as independent words, as in 'That film was absolutely mega!' or 'The antis are out in force'.

**Based on the passage, identify TWO words in (2) which can be considered as compounds. Explain why, discussing the stress type of anti-.**

_____

_____

_____

_____

_____

**25** **Read the passage and fill in the blank with the ONE most appropriate word.** [2 points]

The Sonority Sequencing Generalisation provides one guide to drawing syllable boundaries; leaving aside the exceptional case of /s/ in clusters, we find that legal syllables exhibit a sonority profile which ascends from the left-hand margin of the onset, up to a sonority peak in the nucleus, and subsequently descends to the right-hand margin of the coda. However, there is another, equally important principle governing syllable division, namely Onset Maximalism.

In a word like *falter*, we cannot straightforwardly assign the medial /lt/ to the second syllable. The Sonority Sequencing Generalisation would allow the syllable boundary to follow /lt/ (compare *fault*, a well-formed monosyllabic word), but Onset Maximalism forces the /t/ at least into the onset of the next syllable. The syllable boundary cannot, however, precede the /l/ because /lt/ is not a possible word-initial cluster in English, and it consequently cannot be a word-internal, syllable-initial cluster either.

On the other hand, in *bottle* our immediate reaction might be *bo.ttle*, which fits both the Sonority Sequencing Generalisation and Onset Maximalism. However, we then face a problem with the first syllable, which would on this analysis consist only of /bɒ/; a single short vowel cannot make up the rhyme of a stressed syllable. The first syllable clearly needs a coda; but *bott.le* is not quite right either, since native speakers, asked to check syllable boundaries by saying each syllable in the word twice, typically say *bot-bot-tle-tle*. The same is true of other words with the same problematic structure, like *syllable* in fact, which comes out as *syl-syl-la-la-ble-ble*; it may not be coincidental that these are written with double medial consonants. The usual solution here is to analyse the /t/ of *bottle* as the _____ consonant: that is, as belonging simultaneously in both the coda of the first syllable, and the onset of the second. This does not conflict with either the Sonority Sequencing Generalisation or Onset Maximalism, but also accords with native speakers' intuitions and the stress patterns of English.

**26** Read the passages and follow the directions. [4 points]

─────────────────────── ┤ A ├ ───────────────────────

A syllabic consonant can occur in certain phonetic environments where, in very slow speech, there would be a schwa as a syllable centre. As a syllabic consonant always forms the centre of a syllable, it has the phonological characteristics of a vowel, but, of course, it retains the phonetic characteristics of a consonant. A syllabic consonant and a corresponding non-syllabic consonant cannot usually distinguish meaning, which means that they must be regarded as allophones of the same phoneme. A syllabic consonant is indicated by a small vertical line, [ ˌ ]. There are three consonants, /m, ŋ, r/, which can be transformed into syllabic consonants.

Although the syllabic [m̩] and [ŋ̩] are not uncommon, they can occur only as a result of phonetic processes.

(1) happen [hæpm̩]    thicken [Ɵɪkŋ̩]    broken [bɹokŋ̩]

While the syllabic [ɾ̩] is very common in many rhotic accents, it is rare in non-rhotic accents, where the /r/ phoneme has disappeared almost entirely (except before a vowel). The words *particular* and *perhaps*, for example, are often pronounced [pɾ̩tɪkjəlɾ̩] and [pɾ̩hæps] in General American English whereas in Received Pronunciation (RP) they are usually pronounced [pətɪkjələ] and [pəhæps]. There are only two environments in which the syllabic [ɾ̩] can occur in RP, and even in those environments it is usually optional.

Firstly, the syllabic [ɾ̩] can occur when /r/ is preceded by one consonant (and followed by a vowel) in unstressed syllables:

(2) flattery [flætɾ̩ɪ]   watering [wɔtɾ̩ɪŋ]   preference [pɾɛfɾ̩əns]

Secondly, the syllabic [ɾ̩] can occur in another environment as shown in (3).

(3) history [hɪstɾ̩ɪ]   wanderer [wɑndɾ̩ə]   blustery [blʌstɾ̩ɪ]

┤ B ├

(a) Assimilation: An aspect of connected speech, where one sound, usually a consonant becomes more like, or identical with, a neighbouring sound regarding one or more of the distinctive features

(b) Dissimilation: The process whereby one sound becomes less like a neighbouring sound or a sound in close proximity, often to achieve greater ease of pronunciation, and also greater clarity

(c) Elision: The omission of one or more sounds in connected speech

(d) Intrusion: The insertion of a sound that is not represented in the spelling and has no historical justification

Based on the passages, first, identify TWO phonetic processes in <B> which the words in (1) result from. Second, state the environment where the syllabic [r] can occur in (3).

_____

_____

_____

_____

_____

**27** **Read the passage and follow the directions.** [4 points]

┤ A ├

Nonnative speakers testify to the difficulty they often experience in trying to master the stress patterns of English words. Nonetheless, there is considerable regularity in English word stress patterns. Let us begin by considering words which clearly do not have prefixes or suffixes in present-day English.

Monosyllabic words of a lexical category (such as nouns, verbs, adjectives and adverbs) are unproblematic: there is only one syllable for the primary stress to fall on as in *box*, *run*, and *big*. Let us move on to morphologically simple polysyllabic words.

The basic Germanic pattern is trochaic. For words of more than two syllables, this means having primary stress on the antepenultimate syllable as in (1):

(1) camera      cinema      custody      elephant
    emperor     harmony     library      melody

However, there is a substantial class of exceptions to this basic pattern, in which polysyllabic nouns have ultimate stress. A set of polysyllabic nouns stressed on the ultimate syllable have been borrowed from French.

(2) cigarette      bagatelle      picturesque      connoisseur

Words such as these are mostly morphologically simple in contemporary English. That is, they do not really have a suffix: while there is a morpheme *cigar*, a cigarette is not a small cigar, for instance.

There is a set of nouns which have consonant clusters after the penultimate vowel, and these have penultimate primary stress as in (3).

(3) advantage      apartment      disaster      objective

There is also a set of nouns which have three or more syllables and which end in *-ics*. These too tend to have penultimate stress.

(4) acoustics     electrics     linguistics    logistics     statistics

  Finally, there is a set of loanwords ending in a vowel which depart from the basic antepenultimate pattern, and take penultimate stress.

(5) banana     bikini     mosquito    chorizo     karate
    martini     potato     samosa    tomato     volcano

| B |

academy   consensus   deficit   lemonade   paradise   antelope   strategy

Based on the passage, identify TWO words in <B> which do not have primary stress on the antepenultimate syllable. Then, state the stress pattern of each word, ONLY using the terms in the passage <A>.

**28** Read the passage and fill in each blank with ONE word from the passage. Change the word form(s) if necessary. Write your answers in the correct order. [2 points]

---

Our knowledge of acoustic phonetics and other aspects of sound behaviour can be combined to produce a sonority scale like the one given in (1). Here, the most sonorous sounds appear at the top, and the least sonorous at the bottom. Some English examples are given for each category.

(1) Low vowels                          [ɑ æ] ⋯
      High vowels                  [i u] ⋯
      Glides                          [j w]
      Liquids                        [l ɹ]
      Nasals                        [m n ŋ]
      Voiced fricatives          [v z] ⋯
      Voiceless fricatives       [f s] ⋯
      Voiced plosives            [b d g]
      Voiceless plosives        [p t k]

The general rule expressed by the Sonority Sequencing Generalisation is that syllables should show the sonority curve in (2).

(2)

         t        ɹ        ʌ       m       p

The nucleus constitutes the sonority peak of the syllable, with sonority decreasing gradually towards the margins. In syllables like *trump, prance, plant,* the outermost consonants, at the beginning of the onset and the end of the coda, are at the bottom end of the sonority scale, while less marginal consonants, adjacent to the vowel, are also closer to the vowel in their sonority value. Lack of adherence to the Sonority Sequencing Generalisation therefore rules out _____①_____ like *[lp], *[jm], *[ɹg], although onsets with the same segments in the opposite order are found in *play, muse, grey.* Similarly, universal sonority restrictions mean English rules out _____②_____ like *[pm], *[kl], *[mr], although again clusters with the opposite order, which do show descending sonority, are attested in *lamp, silk, harm* (the last in rhotic accents only).

## 29 Read the passage and follow the directions. [4 points]

Every language has many phonological rules. In addition to seeing that they apply to natural classes of segments, we can classify phonological rules according to the kind of process that they involve. Two major types of processes are discussed, along with examples from the phonology of English.

Phonological rules of insertion cause a segment not present at the phonemic level to be added to the phonetic form of a word. An example of this kind of rule from English is voiceless stop insertion. Between a nasal consonant and a voiceless fricative, a voiceless stop is inserted. Thus, for instance, the voiceless stop insertion rule may apply to the words in (1).

(1) dance /dæns/ → [dænts]
    strength /stɹɛŋθ/ → [stɹɛŋkθ]
    hamster /hæmstɹ/ → [hæmpstɹ]

Deletion rules eliminate a sound that was present at the phonemic level. Such rules apply more frequently to unstressed syllables and in casual speech. English examples include /h/-deletion. /h/ may be deleted in an unstressed syllables. The /h/-deletion rule would apply to a sentence. Take a look at the sentence in (2).

(2) He, not she, handed her his hat.

Deletion is common in fast speech because it saves time and articulatory effort. Sounds like [h] that are not very perceptible are often the "victims" of deletion because speakers can save time and effort by deleting them without sacrificing much information. That is, the listener may not be relying on these sounds in order to understand what the speaker is saying.

Another common type of deletion is dissimilatory deletion. Like dissimilation, this process involves two close or adjacent sounds, but rather than one sound becoming less similar, as in dissimilation, one of the sounds is simply deleted. This often affects [ɹ] in English.

(3) prerogative /pɹɹɑgətɪv/ → [pəɹɑgətɪv]

    governor /gʌvəɹnəɹ/ → [gʌvənɹ]

    library /lɑɪbɹɛɪɪ/ → [lɑɪbɛɪɪ]

Based on the passage, first, identify TWO words in (2) where /h/-deletion occurs. Second, considering the data in (1), state ONE more condition where a voiceless stop can be inserted.

_____

_____

_____

_____

_____

**30 Read the passage and follow the directions.** [4 points]

In reality, there is often more than one process that occurs between a given phonemic form and the phonetic output. This can be seen particularly easily with regard to the English rules that involve stress, such as flapping, aspiration, /h/-deletion, and vowel reduction. In most of these cases, since the processes are independent of each other, we can conceive of multiple rules applying at the same time without a problem. For example, in (1) we can see that there is no need to order flapping and vowel reduction with respect to each other in the pronunciation of *photograph*. Since flapping does not affect the environment in which vowel reduction takes place, nor vowel reduction the environment in which flapping takes place, applying one rule before the other does not change the outcome.

(1) a. phonemic form:　　　　/ˈfotoɹæf/

　　　flapping:　　　　　ˈfoɾoˌgɹæf

　　　vowel reduction:　　ˈfoɾəˌgɹæf

　　　phonetic form:　　　[ˈfoɾəˌgɹæf]

　　b. phonemic form:　　　/ˈfotoɹæf/

　　　vowel reduction:　　ˈfotəˌgɹæf

　　　flapping:　　　　　ˈfoɾəˌgɹæf

　　　phonetic form:　　　[ˈfoɾəˌgɹæf]

But there are other cases in which the interaction among phonological rules is more complex. We can illustrate this by looking at the interaction of flapping in English with the following rule that affects the pronunciation of the diphthong /aɪ/ in some dialects.

(2) Diphthong-raising: The diphthong /aɪ/ is pronounced as [əɪ] when it occurs before a voiceless sound (i.e., the initial low vowel /a/ of the diphthong /aɪ/ is "raised" to the mid vowel [ə] before a voiceless consonant).

For speakers with this rule, the vowels in the words *write* [ɹəɪt] and *ride* [ɹaɪd] differ because of the voicing contrast between [t] and [d]. But in the related words *writer* and *rider*, the /t/ and /d/ appear between a stressed vowel and an unstressed vowel, which is the environment in which the flapping rule applies. In this case, applying the rules in different orders would result in two different pronunciations, as seen in (3) for the word *writer*.

(3) a. phonemic form:           /ˈɹaɪtəɹ/
     flapping:
     raising:
     phonetic form:
  b. phonemic form:           /ˈɹaɪtəɹ/
     raising:
     flapping:
     phonetic form:

**Based on the passage, first, identify the order in (3) which gives the correct phonetic form [ɹəɪɾəɹ], not [ɹaɪɾəɹ]. Second, explain why the reverse order cannot give the correct form.**

_____

_____

_____

_____

_____

**31** Read the passage and fill in each blank with the appropriate feature from the passage. Write your answers in the correct order. [2 points]

Stops and vowels differ from each other in four features.

A vowel is resonant, the result of periodic waves; when a vowel is articulated, particles of air vibrate in regular, repetitive patterns. A stop is essentially an instant of silence. If air particles are vibrating at all, there is no regular pattern. To express this difference we say that vowels are [+ sonorant] and stops are [− sonorant].

A vowel is the center or peak of its syllable, more prominent than what precedes or follows in the syllable. When two or more adjoining syllables differ in loudness or pitch, the difference is in their respective vowels. In a two-syllable word like *baby* the first syllable is more prominent than the second, and that difference is due to the comparative prominence of their vowels. Stops have no role in relative prominence or change of pitch. Thus we say that vowels are [+ syllabic] and stops are [− syllabic].

When a vowel is articulated, air comes continuously out of the mouth. The nature of a stop is that air is stopped—prevented from escaping. We say that vowels are [+ continuant] and stops are [− continuant].

When a stop is articulated, either the lower lip or some part of the tongue is in contact with some other part of the mouth—the upper lip or some part of the roof of the mouth. When a vowel is articulated, there is no interruption of the air stream. This distinction is captured with a feature [consonantal]. When there is some interruption of the breath stream, as there is for stops, the segment is [+ consonantal]. Vowels are [− consonantal].

The other four classes of speech sounds, fricatives, nasals, liquids, and glides, are partly like stops and vowels but of course are also different from them and from one another. Fricatives are segments like the [f v s z] of *feel, veal, seal, zeal,* respectively. They are articulated by squeezing the outgoing air stream between an articulator (the lower lip or some part of the tongue) and a point of articulation (the upper lip or some part of the roof of the mouth) so that turbulence or friction —rubbing—results. Fricatives are like stops in three features but differ in one. Like stops, they are the result of aperiodic vibration, therefore [− sonorant]; they require some interruption of the air stream, so they are _____①_____; they are not typically the peaks of syllables and so are designated _____②_____. Finally, unlike stops, fricatives are [+ continuant] since air is flowing continuously out of the mouth.

**32** **Read the passages and follow the directions.** [4 points]

─┤ A ├─

English does not exploit, in the word and the syllable, all the possible combinations of its phonemes. A knowledge of the word initial sequence(s) will usually give a guide to the point of phonological syllable boundary.

Initial CC clusters pattern as in (1):

(1) Word Initial CC

| /l/ | | /r/ | | /w/ | |
|---|---|---|---|---|---|
| pl- | play | pr- | prill | *pw- | |
| *tl- | | tr- | trill | tw- | twill |
| kl- | clay | kr- | cray | kw- | quill |
| bl- | blue | br- | brew | *bw- | |
| *dl- | | dr- | dry | dw- | dwell |
| gl- | glen | gr- | grey | gw- | Gwen |
| fl- | fly | fr- | fry | *fw- | |
| *Θl- | | Θr- | thrart | Θw- | thwart |
| sl- | slay | *sr- | | sw- | sway |

Initial CCC clusters pattern as follows:

(2) Word Initial CCC

| /l/ | | /r/ | | /j/ | | /w/ | |
|---|---|---|---|---|---|---|---|
| spl- | splash | spr- | spring | spj- | spew | *spw- | |
| *stl- | | str- | string | *stj- | | *stw- | |
| skl- | sclerosis | skr- | scrape | skj- | skewer | skw- | squeeze |

Triple onsets can be described as an addition of /s/ as $C_1$ to a voiceless stop + a/an _____ double onsets.

---

**┤ B ├**

Phonologists propose a set of unary place features based on active articulator.

[labial] Definition: constriction at the lips
　　　　Natural class: bilabials and labiodentals
[coronal] Definition: constriction made with the tongue front
　　　　　Natural class: dentals, alveolars, alveopalatals, retroflexes, palatals
[dorsal] Definition: constriction made with the tongue body
　　　　Natural class: palatals, velars and uvulars
[laryngeal] Definition: constriction at the glottis
　　　　　Natural class: [h] and [ʔ]

---

Based on the passages, first, fill in the blank with the ONE most appropriate word. Second, state a $C_1$ consonant which [w] cannot follow in initial CC clusters in (1), using ONE place feature in <B>.

_____

_____

_____

_____

_____

**33** Read the passage and fill in the blank with ONE word from the passage.

[2 points]

We use the term *discourse* to refer to any act of speech which occurs in a given place and during a given period of time. The word *text* is used by some authors with this meaning. We are concerned mostly with spoken discourse. A written discourse may be the record of something that has been spoken, or it may originate for the purpose of being performed aloud, like a speech or play, or it may exist without ever having been spoken or intended to be spoken, like most articles and books.

A discourse consists of at least one *utterance*, which is defined as a stretch of speech produced by a single speaker, with silence before and after on the part of that speaker. Two utterances in a discourse may be (partly) simultaneous, but only when two people speak at the same time. By definition one person cannot produce two utterances at the same time, though of course speakers may make several false starts and may not complete what they intended to say.

An utterance consists of at least one *tone unit*, a stretch of speech which has a melody or intonation, one of a fairly small inventory of intonation contours that exist in the language. The melody results from the physical fact that the speaker's vocal cords vibrate at different frequencies in the articulation of the tone unit, producing parts of it at different pitches.

A tone unit consists of at least one _____. It is an element which is recognized in all descriptions of speech, and yet one that is hard to define. It consists of a vowel sound, usually with consonants before and after it. When a tone unit consists of several syllables, which is usually the case, they differ in prominence. Relative prominence is due to some combination of factors: greater force with which air is expelled from the lungs, higher pitch or changing pitch, the duration, or timing, of the syllable.

_____

_____

## 34 Read the passage and follow the directions. [4 points]

Native speakers of some varieties of Scottish English habitually utter the speech sounds '[ɾ]' and '[l]', i.e. the voiced alveolar tap and the voiced lateral approximant. So do speakers of Korean. Here are some examples of Scottish English and Korean words which contain those sounds:

(1) [ɾ] and [l] in Scottish English and Korean

    a. Scottish English          b. Korean

       [læm] lamb             [mul] 'water'

       [ɾæm] ram              [mulkama] 'place for water'

       [lɪp] lip                [muɾe] 'at the water'

       [ɾɪp] rip                [mal] 'horse'

       [bɛɾi] berry           [malkama] 'place for horse'

       [bɛli] belly           [maɾe] 'at the horse'

While speakers of Scottish English and Korean habitually utter both sounds, many native speakers of Korean who are learning to speak this variety of Scottish English would find the distinction between [l] and [ɾ], when they speak Scottish English. On the face of it, this is puzzling because Korean speakers have no difficulty in uttering the two sounds. So wherein does the problem reside?

The difficulty is of a mental nature. In Scottish English, the two sounds may occur in the same places within a word. Furthermore, two words may differ solely with respect to the segments [ɾ] and [l]: there are minimal pairs involving the two sounds ([ɾæm] vs [læm], for instance). In this variety of Scottish English, [ɾ] and [l] are in parallel distribution. In Korean, [ɾ] and [l] may never occur in the same place. They are in complementary distribution: where one occurs, the other never does, and vice versa. Because of this, it is impossible to find minimal pairs involving these two sounds in Korean. The two sounds are also phonetically similar. Therefore the two sounds are realizations of the same phoneme in Korean.

Korean and this variety of Scottish English do not differ at the allophonic level: both have [ɾ] and [l]. But they do differ at the phonemic level: the Scottish English speaker has a mental distinction which the Korean speaker lacks; the Korean speakers' problem is thus mental in nature, not articulatory. We have said that it is entirely predictable which allophone of the Korean /l/ phoneme will occur in a given context. We may express that generalization in terms of a phonological rule, as follows:

(2) /l/ realization in Korean

    /l/ is realized as [ɾ] _____.

**Based on the passage, first, identify ONE Language (i.e., Scottish English or Korean) in which the distinction between [ɾ] and [l] is contrastive. Second, complete the rule in (2), using TWO words.**

_____

_____

_____

_____

_____

## 35 Read the passage and follow the directions. [4 points]

┤ A ├

In many languages, including English, one or more of the syllables in every content word are stressed. A stressed syllable, which can be marked by an acute accent (´), is perceived as more prominent than an unstressed syllable. Stress can be contrastive in English. It can distinguish between nouns and verbs such as the noun *cónflict*, and the verb *conflíct*. In this pair, the noun has the stress on the penult and the verb has it on the ult. It may also distinguish between words of other categories, such as the adjective *inválid* (not valid) and the noun *ínvalid* (a sickly person).

Some words may contain more than one stressed vowel, but exactly one of the stressed vowels is more prominent than the others. The vowel that receives primary stress is marked by an acute accent (´). The other stressed vowels are indicated by grave accents (`) over the vowels (these vowels receive secondary stress).

(1) rèsignátion      lìnguístics      sỳstemátic
    fùndaméntal    ìntrodúctory    rèvolútion

Generally, speakers of a stress-timed language like English (as opposed to French, say) know which syllable receives primary stress, which one receives secondary stress, and which one is unstressed. It is part of their implicit knowledge of the language. It's usually easy to distinguish between stressed and unstressed syllables because the vowels in unstressed syllables are pronounced as schwa [ə] in English except at the ends of certain words such as *confetti*, *laboratory*, and *motto*. It may be harder to distinguish between primary and secondary stress. If you are unsure of where the primary stress is in a word (and you are a native or near-native speaker of English), try shouting the word as if talking to a person across a busy street. Often, the difference in stress becomes more apparent.

The stress pattern of a word may differ among English-speaking people. For example, the British and American vowels differ in the word *laboratory*. In most varieties of American English the word *láboratòry* [lǽbərətʰɔri] has two stressed syllables, but in most varieties of British English it receives only one stress [ləbɔ̀rətri].

Stress is a property of the syllable rather than a segment; it is a prosodic or suprasegmental feature. To produce a stressed syllable, one may change the pitch (usually by raising it), make the syllable louder, or make it longer. We often use all three of these phonetic means to stress a syllable.

---

**⊢ B ⊣**

(a) Don't <u>pervert</u> the idea.

(b) He'll <u>subject</u> us to criticism.

(c) This new will <u>damage</u> his reputation.

---

**Based on the passage, identify TWO sentences in <B> in which the underlined words have the same stress pattern. Second, explain why, stating the part of speech and stress position of the underlined words, using the term in the passage.**

_____

_____

_____

_____

_____

**36** Read the passage and fill in each blank with the appropriate feature from the passage. Write your answers in the correct order. [2 points]

Different kinds of speech sounds and different manners of articulating are different ways of manipulating the air stream. We recognize six kinds of speech sounds: vowels, glides, nasals, liquids, fricatives, and stops.

Some articulatory features are distinctive and others are redundant. There are four features for distinguishing classes of speech sounds: [sonorant], [syllabic], [continuant] and [consonantal]. We need to recognize that even features which are distinctive in some areas may be used redundantly in other areas. Four features, with plus and minus values, would be enough to distinguish classes of speech sounds.

The feature [+ syllabic] is sufficient to designate the class of vowels; no other class has this feature. So the other features, [+ sonorant, + continuant, − consonantal], while they describe true facts about the pronunciation of vowels, have no role in telling how vowels are different from other classes of segments. For classification, one feature is distinctive, the other features are redundant. We can express this fact in a redundancy statement like this:

Whatever is [+ syllabic] is redundantly [+ sonorant, + continuant, − consonantal].

Or more briefly like this:

If [+ syllabic], then [+ sonorant, + continuant, − consonantal].

For glides we need two features together, ____①____ and ____②____, for a distinctive label. The feature ____①____ distinguishes vowels and glides together from other classes, and the feature ____②____ distinguishes glides from vowels.

## 37 Read the passage and follow the directions. [4 points]

────────────────┤ A ├────────────────

In English, the tonic falls on what is known as the last lexical item (LLI). Recall that words can be classified into two broad groupings: words of a lexical category and words of a functional, or grammatical, category. For example, the LLI is the noun *doctor* in (1), the adjective *pregnant* in (2), the verb *cheats* in (3), and the adverb *gracefully* in (4):

(1) 'Mary 'went to the \\**doc**tor.
(2) Is 'Mary ╱**preg**nant?
(3) My 'husband \\**cheats**.
(4) His 'lover 'walks \\**grace**fully.

It is common in English to shift the tonic away from the default position, for various purposes. Consider the following possible intonational patterns for the sentence *John is taking the train to London*:

(5) 'John is 'taking the 'train to \\**Lon**don.
(6) 'John is 'taking the \\**train** to 'London.
(7) \\**John** is 'taking the 'train to 'London.

In (5), we have the default pattern for tonic placement, with the tonic on the stressed syllable of the LLI. In (6), we have contrastive intonation: the train is being contrasted with some other mode of transport, such as the plane. In (7), the speaker is stressing the fact that it is John, not someone else, who is taking the train to London.

It is common to find that LLIs which are in syntactic units which have an adverbial function, and which convey information relating to time, fail to take the tonic, as in (8):

(8) 'John's 'going to \\**Lon**don on 'Saturday.

Here, *Saturday* is the LLI, but since the prepositional phrase *on Saturday* is a final temporal adverbial, the LLI within that adverbial expression fails to take the tonic. If we were to place the tonic on *Saturday*, that would constitute a case of contrastive intonation:

(9) 'John's 'going to 'London on \\**Sa**turday
    (as opposed to some other day of the week).

---

┤ B ├

(a) Bill gave it to her.
(b) Mary gave John the camera.

---

**Based on the passage, first, identify the word which has the tonic (accent) in each sentence in <B>. Second, explain why, using the terms in <A>.**

_____

_____

_____

_____

_____

**38** **Read the passage and follow the directions.** [4 points]

Segments may be more or less nasalised, labialised or fronted, and this gradience of many allophonic features may lead to the oversimplified conclusion that in certain cases the allophonic rule in question optionally fails to apply when in reality, on closer inspection, it may well be implemented to a very slight extent. It makes sense, then, to concentrate our search for a genuinely optional rule on a phonetic feature that is intrinsically binary, such as the release characteristics of oral stops. Such stops may be either released (as so far we have always assumed they are) or unreleased. There is no intrinsic gradience in this feature. Here are some examples of unreleased stops, indicated by a superscript 'minus' after the stop:

(1) captain [kæp⁻tən]

hatpin [hæt⁻pɪn]

blackboard [blæk⁻bɔd]

obtain [əb⁻ten]

good dog [gʊd⁻dɒg]

rugby [rʌg⁻bɪ]

Unreleased stops occur in another context:

(2) cap [kæp⁻]

hat [hæt⁻]

black [blæk⁻]

cab [kæb⁻]

good [gʊd⁻]

rug [rʌg⁻]

What is important here is that in both contexts the release of stops is, in phonological terms, optional: released and unreleased stops in such contexts are in _____ variation. Thus [t] and [t˺] do not contrast, despite their parallel distribution, because they are not utilised in minimal pairs. However, this notion of _____ variation is only valid when the range of possible variables that may determine allophony is restricted to purely phonological ones, excluding nonlinguistic factors: such stops are most likely to be released in slow, careful speech; they are commonly unreleased in casual or fast speech, and some speakers habitually have more unreleased stops than others.

**Based on the passage, first, fill in each blank with the ONE most appropriate word. (Use the SAME answer for both blanks.) Second, state the context where unreleased stops occur in (1).**

_____

_____

_____

_____

_____

**39** Read the passage and fill in each blank with the ONE most appropriate word. Write your answers in the correct order. [2 points]

Say the phrase *kitchen cupboard* to yourself, and think about the first sounds of the two words. Despite the difference in spelling, native speakers will tend to think of those initial consonants as the same—both are [k]s. However, if you say the phrase several times, slowly, and think uncharacteristically carefully about whether your articulators are doing the same at the beginning of both words, you will find that there is a discernible difference. For the first sound in *kitchen*, your tongue will be raised towards the roof of your mouth, further forward than for the beginning of *cupboard*; and for *kitchen*, your lips will be spread apart a little more too, while for *cupboard* your mouth will be more open. This difference is even clearer from the phrase *car keys*, this time with the first word having the initial sound produced further back in the mouth, and the second further forward.

In IPA terms, these can be transcribed as [k], the *cupboard* sound, and [c], *the kitchen* one. However, in English [k] and [c] do not signal different meanings as [k] and [t] do in *call* versus *tall*; instead, we can always predict that [k] will appear before one set of vowels, which we call back vowels, like the [ʌ] of *cupboard* or the [ɑː] a Southern British English speaker has in *car*, while [c] appears before _____①_____ vowels, like the [ɪ] of *kitchen* or the [i] in Southern British English *keys*. Typically, speakers control predictable differences of this type automatically and subconsciously, and sometimes resist any suggestion that the sounds involved, like [k] and [c] in English, are different at all, requiring uncharacteristically close and persistent listening to tell the two apart. The difference between [k] and [c] in English is redundant; in phonological terms, this means the difference arises automatically in different contexts, but does not convey any new information. Those realisations, here [k] and [c], are allophones of the phoneme /k/. To qualify as allophones of the same phoneme, two (or more) phones, that is sounds, must meet two criteria. First, their distribution must be predictable: we must be able to specify where one will turn up, and where the other; and those sets of contexts must not overlap. If this is true, the two phones are said to be in _____②_____ distribution. Second, if one phone is exceptionally substituted for the other in the same context, that substitution must not correspond to a meaning difference.

**40** Read the passage and follow the directions. [4 points]

The location of stress matters in an aspiration rule. A voiceless consonant is not aspirated in syllable-initial position if the consonant is followed by an unstressed vowel. In other words, the rule for assignment of aspiration should be stated as follows: voiceless stops become aspirated at the beginning of a stressed syllables.

The dependence of aspiration on the location of stress leads to discovering further evidence for an aspiration rule. Certain word-formation processes in English change the location of stress. For example, in 'atom' the stress is on the first syllable of the root and in the related adjective 'atomic' the stress is on the second syllable. The pairs of words in (1) further illustrate the property of stress shifting, where the verbs on the left have stress on the second syllable of the root but the nouns derived from these verbs on the right have no stress on the second syllable.

(1) [əpʰláɪ]      apply        [æ̀pləkʰéʃn̩]      application
    [səpʰóz]     suppose      [sʌ̀pəzíʃn̩]       supposition
    [əkʰwáɪr]    acquire      [æ̀kwəzíʃn̩]       acquisition

As predicted by our rule for aspiration, the phonetic presence or absence of aspiration on the medial stop of the root may alternate within a given root, according to where the stress appears in the root.

Another set of examples involves the word-formation process adding the object-nominalization suffix -ee and the subject-nominalization suffix -er to a verb, to form a noun referring to the direct object of the action and to the subject of the action, respectively.

(2)

| Verb | Subject noun | Object noun | |
|---|---|---|---|
| [grǽnt] | [grǽntər] | [grǽnt̬i] | grant |
| [ʃíft] | [ʃíft̬ər] | [ʃíft̬i] | shift |
| [hélp] | [hélpər] | [hélpi] | help |
| [ʧʰók] | [ʧʰókər] | [ʧʰoki] | choke |
| [stráɪk] | [stráɪkər] | [straɪki] | strike |
| [ətʰǽk] | [ətʰǽkər] | [ətǽki] | attack |

Based on the passage, state whether the underlined stops in *Object noun* in (2) are aspirated or not. Then, explain why, discussing stress shifting in the word-formation process.

_____

_____

_____

_____

_____

**41** **Read the passage and follow the directions.** [4 points]

When words consist of more than one syllable, when they are multisyllabic or polysyllabic, the problem of syllabification arises. Should the consonants /kstɹ/ in the word *extreme* /ɪkstɹim/ be analysed as coda consonants of the first syllable, as onset consonants of the second syllable or should they be split up somehow to fill both positions? Phonologists have proposed that these consonants are distributed according to the maximum onset principle. This principle states that intervocalic consonants are syllabified as the onset of the following syllable as far as the phonotactic constraints of the language allow it. This means that the two syllables of *extreme* are split up into /ɪk.stɹim/. /stɹ/ is syllabified as the onset of the second syllable, since this conforms to the phonotactic rules of onset clusters. /kstɹ/ violates these rules, so that /k/ has to be syllabified as the coda of the first syllable.

In some cases, the maximum onset rule leads to questionable results. For example, the words *apple* and *epic* would have to be syllabified into /æ.pl/ and /ɛ.pɪk/, which violates the rule that stressed syllables have to consist of at least a long vowel or a short vowel plus a consonant. /æ/ and /ɛ/ are short vowels and, according to this rule, cannot stand on their own in a syllable. A way around this problem is to propose that the /p/ in both cases is an ambisyllabic consonant, i.e. that it belongs simultaneously to the coda of the first and the onset position of the second syllable.

(1)

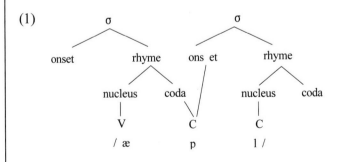

In connected speech, the problem of syllabification arises also across word boundaries. Speakers often produce speech that contains resyllabification, where one or more consonants of one word are attached to the following word. Resyllabification also follows the maximum onset principle. This can be seen for example in the phrase *have it*, which is usually resyllabified into [hæ.vɪt]. The last consonant of the word have is produced as the onset of the second syllable.

The 'linking /r/' in non-rhotic accents can also be described as resyllabification. In non-rhotic accents of English, coda /ɹ/ is not pronounced. /ɹ/ is pronounced, however, when the /ɹ/ is resyllabified as an onset consonant of the following syllable. Now consider the data in (2).

(2) pai<u>r</u>ing
    fa<u>r</u> away
    Pete<u>r</u> and Ma<u>r</u>y

Based on the passage, first, identify ONE word in (2) where /ɹ/ is not resyllabified. Second, state the condition where /ɹ/ is resyllabified as an onset of the following syllable in non-rhotic accents of English.

_____

_____

_____

_____

_____

**42** Read the passage and fill in the blank ① with ONE word from the passage and the blank ② with the appropriate feature from the passage. Write your answers in the correct order. [2 points]

Stops, fricatives, nasals, and liquids are all [+ consonantal]; in their articulation the lower lip or some part of the tongue impedes the flow of air in some way, in some part of the mouth. The four classes together are called consonants. Vowels and glides are articulated without such impedance; they are [− consonantal]. For vowels and glides it is the shape of the oral cavity in which air is flowing freely that determines the quality of the sound produced. Glides are like certain vowels in their production, but they are like _____①_____ in the positions they occupy in syllables and larger units.

The four classes of consonants differ from one another in their manner of articulation, specifically in whether or not the articulation is characterized by periodic vibration of air particles and in whether or not the air stream is escaping from the mouth during the articulation. We can express these differences with the features [sonorant] and [continuant] below.

| liquids | nasals | fricatives | stops |
|---|---|---|---|
| + sonorant | + sonorant | − sonorant | − sonorant |
| + continuant | ② | + continuant | − continuant |

Liquids and nasals are 'musical' like vowels. Although the air stream is obstructed in some way, the vocal tract still acts as a resonance chamber in which air particles flow in periodic waves. Obstruent consonants — fricatives and plosives — are articulated with total or near-total obstruction of the air stream so that resonance is minimal or absent. For liquids and fricatives air flows out from the mouth during articulation; thus any of these consonants can be held — continued — as long as the lungs provide air. Nasals can also be prolonged since air escapes during their articulation, but through the nasal cavity alone. A stop, since it involves complete obstruction of the breath stream, is essentially an instant of silence.

**43** **Read the passage and follow the directions.** [4 points]

The normally accepted definition of the foot is that each phonological foot starts with a stressed syllable, and continues up to, but not including, the next stressed syllable. Feet can be classified into types, three of which are shown in (1).

(1)

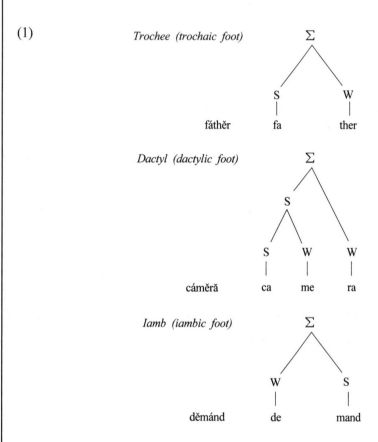

The English process of Iambic Reversal seems designed precisely to avoid either lapses, where too many unstressed syllables intervene between stresses, or clashes, where stresses are adjacent, with no unstressed syllables in between at all. It affects combinations of words which would, in isolation, have final stress on the first word, and initial stress on the second. For instance, (2) shows that the citation form of *thirteen* has final stress.

(2) A: How many people turned up?

    B: ˌThir'teen

However, take a look at the following case when final-stressed words like *thirteen* form phrases with initial-stressed ones like *players*, as illustrated in (3).

(3)  W S      S W      S W     S W
     thirteen    players  →  thirteen    players

If these words retained their normal stress pattern, we would find clashing sequences of WSSW, as shown on the left of (3); consequently, the prominence pattern of the first word is reversed. The result is a sequence of two trochaic feet, SWSW.

Now, consider the example in (4).

(4) champagne cocktails

Based on the passage, first, identify whether Iambic Reversal occurs in the phrase 'champagne cocktails' in (4). Second, if so, state the reason why it occurs and the process of stress alternation.

_____

_____

_____

_____

_____

## 44 Read the passage and follow the directions. [4 points]

Although the word *stem* has multiple meanings in linguistics, it is the minimal constituent within a word that can stand as an independent word. Thus, in *jumping* [[ dʒʌmp ]ᵥ ɪŋ ]ₙ, the stem is [ dʒʌmp ]ᵥ. In *identifier* [[[ aɪdɛnt ] ɪfaɪ ]ᵥ ɚ ]ₙ, the stem is [ aɪdɛntɪfaɪ ]ᵥ. Although we can recognize a smaller root morpheme [ aɪdɛnt ] within this word (compare *identity, identical*), we will not consider it to be the stem, since it cannot occur as an independent word.

Consider now an example of a stem-bounded rule. The following rule occurs in some version in a number of English dialects:

(1) Pre-/l/ Monophthongization

    oʊ → o / ___ l

(2) /oʊ/ before /l/: [o]           /oʊ/ in other environments: [oʊ]

    hole [hol]                     Poe [poʊ]

    poultry [polʧɹi]            moat [moʊt]

    mole [mol]                 propane [pɹoʊpeɪn]

    mold [mold]               toad [toʊd]

The above are all simple, monomorphemic forms. The more subtle effects occur when we add suffixes to stems that end in /oʊ/ or in /oʊ/ plus /l/.

(3) slow-ly [sloʊli]    toe-less [toʊləs]    low-land-s [loʊləndz]

(4) goal-ie [goli]    hole-y [holi]    roll-ing [ɹolɪŋ]

It can be seen that underlying /oʊ/ gets monophthongized only if it is in the same stem as the immediately following /l/.

Now consider the following examples of Vowel Nasalization:

(5) Venus [vĩnəs]             freeness [fɹinəs]

    bonus [bõũnəs]         slowness [sloʊnəs]

    Uranus [jʊɹêĩnəs]     greyness [gɹeɪnəs]

    Linus [lãĩnəs]          dryness [dɹaɪnəs]

Based on the passage, state the environment where the Vowel Nasalization occurs in (5), ONLY using the terms in the passage.

_____

_____

_____

_____

_____

**45** Read the passage and fill in the blank ① with ONE word from the passage and the blank ② with the ONE most appropriate word. Write your answers in the correct order. [2 points]

> We can classify the suffixes as:
>
> (a) stress-bearing suffixes;
> (b) stress-shifting suffixes;
> (c) stress-neutral suffixes.
>
> The common element between groups (a) and (b), when added to a root, is that they change the location of the stress from its original position. Stress-bearing suffixes attract the stress to themselves, while stress-shifting suffixes move the stress to some other syllable. Groups (b) and (c) have the common element of not carrying stress.
>
> Below are some common derivational suffixes:
>
> | (1) | -ade | lemon — lemonade |
> |---|---|---|
> | | -aire | million — millionaire |
> | | -ation | realize — realization |
> | | -ee | absent — absentee |
> | | -eer | mountain — mountaineer |
> | | -ese | Japan — Japanese |
> | | -esque | picture — picturesque |
> | | -ette | kitchen — kitchenette |
> | | -itis | larynx — laryngitis |
> | | -ific | honor — honorific |
>
> Expectedly, these stress- ____①____ suffixes always constitute ____②____ syllables considering syllable weight. The items above with suffixes should not be confused with the same/similar-looking monomorphemic forms such as *brigade, jamboree, grotesque, brunette, bursitis,* etc.

_____

_____

**46 Read the passages and follow the directions.** [4 points]

───────────────────┤ A ├───────────────────

A morpheme is said to alternate when it appears in different forms in different contexts. The analysis of alternations is one of the central areas of phonology. Alternation often arises because of the way that phonology interacts with morphology.

We will be observing the relationship of three phonological rules with two rules of derivational morphology, given below in (1).

(1) a. *-able* Affixation: Verb + əbəl → Adjective

"able to be Verbed"

 b. *-ation* Affixation: Verb + 'eʃən → Noun

"the process or product of Verbing"

The reason morphological rules are of phonological interest is that they can rearrange the phonological environments of the phonemes. The segments of prefixes and suffixes can themselves be part of the environment of a phonological process. Consider the following data in (2):

(2) note　　　　　notable　　　　　notation

Let us consider the particular allophone of /t/ that emerges in these forms. In *note* occurring by themselves, the /t/ phoneme is at the end of a word. It is thus eligible for Preglottalization, and emerges as the allophone [ˀt].

Once the morphology has arranged the appropriate suffixes, the phonological form of words is accommodated to the new environments that are created. The selection of the proper allophone of /t/ is not established for the stem /not/ once and for all, but rather is determined on the basis of the environment in which the stem-final /t/ appears.

Referring to the definition of alternation, we see that the morpheme *note* does indeed alternate: depending on the context (which the morphology creates for them), they take on different forms. For example, the phonological form of the word *note* is ['noˀt].

---
### | B |

Here are some phonological rules of English, all of which apply to the phoneme /t/ and give rise to alternation:

(1) Preglottalization: A voiceless stop is preglottalized [ˀp, ˀt, ˀk] when in final position.

(2) Glottal stop replacement: The glottal stop replacement [ʔ] requires the target /t/ to be in a syllable-final position.

(3) Tapping: The /t/ phoneme is realized as a tap [ɾ] just in case it occurs between two vowels of which the second is stressless.

(4) Aspiration: Voiceless stops are aspirated [pʰ, tʰ, kʰ] when they precede a stressed vowel and are not preceded by /s/.

---

Based on the passages, first, state the phonological forms of the words 'notable' and 'notation' with the proper allophone of /t/ and the primary stress mark, ONLY using phonetic symbols shown in the passages. Second, state which phonological rule in <B> is applied in each word.

_____

_____

_____

_____

_____

**47** **Read the passage and follow the directions.** [4 points]

┤ A ├

The prominence patterns of compounds systematically have nonphrasal stress patterns as shown in (1):

(1) a. [ 'AB ]
    greenhouse
    filing cabinet
  b. [[ 'AB ] C ]
    blackboard eraser
    house-warming party
  c. [ A [ 'BC ]]
    government working party
    university works department
  d. [[ ,AB ] [ 'CD ]]
    engine oil filler cap
    car maintenance training course
  e. [[ A [ 'BC ]] D ]
    parish coffee-morning committee
    university car-park inspector

The prominence patterns displayed in (1) fall into groups, clearly determined by internal syntactic structure, suggests the possibility of a generalisation. Let us simplify matters by merely looking at (1a-c) in the first instance.

The form of metrical trees for compounds is determined by the internal structure. Note that in each case the metrical tree is a copy of the internal syntactic structure of the compound, and that the prominence relations in the metrical tree express the stress patterns indicated in (1).

(2)  a.           b.           c.

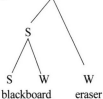

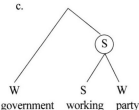

This more restricted set of data reveals the generalisation. Looking again particularly at the behaviour of the right-hand node in each pair, we notice that this node is not invariably strong but only under certain conditions:

(3) Compound Prominence Rule

In a pair of sister nodes $[N_1\ N_2]_L$, where L is a lexical category, $N_2$ is strong if it branches above the word level.

In (2b), for example, $N_1$ is *blackboard* and $N_2$ is *eraser*. Since $N_2$ does not branch above the word level, $N_2$ is not strong. In contrast, in (2c) $N_1$ is *government* and $N_2$ is *working party*. Since $N_2$ branches above the word level, $N_2$ becomes strong.

---

**⊦ B ⊢**

(a) home word-processing equipment

(b) schools liaison committee meeting

(c) Labour party finance committee

(d) arts faculty entrance test

(e) schools liaison committee

(f) word-processing equipment

---

Based on the passage, first, divide the examples in \<B\> into two groups of the same internal structure. Second, identify the internal structure of each group, using the numbers (1a)—(1e) in \<A\>.

_____

_____

_____

_____

_____

**48** Read the passage and fill in each blank with the appropriate feature. Write your answers in the correct order. [2 points]

---

Liquids, the consonants which begin the words *led* and *red*, for instance, were shown to be

[± syllabic]
[+ consonantal]
[+ continuant]
[+ sonorant]

We can now add two other features which the liquids share: they are [+ voice] and [− sibilant].

How do /l/ and /r/ differ from each other? Phonologists who use the features [anterior] and [coronal] say that /l/ is [+ anterior] and /r/ is _____①_____ since /l/ is sometimes articulated with the tip of the tongue on the alveolar ridge and /r/ is never articulated so far forward. However, both consonants are articulated in different parts of the mouth; neither the articulator nor the place of articulation is truly distinctive for these two consonants. What distinguishes them from each other is the shape of the tongue. One of them, /l/, is articulated with the sides of the tongue curled in and air escaping over the sides. We say that /l/ is [+ lateral].

For /r/ the tongue is also curled but in a different way; the whole body of the tongue is pulled back and bunched up, with a slight groove in the very tip—not a groove along the center line of the surface, which would make it a sibilant. Typically, there is also some rounding of the lips. Instead of pulling the tongue back and humping it up, some speakers turn the tongue-tip backward; hence the term 'retroflex' has been used by some phoneticians, but this name is not appropriate for the most usual articulation. Various appropriate names might be used to describe the physical facts of articulation. To place /r/ in a system of distinctive features it is enough to say that it is _____②_____.

---

## 49 Read the passage and follow the directions. [4 points]

English has rules of phonological neutralization. The one to be discussed here takes the form of a deletion: the contrast that is wiped out is that of /t/ with zero. Consider first some minimal pairs demonstrating this contrast. We are particularly interested in cases where the /t/ follows an /n/:

(1) plant [plænt]    vs.    plan [plæn]

     stunt [stʌnt]    vs.    stun [stʌn]

     bent [bɛnt]    vs.    Ben [bɛn]

There are also a fair number of near-minimal pairs:

(2) Bentley ['bɛntli] vs.    Henley ['hɛnli]

     until [ən'tɪl]    vs.    anneal [ə'nil]

Since all of the examples on the left-hand side are selected to have /t/ preceded by /n/, we can also describe the contrast by saying that /nt/ contrasts with /n/.

Now, let us consider a number of groups of words that share the same morphological stem. The pronunciations given are not common to all dialects of English, but are common in North America.

(3) plant ['plænt]    planter ['plænɚ]

     plan ['plæn]    planner ['plænɚ]

     stunt ['stʌnt]    stunting ['stʌnɪŋ]

     stun ['stʌn]    stunning ['stʌnɪŋ]

     punt ['pʌnt]    punting ['pʌnɪŋ]

     pun ['pʌn]    punning ['pʌnɪŋ]

Our assertion is that, at least for some speakers and in some speech styles, *planter* is pronounced identically to *planner*, and similarly for the other pairs. The rule involved, to which we will now turn, is evidently a neutralizing one.

From the data, we know that the /t/ is maintained after /n/ when the /t/ is at the end of a word (['stʌnt]); moreover, in the relatively few cases where an /nt/ sequence is followed by a consonant (others include *entry* ['ɛntɹi], *antler* ['æntlɚ] and *Antwerp* ['æntwɚp]), the /t/ survives. Additional data given below indicate that stress also plays a role:

(4) mental ['mɛnəl]          mentality [mɛn'tælɪɾi]

   scientist ['saɪənəst]     scientific [ˌsaɪən'tɪfɪk]

Thus we can state the rule as follows:

(5) /t/ is deleted when _____.

Neutralization creates ambiguous utterances; thus on hearing [ðeɪɑɹ'plænɪŋə'gɑɹdən] from a native speaker of this dialect, only context or further queries can determine the speaker's intent.

Based on the passage, first, complete the rule by filling in the blank in (5). Second, state the TWO possible interpretations of [ðeɪɑɹ'plænɪŋə'gɑɹdən] (i.e., write the two sentences for the given utterance).

_____

_____

_____

_____

_____

**50** Read the passage and fill in the blank ① with the ONE most appropriate word and the blank ② with ONE word from the passage. Write your answers in the correct order. [2 points]

Complementary distribution is a fundamental concept of phonology, and interestingly enough, it shows up in everyday life. Table 1 shows that aspirated and unaspirated voiceless stop consonants are in complementary distribution. In general, then, the allophones of a phoneme are in complementary distribution— never occurring in identical environments.

| Syllable-Initial before a Stressed Vowel | | | After a Syllable-Initial /s/ | | | Nonword* | | |
|---|---|---|---|---|---|---|---|---|
| [pʰ] | [tʰ] | [kʰ] | [p] | [t] | [k] | | | |
| *pill* | *till* | *kill* | *spill* | *still* | *skill* | [pɪl]* | [tɪl]* | [kɪl]* |
| [pʰɪl] | [tʰɪl] | [kʰɪl] | [spɪl] | [stɪl] | [skɪl] | [spʰɪl]* | [stʰɪl]* | [skʰɪl]* |
| *par* | *tar* | *car* | *spar* | *star* | *scar* | [paɹ]* | [taɹ]* | [kaɹ]* |
| [pʰaɹ] | [tʰaɹ] | [kʰaɹ] | [spaɹ] | [staɹ] | [skaɹ] | [spʰaɹ]* | [stʰaɹ]* | [skʰaɹ]* |

<Table 1. Distribution of Aspirated Voiceless Stops>

Two sounds are in complementary distribution if /X/ never appears in any of the phonetic environments in which /Y/ occurs.

Complementary distribution alone is insufficient for determining the allophones when there is more than one allophone in the set. The phones must also be phonetically similar, that is, share most phonetic features.

In English, the velar nasal [ŋ] and the glottal fricative [h] are in complementary distribution; [ŋ] does not occur word-initially and [h] does not occur word-finally. But they share very few phonetic features: [ŋ] is a voiced velar nasal stop; [h] is a voiceless glottal fricative. Therefore, they are not allophones of the same phoneme; [ŋ] and [h] are allophones of _____①_____ phonemes.

Two or more sounds are allophones (positional variants) of the _____②_____ phoneme, if (a) they are in complementary distribution, and (b) they are phonetically similar.

**51** **Read the passage and follow the directions.** [4 points]

Languages are permeated with variation: we frequently say the same thing in different ways. The variation in phonology takes two forms. One is the phenomenon of *phonological doublets*, in which one word happens to have two different phonemic forms. For instance, in many people's speech, the word in (1) can be pronounced either way.

(1) economics   [ˌikəˈnɑmɪks], [ˌɛkəˈnɑmɪks]

This does not refer to instances in which different people say certain words differently; rather, a doublet is a case where one and the same person uses both variants. The usual treatment of phonological doublets posits that in the lexicon (the mental store of words in the mind/brain), they have just one listing for their syntactic properties and meaning, but more than one phonemic representation.

The other kind of variation in phonology is when a single phonemic representation gives rise to more than one phonetic form; this is called *free variation*. Here is one example found in the speech of many Americans. In the dialect in question, the vowel phoneme /æ/ has a diphthongal allophone I will transcribe as [ɛ̃ə]. Some data on the distribution of [ɛ̃ə] vs. [æ] are given below:

(2) [æ]                          [ɛ̃ə]

   lap /læp/ [læp]               man /mæn/ [mɛ̃ə̃n], [mæ̃n]

   pal /pæl/ [pæl]               Spanish /spænɪʃ/ [spɛ̃ə̃nɪʃ], [spæ̃nɪʃ]

   pack /pæk/ [pæk]              dance /dæns/ [dɛ̃ə̃ns], [dæ̃ns]

   lab /læb/ [læb]               flannel /ˈflænəl/ [ˈflɛ̃ə̃nəl], [ˈflæ̃nəl]

To summarize the pattern: if an /n/ follows /æ/, then there are two outputs, one with [ɛ̃ə̃] and one with [æ̃]. Otherwise, the observed allophone is [æ]. This [ɛ̃ə̃]~ [æ̃] pattern is systematic; it holds not just for these four words, but for any word in this dialect in which /æ/ precedes /n/.

In analyzing the data, we should first dispose of the distribution of nasality. The nasalization seen on both [ɛ̃ə̃] and [æ̃] is plainly the consequence of Vowel Nasalization. More crucial is the free variation between the monophthongal and diphthongal allophones. These cannot be phonological doublets because they are part of a systematic pattern rather than being idiosyncratic. We need to express the variation with a rule.

An appropriate analysis, then, would be as follows. We set up /æ/ as the basic form of the phoneme, and include the following rule.

(3) /æ/ Diphthongization

$$\text{æ} \rightarrow \text{ɛə} \ / \ \underline{\qquad} \ \text{n}$$

The phoneme /æ/ can be realized as [ɛə] when it precedes /n/.

Based on the passage, first, identify the variation form of the words 'envelope' and 'ban', respectively (i.e., either phonological doublets or free variation). Second, explain why, ONLY based on the description in the passage.

_____

_____

_____

_____

_____

**52** **Read the passage and follow the directions.** [4 points]

| A |

Each set of data in (1) exemplifies an alternation of two phonemes, which takes place when an affix is added to the end of the word.

(1) a. medic — medicine          b. democrat — democracy

    toxic — toxicity                  subvert — subversive

    classic — classicist              pirate — piracy

    critic — criticism                complacent — complacency

  c. suffice — sufficient          d. revise — revision

    race — racia                      enclose — enclosure

    depress — depression              confuse — confusion

    sense — sensual                   erase — erasure

The alternations exemplified in this data are quite regular, and can be expressed in the form of a rule; for example, in (1a), /k/ becomes /s/ when the affix begins with the vowel /ɪ/. Similarly, in (1b), /t/ becomes /s/ under the same condition. We can combine these two rules as in (2):

(2) $Rule\ 1\ \begin{Bmatrix} k \\ t \end{Bmatrix} \rightarrow s\ /\ \_\_\_ + \text{ɪ}$

(1c) and (1d) illustrate a different rule; /s/ changes to /ʃ/, and /z/ changes to /ʒ/. It seems that this change takes place when the affix begins with /ɪ/ or /j/, followed immediately by a vowel. But when the preceding consonant is /s/, the sequences /sɪ/ or /sj/ coalesce into /ʃ/. Similarly, the sequences /zɪ/ or /zj/ coalesce into /ʒ/. This happens only when another vowel follows immediately. The rule can be formulated as in (3):

(3) $Rule\ 2\ \begin{Bmatrix} s \\ z \end{Bmatrix} + \begin{Bmatrix} \text{ɪ} \\ j \end{Bmatrix} + \begin{Bmatrix} \text{ʃ} \\ 3 \end{Bmatrix}\ /\ \_\_\_ V$

Now look at the following data in (4). From the data given, work out which two phonemes are in alternation:

(4) a. relate — relation
     confident — confidential
     convert — conversion
     infect — infectious

   b. magic — magician
     music — musician
     silica — siliceous

Set (4a) illustrates a relationship between /t/ and /ʃ/; set (4b) a relationship between /k/ and /ʃ/. The environment requires an affix which begins with /ɪ/ or /j/, followed immediately by a vowel, as in sets (1c) and (1d) above. The rule for (4a) and (4b) combined is therefore as follows:

(5) $Rule\ 3\ \begin{Bmatrix} k \\ t \end{Bmatrix} + \begin{Bmatrix} 1 \\ j \end{Bmatrix} \rightarrow \int / \underline{\quad} V$

| B |
|---|

| | | |
|---|---|---|
| logician | fanaticism | incision |
| malicious | permissive | presidential |

Based on the passage, first, identify TWO words in <B> that Rule 3 is applied. Second, state how the rule is applied to each word, just as described in the passage.

_____

_____

_____

_____

_____

**53** Read the passage and fill in each blank with the ONE most appropriate word. Write your answers in the correct order. [2 points]

> Assimilation rules in languages reflect coarticulation—the spreading of phonetic features either in the anticipation or in the perseveration of articulatory processes. The auditory effect is that words sound smoother.
>
> There are many assimilation rules in English and other languages. The voiced /z/ of the English regular plural suffix is changed to [s] after a voiceless sound, and that similarly the voiced /d/ of the English regular past-tense suffix is changed to [t] after a voiceless sound. These are instances of voicing assimilation. In these cases the value of the voicing feature goes from [+ voice] to [− voice] because of assimilation to the [− voice] feature of the final consonant of the stem, as in the derivation of *cats*:
>
> (1) /kæt + z/ → [kæts]
>
> We saw a different kind of assimilation rule. Regressive assimilation helps explain the various allomorphic forms of the English negative prefix: *in-, im-, ir-, il-*. Note that the unmarked prefix *in-* occurs in all cases except when the following sound is a bilabial or a liquid: *indecent, inept, invalid*. However, when the following sound is a bilabial, the organs of speech approach a position closer to that of the conditioning sound to produce [ɪm-], as in *impossible* or *immobile* and to produce [ɪŋ-], as in *incongruous* or *incorrect*. In these cases, the negative morpheme prefix spelled *in-* or *im-* agrees in _____①_____ of articulation with the word to which it is prefixed. Similarly, when followed by the liquids /l/ and /r/, the negative prefix is conditioned or changed to *il-* and *ir-* respectively, as in *illogical* and *irrational*. In these data, the negative morpheme prefix agrees in _____②_____ of articulation.

**54** **Read the passage and follow the directions.** [4 points]

The core of the Scottish Vowel-Length Rule (SVLR) has been stated as follows: while lax vowels are invariably short, tense vowels are either long or short, depending on their contexts. Long realisation of tense-vowel phonemes is somehow related to their position: either word or morphological boundary. Consider the following examples:

(1) a. Long vowel                    Short vowel
     /i/ breathe leave ease ear see    Leith leaf leash leap feel keen
     /e/ wave maze bear day            pace waif fake fade fail name
     /a/ halve vase par spa            half pass path mad cap calm
     /u/ smooth groove sure shoe       youth hoof use loot fool tune
     /o/ loathe grove pose shore go    loaf close loath coat foal foam
     /ɔ/ pause paw                     cough loss bought cot call done

   b. Short vowel
     /ɪ/ give fizz pith dish fill lip fin
     /ɛ/ rev Des her mess pet tell ten
     /ʌ/ love does duff lush pull cup pun

Example (1a) shows the distribution of long and short realisations of the tense-vowel phonemes: they are realised as long before a/an ____①____ boundary, a non-lateral /r/ and the other environment, but they are short elsewhere. The lax vowel phonemes are realised as short in all contexts, including those where tense vowels would be long (love, live, rev etc.).

Of the three diphthongs of Scottish Standard English (SSE), /aɪ aʊ ɔɪ/, the first one somewhat surprisingly is subject to SVLR. Here are some examples:

(2) 'long' [a·ɪ]                      'short' [ʌɪ]
     drive rise writhe shy            life rice light file fine

SVLR has presented a problem for the analysis: /aɪ/ is the only diphthong that undergoes SVLR.

Now consider the following data in (3). SVLR occurs in a/an _____②_____ boundary rather than the position before a pause or at the end of an utterance:

(3) a. Long vowel

    kneed brewed stayed

    towed gnawed baad sighed

    freely slowness

b. Short vowel

    need brood staid

    toad nod bad side

    Healey bonus

**Based on the passage, first, fill in each blank with ONE word from the passage. Write your answers in the correct order. Second, state one more environment where tense-vowel phonemes are realised as long in (1).**

---

---

---

---

---

## 55 Read the passage and follow the directions. [4 points]

---| A |---

The words listed in (1) below have final stress (as marked) for many speakers.

(1)  a. ca'det　　　b. ˌmar'quee　　c. ba'lloon　　d. e'llipse
　　　ca'nal　　　　de'gree　　　　ˌar'cade　　　la'ment
　　　ga'zette　　　ca'noe　　　　ˈra'vine　　　ri'poste
　　　ˌmarzi'pan　　ˌbou'quet　　　ˌcham'pagne　ˌcomman'dant
　　　ˌcatama'ran　　　　　　　　ˌlam'poon
　　　　　　　　　　　　　　　maga'zine

The syllable-weight requirement for stressed syllables makes the prediction that there are no final-stressed words in English that end in a light syllable—just as there are no monosyllabic words consisting of a light syllable. This prediction is correct: no English word with final stress ends in a lax vowel. All the examples in (1) end in heavy syllables: (1a) ends in VC, (1b) in V:, (1c) in V:C and (1d) in V(:)CC. This fact confirms the correlation between syllable weight and stress. Another observation regarding this correlation can be made among the bisyllabic words in (1).

What the list in (1) does not reveal is the fact that nouns with final stress are comparatively rare in English; indeed, the length of this list is somewhat misleading. Many of the examples given there are rather uncommon loan words, and it would be difficult to compile such a collection if one were to exclude such rare words, just as it would be to double the list.

The reader may well have disagreed with some of the stress patterns given in (1): for example, in some dialects (or for certain speakers, or in colloquial speech) we find ˈcommanˌdant, ˈmarziˌpan, ˈarcade, ˈbouˌquet etc. Notice also the variable stress patterns in the following words, not listed in (1):

(2) finance: [fi'nans] or [ˌfaɪ'nans] or ['faɪˌnans]
　　romance: [rə'mans] or [ˌro'mans] or ['roˌmans]

As a result of these stress shifts (speaker-, dialect-, style- or contextspecific), then, the class of end-stressed nouns is unstable. Now consider common class of nouns that constantly have a primary-secondary stress pattern, as in (3):

(3) 'rab͵bi      'syn͵tax      'chromo͵some
     'kum͵quat      'tex͵tile      'nightin͵gale

---

**B**

Consider the following nouns in (4):

(4) artiste      hotel        camomile
     brigade      bamboo     convoy

Based on the passage, first, identify TWO words in &lt;B&gt; which show the same stress pattern as in (3). Second, state the requirement where secondary stress occurs on the first syllable among the bisyllabic examples in (1).

_____

_____

_____

_____

_____

**56** Read the passage and fill in each blank with ONE word from the passage. Write your answers in the correct order. [2 points]

---

One of the most important factors in locating stress within the word is syllable structure. Consider the stress placement in the nouns listed below, where syllable boundaries are indicated by dots.

(1) e.le.phant
   wa.lla.by
   al.ge.bra
   oc.to.pus
(2) hy.e.na
   com.pu.ter
   po.ta.to
   ko.a.la
(3) ve.ran.da
   u.ten.sil
   con.vic.tion
   pen.tath.lon

In (1), the words have _____①_____ stress, whereas those in (2) and (3) have stress on the penultimate syllable. For the majority of nouns in English, stress is determined by the nature of the penultimate syllable, or more specifically the nature of the rhyme of the penultimate syllable, since what (if anything) is in the onset is irrelevant to stress placement. In (1) the penultimate rhyme is just a short vowel nucleus, whereas in (2) the penultimate rhyme has a long vowel or a diphthong in the nucleus and in (3) the penultimate rhyme is a short vowel nucleus followed by a consonant in the coda. So there is more 'phonological material' in the rhymes of the penultimate syllables in the words in (2) and (3).

---

Syllables (or rhymes) consisting of long vowels, diphthongs or those with codas, such as those exemplified by the penults in (2) and (3) are known as heavy; syllables with rhymes consisting only of a short vowel are known as light. For the majority of English nouns of more than two syllables, if the penultimate syllable is heavy, it takes stress; if the penultimate syllable is light, stress is placed one syllable to the left, on the antepenultimate (even if this is also light). In two syllable words, the words typically have stress on the _____②_____ syllable irrespective of its weight, as shown in (4).

(4) muskrat        turnip        parrot        cobra

**57** **Read the passage and follow the directions.** [4 points]

Nasal consonants are particularly susceptible to assimilation. In morpheme-final clusters, the nasal is always homorganic with the following plosive, that is, they share the same place of articulation.

However, the process is even more extensive than this. We can see from this data that the nasal's locus of articulation varies quite precisely according to the following obstruent. Look at the following data:

(1) lamp       [-mp]       (bilabial)

 lymph       [-ɱf]       (labio-dental)

 tenth       [-n̪θ]       (dental)

 hint       [-nt]       (alveolar)

 inch       [-ɲʧ]       (palato-alveolar)

 wink       [-ŋk]       (velar)

Nasal assimilation is sensitive not only to the locus of the following obstruent, but also to the (wider) environments in which it occurs. The examples in (1) above illustrate its operation within the morpheme.

Nasal assimilation operates across syllable boundaries, as in *amphora* ([-ɱf-]); and it also operates in the following environment as in (2).

(2) [ʌmprədʌktiv]       unproductive

 [ʌmbitn̩]       unbeaten

 [ɪŋkəplit]       incomplete

 [ʌŋgreʃəs]       ungracious

In this case the assimilation is optional: pronunciations with [ɪn-, ʌn-] are also possible. There is also optional assimilation as shown in (3):

(3) [ɪɱ fækt]       in fact

 [ɪŋ kes]       in case

 [ʧeŋ gæŋ]       chain gang

Yet, despite the fact that nasal assimilation occurs across some boundaries, it does not occur before a/an _____ suffix and a past tense suffix even though the nasal precedes the obstruent, as shown in (4):

(4) [rɪŋz]      rings

    [sɪŋz]      sings

    [sʌmz]      sums

    [rɪŋd]      ringed

    [rɑŋd]      wronged

**Based on the passage, first, fill in the blank with the ONE most appropriate word. Second, state each environment where nasal assimilation optionally occurs in (2) and (3).**

_____

_____

_____

_____

_____

## 58 Read the passages and follow the directions. [4 points]

┤ A ├

A stop is a sound that involves complete closure of the oral cavity. The articulators come so close together that no air can escape between them.

In continuants, on the other hand, the air stream is not totally blocked in the oral cavity—it can escape continuously through the mouth. The consonants in *sue, zoo, lie, you, thigh,* etc. are continuants.

Note that definitions of stops and continuants are mutually exclusive: any sound that is not a stop is a continuant, and vice versa. We may therefore distinguish speech sounds in terms of the binary feature [+ continuant] vs [− continuant]. Example (1) below gives some examples of this phonetic distinction:

(1) [+ continuant]        [− continuant]

    rye, lie, you, woo       pea, tea, key

    thigh, thy, sue, zoo, etc.    buy, die, guy

    all vowels               my, nigh, etc.

Obviously, this distinction alone does not suffice to characterise manners of articulation in precise phonetic terms. A sonorant is a sound whose phonetic content is predominantly made up by the sound waves produced by its voicing. In other words, sonorants are characterised by 'periodic acoustic energy'. There are no voiceless sonorants because, simply speaking, the removal of voicing from a sonorant makes it nondistinct from other members of this set and practically inaudible.

In contrast, obstruent articulation involves an obstruction of the air stream that produces a phonetic effect independent of voicing. Obstruents can typically occur in voiced and voiceless variants. Sonorants are always voiced.

Again, the two categories, sonorant and obstruent, have been defined in a mutually exclusive way: any nonsonorant is automatically an obstruent and vice versa. We may simplify our terminology and characterise speech sounds as either [+ sonorant] or [− sonorant]. The list in (2) below gives some English examples of both.

(2) [+ sonorant]    [− sonorant]

    my, nigh    pea, tea, key

    lie, rye    buy, die, guy

    you, woo    thigh, sue, etc.

    all vowels    thy, zoo, etc.

Together, the two features make up manners of articulation or, to put it the other way around, what we refer to as manners of articulation are combinations of the basic properties that the two features describe.

---

**B**

Two features, each of them binary, can be combined with each other in four different ways. In the case of the features [Sonorant] and [Continuant], the four combinations given in (3) below are possible; any given sound will fit into one of these four categories:

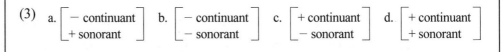

(3)  a. $\begin{bmatrix} - \text{continuant} \\ + \text{sonorant} \end{bmatrix}$  b. $\begin{bmatrix} - \text{continuant} \\ - \text{sonorant} \end{bmatrix}$  c. $\begin{bmatrix} + \text{continuant} \\ - \text{sonorant} \end{bmatrix}$  d. $\begin{bmatrix} + \text{continuant} \\ + \text{sonorant} \end{bmatrix}$

**Based on the passages, first, identify the feature combinations of all stop sounds, using the number (3a—3d) in <B>. Second, state ONE natural class of consonant sounds that the feature combination (3d) refers to.**

_____

_____

_____

_____

_____

**59** Read the passage and follow the directions. [4 points]

The rhyme of a syllable is a unit that consists of the peak and the coda. But one question arises here: why do we need to recognise the rhyme as a phonological unit? Why do we not simply analyse a syllable (such as *clamp*) as in (1a) and propose instead the rather more complex analysis (1b)?

(1)

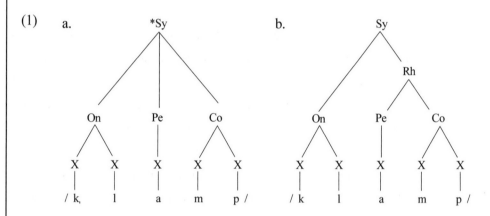

Note: Sy = Syllable, On = Onset, Pe = Peak, Co = Coda, Rh = Rhyme

The reason for having the rhyme as a unit is that peak and coda 'function together' rather than separately in a number of ways. In the case of monosyllabic words, it can be shown that it is the number of X-positions in the rhyme that determines whether or not a syllable is well-formed. Consider the following examples:

(2) a. eye    b. sit    c. seal    d. clamp    e. */klaɪmp/    f. finds

Ignoring the example in (2f), we find that (2a-d) are well-formed syllables while (2e) is not. Here are their full analyses in terms of the notation developed above:

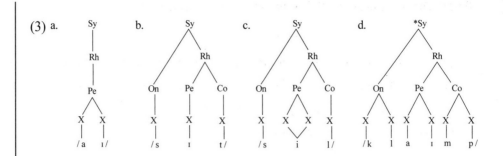

Provided we can account for *finds* and *seals* by different means, we can make the generalisation that well-formed syllables contain no more than three X-positions in the rhyme. Notice how peak and coda interact in this calculation of maximal syllables: it makes no difference to the well-formedness of a syllable whether the peak contains two X-positions and the coda one, or vice versa. It is the sum of X-positions in peak plus coda that counts, not the way in which these X-positions are distributed. This is the reason for introducing the rhyme into our model of syllable structure: without the rhyme, it would be rather difficult to make generalisations about maximal syllables.

**Based on the passage, identify whether /ɛlm/ and /silm/ are well-formed or not, and then explain why, including the sum of X-positions of each word in the rhyme.**

_____

_____

_____

_____

_____

**60** Read the passage and fill in the blank with the TWO most appropriate words. Write your answer with the natural class. [2 points]

> Coalescent assimilation is a type of reciprocal assimilation. Figure 1 illustrates how the first and second sounds in a sequence come together and mutually condition the creation of a third sound with features from both original sounds.
>
> **Sound A** + **Sound B**
>
> ↘ ↙
>
> **Sound C**
>
> *Figure 1 The process of coalescent assimilation*
>
> The consonants /s, z/ may undergo palatalization and turn into [ʃ, ʒ] respectively, when they occur before the palatal glide /j/. Consider the following examples:
>
> (1) I miss_you                [ʃ]
>
>     this_year            [ʃ]
>
>     I please_you        [ʒ]
>
>     Who's_your boss?    [ʒ]
>
> Also noteworthy is the fact that /t, d/ may turn into palato-alveolar affricates when they are followed by the palatal glide /j/ in the following word.
>
> (2) Would_you mind moving?    [dʒ]
>
>     proce_dure                [dʒ]
>
>     ate_your dinner       [tʃ]
>
>     sta_ture                  [tʃ]
>
> Thus, we can put together the data in (1) and (2), and state the rule as in (3):
>
> (3) _____ become palatoalveolars when followed by a word that starts with the palatal glide /j/.

**61** **Read the passage and follow the directions.** [4 points]

┤ A ├

It has been apparent that monosyllabic words can violate the core-syllable pattern: for example, the problems are posed by the initial /s/ in *spring* and by the final /s/ in *clamps*. As regards the rhyme, both of the two constraints on the form of this phonological unit can be violated: there may be more than three X-positions in the rhyme, and there may be violations of our generalisation that sonority decreases from left to right. Both these pattern violations are exemplified by the final consonant in *clamps*.

Consider the examples of *Three-X exceeded* and *Sonority violated* pattern violations in (1).

(1)

| Three-X exceeded | Sonority violated | Both | Offending segment |
|:---:|:---:|:---:|:---:|
| mind | begged | lobed | /d/ |
| paint | dropped | text | /t/ |
| Glides | adze | minds | /z/ |
| bounce | fox | drinks | /s/ |
|  | width | length | /Ө/ |
| lounge |  |  | /dʒ/ |

Note that it is common for segments at the end of the rhyme to violate both constraints: they may exceed the limit of three X-positions and violate the sonority generalisation. Note also that in some cases, offending segments are inflexional endings (for plural or past tense) while in others they are not. The examples in (1) show clearly that we have to allow for certain consonants to occur after the final consonant of an otherwise well-formed core syllable.

All the examples listed in (1) contain one or more consonants that cannot be part of the core syllable. Here are two examples that contain more than one such consonant: *minds* and *texts*.

(2)

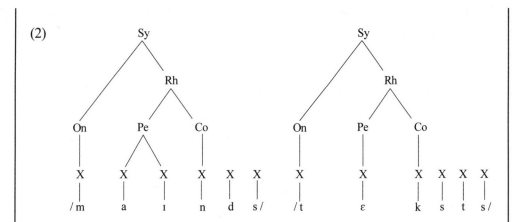

In *minds*, the /n/ must be the final segment of the core syllable because it is the third X in the rhyme, while in *texts*, the /k/ is the final segment of the core syllable because the following /s/ fails to conform with the sonority generalisation.

   It would seem at first sight, then, that the constraints on the structure of the rhyme are invalid. However, what makes our previous generalisations still valid is the fact that the segments that can be appended to the core syllable fall into a very clearly defined class. To accommodate the cases listed in (1), we allow a rhyme to contain a core rhyme plus further X-positions, which must contain certain natural class, and which we shall refer to as the appendix.

---

| B |

| globes | beans | flounce | fifth |
| hinge | filed | coax | hoofed | lads |

Based on the passage, first, identify ALL and ONLY words in <B> which violate both of the two constraints, *Three-X exceeded* AND *Sonority violated*. Second, state the natural class that can be appended to the core syllable, considering the data in (1).

_____

_____

_____

_____

_____

**62** Read the passage and fill in each blank with the appropriate feature. Write your answers in the correct order. [2 points]

---

Fricatives are segments like the [f v s z] of *feel, veal, seal, zeal,* respectively. They are articulated by squeezing the outgoing air stream between an articulator (the lower lip or some part of the tongue) and a point of articulation (the upper lip or some part of the roof of the mouth) so that turbulence or friction—rubbing —results. Fricatives are like stops in three features but differ in one. Like stops, they are the result of aperiodic vibration, therefore [− sonorant]; they require some interruption of the air stream, so they are [+ consonantal]; they are not typically the peaks of syllables and so are designated [− syllabic]. Finally, unlike stops, fricatives are [+ continuant] since air is flowing continuously out of the mouth. Say *cup* and see if you can prolong the final sound; say *cuff* and hold the last sound as long as you can.

Nasals are segments like the [m] of *mitt* and the [n] of *knit,* sounds made by stopping the flow of air somewhere in the mouth but letting it exit through the nose. Nasals are musical—[+ sonorant]—as every singer and teacher of singing knows. Since the air stream is interrupted in the mouth, they are [ ① ]. Since air does not escape through the mouth, they are [ ② ]. This is a matter of definition; [+ continuant] is defined to mean 'with air flowing out the mouth'; actually a nasal can be prolonged because air is flowing continuously through another exit. Say *come* and make the last sound continue as long as you have breath. Last, we classify nasals as both plus and minus syllabic—[± syllabic]. They are usually not the peak of a syllable, but they can be, as in the word *kitten.*

Liquids include the [l] of *lead* and the [r] of *read.* In their articulation the tongue is raised, partly impeding the flow of air, but the tongue is shaped in such a way that air flows around it, creating particular patterns of vibration. Because of the impedance liquids are classed as [+ consonantal]; because of the periodic vibration they are [+ sonorant]; because air flows freely they are [+ continuant]. Finally, like nasals, they are [± syllabic]—usually not the peak of a syllable but sometimes the peak, as in *metal* and *manner.*

---

## 63 Read the passage and follow the directions. [4 points]

┤ A ├

Take a look at some words that are morphologically complex in that they consist of roots and suffixes. We shall distinguish between two types of suffixes: inflexional and derivational. Inflexional suffixes produce different forms of the same word: for example, the plural form (*cameras*) of *camera*, the present participle form (*developing*) of the verb *develop*, the past tense of verbs (*commented*) and so on. Derivational suffixes, in contrast, produce new words; along with compounding (as in *fireplace*, *snowball*), the derivational morphology forms part of the word-formation devices in the grammar. Thus the suffix *-less* attaches to a noun base and forms adjectives (*penniless*, *driverless*, *luckless*); *-ly* attaches to adjectives and forms adverbs (*nicely*, *carefully*); *-ee* attaches to verbal bases and forms nouns (*employee*, *payee*) and so forth.

(1)

| Inflexional | Derivational | Derivational |
|---|---|---|
| a. tallies | b. penniless | c. atomic |
| developing | nationhood | solemnity |
| commented | solemnly | substantial |
| furnishes | interpretable | Newtonian |
| cameras | openness | humidity |

On the phonological side, such suffixes may be divided into two classes—stress-shifting and stess-neutral; and, as is shown in (1), this division is not congruent with the division, on the morphological side, into inflexional and derivational suffixes.

Let us deal with stress-neutral suffixes first. Such suffixes have two properties that set them apart from the other, stress-shifting class, Firstly, they never make any difference to the stress pattern of their base, that is, of the word to which they are attached. When, for example, the third person singular -s is added to the verb *tally*, the final syllable becomes heavy (*tallies*); nevertheless, the stress remains on the initial syllable. The second property of stress-neutral suffixes is that such suffixes are always unstressed—even where they constitute heavy syllables, and even where several such suffixes are stacked together. Stress-neutral suffixes, then, are simply appended as unstressed material to an entirely unmodified base.

The behaviour of stress-shifting suffixes is different in both respects. Firstly, the stress pattern of the word may radically differ from that of the base to which stress-shifting suffixes are attached. Secondly, stress-shifting suffixes differ from stress-neutral ones in that they themselves can bear the main stress of the word.

---

| B |

Consider the following data in (2):

(2) *-ant*       ascendant, exhalant, reactant

 *-ette*      usherette, maisonette, launderette

 *-ese*      Japanese, Cantonese, Chinese

 *-esque*     picturesque, picaresque, arabesque

 *-some*      burdensome, toilsome, heartsome

---

Based on the passage <A>, first, state the class of derivational suffixes in (1b) and (1c), using the terms, *stress-shifting* and *stress-neutral*. Second, identify ALL stress-shifting suffixes in (2).

_____

_____

_____

_____

_____

## 64 Read the passages and follow the directions. [4 points]

─────────┤ A ├─────────

The basic generalisation concerning the stress contours of phrases is exemplified by *black bird*: the second (phrase-final) one (*bird*) bears the main stress and the first one (*black*) a lesser stress. Here are some more examples:

(1) a. Noun phrases
    good work
    heavy metal
    scientific investigations

  b. Adjective phrases
    very good
    incredibly heavy
    allegedly scientific

  c. Verb phrases
    drinks heavily
    knows everything
    rested after lunch

  d. Adverb phrases
    rather enthusiastically
    quite clearly
    very well

  e. Sentences
    Roger disapproved
    Cigars stink
    Jennifer smokes

Let us now express these stress patterns in terms of metrical trees. In the construction of such trees, two questions arise: what is the form of the tree, and what are the prominence relations among its branches? The answer to the former question is here trivial: the metrical tree is here automatically a copy of the syntactic structure as the examples shown in (2).

(2)

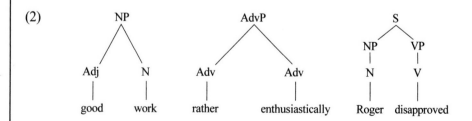

The metrical trees, expressing both structure and prominence relations, then look like in (3):

(3)

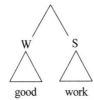
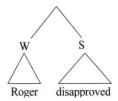

|   |   |   |
| W | S | W | S | W | S |
| good | work | rather | enthusiastically | Roger | disapproved |

The rule that governs such prominence relations among word trees within phrases has the following form:

(4) Phrasal Prominence Rule

In a pair of sister nodes $[N_1\ N_2]_p$, where P is a phrasal category, $N_2$ is strong.

---

**B**

In more complex constructions, the form of the metrical tree is determined by that of the syntactic tree structure. Now consider the construction in (5):

(5) Many students attend lectures regularly.

**Bearing in mind the metrical tree of the construction in (5), first, identify the strongest stress in the noun phrase (i.e., Subject) and the higher verb phrase of the construction in (5), respectively. Second, state which word should be the strongest stress of the WHOLE construction in (5).**

_____

_____

_____

_____

_____

**65** Read the passage and fill in each blank with ONE word from the passage. Write your answers in the correct order. [2 points]

> Vowel articulations are not as easy to feel at first as consonant articulations because the vocal tract is not narrowed as much. To become acquainted with vowel articulation, alternately pronounce the vowels of *he* and *awe*. You will feel the tongue move from a high front to a low back position. Once you feel this tongue movement, alternate between the vowels of *awe* and *at*. You will feel the tongue moving from the low back to low front position. Finally, alternate between the vowels of *he* and *who*. You will notice that in addition to a tongue movement between the high front and high back positions, you are also rounding your lips for the [u].
>
> Vowels for which the tongue is neither raised nor lowered are called mid vowels. The front vowel of English *made* and *fame* is mid, front, and unrounded. The vowel of *code* and *soak* is mid, back, and rounded. The vowels are summed up in table 1. Note that in describing the vowels, the articulatory parameters are presented in the order *height, backness, rounding*.

| TABLE 1. Basic phonetic parameters for describing Canadian English vowels | | |
|---|---|---|
| heat | [i] | high front unrounded |
| fate | [eɪ] | mid front unrounded |
| mad | [æ] | low front unrounded |
| Sue | [u] | high back rounded |
| boat | [ow] | mid back rounded |
| sun | [ʌ] | mid central unrounded |
| cot, caught | [ɑ] | low back ____①____ |

As shown in table 1, in standard Canadian English, there is no difference between the vowels of a pair of words like *cot* and *caught*, both of which contain the vowel [ɑ]. In some dialects of North American English, as well as in many other dialects of English worldwide, the vowel of *caught* (and certain other words such as *law*) is the mid back _____②_____ lax vowel [ɔ].

Note that non-front vowels are traditionally divided into central and back vowels; often the term *back* alone is used for all non-front vowels.

## 66 Read the passage and follow the directions. [4 points]

The IPA represents speech in the form of segments—individual phones like [p], [s], or [m]. Segments are produced by coordinating a number of individual articulatory gestures including jaw movement, lip shape, and tongue placement. Many of these individual activities are represented as smaller subunits called features, of which segments are composed.

Some articulatory features are distinctive and others are redundant. There are four features for distinguishing classes of speech sounds: [sonorant], [syllabic], [continuant] and [consonantal]. We need to recognize that even features which are distinctive in some areas may be used redundantly in other areas.

The feature [+ syllabic] is sufficient to designate the class of vowels; no other class has this feature. So the other features, [+ sonorant, + continuant, − consonantal], while they describe true facts about the pronunciation of vowels, have no role in telling how vowels are different from other classes of segments. For classification, one feature is distinctive, the other features are redundant. We can express this fact in a redundancy statement as in (1):

(1) Whatever is [+ syllabic] is redundantly [+ sonorant, + continuant, − consonantal].

Or more briefly like this:

(2) If [+ syllabic], then [+ sonorant, + continuant, − consonantal].

For glides we need two features together, [− consonantal] and [− syllabic], for a distinctive label. The feature [− consonantal] distinguishes vowels and glides together from other classes, and the feature [− syllabic] distinguishes glides from vowels. So the features [+ sonorant] and [+ continuant] are redundant. The redundancy statement for glides is shown in (3):

(3) If [− consonantal, − syllabic], then [+ sonorant, + continuant].

What is the redundancy statement for nasals?

(4) If [+ sonorant, ____①____], then [____②____, − syllabic].

First, fill in each blank with ONE feature from the passage. Write your answers in the correct order. Second, state the redundancy statement for *Liquids*, starting with the feature *sonorant*, as shown in the passage.

_____

_____

_____

_____

_____

**67** **Read the passage and follow the directions.** [4 points]

The context in which aspiration occurs is the syllable-initial position. The general rule of aspiration is as follows:

(1) Rule 1: Aspiration is strongest in the initial position of stressed syllables.

Let us consider the following examples in (2):

(2) a. pit [pʰɪt]     b. spit [spɪt]     c. bit [bɪt]
    tie [tʰaɪ]         sty [staɪ]        die [daɪ]
    come [kʰʌm]     scum [skʌm]     gum [gʌm]

Aspiration does not occur in the examples in (2b), where voiceless stops are preceded in syllable onsets by /s/. Hence, the /p/ is aspirated in *pit* but not in *spit*, in *tie* but not in *sty*, etc. There is also no aspiration of the voiced stops in (2c)—aspiration is clearly restricted to voiced stops.

Consider the further examples in (3) where aspiration also occurs:

(3) polite [pʰəlaɪt]     vacuum [vakʰjuəm]     pickle [pʰɪkʰəl]

These data imply the following rule:

(4) Rule 2: Aspiration also occurs in _____.

The production of the sonorant falls partly or completely within the aspiration period of the stop, and devoicing of the sonorant occurs:

(5) Rule 3: A sonorant is devoiced when it follows a voiceless aspirated stop in syllable onset position.

Now consider the data in (6):

(6) a. pray /preɪ/       b. spring /sprɪŋ/       c. apron /eprən/
       play /pleɪ/          split /splɪt/             applaud /əplɔd/
       crew /kru/          screw /skru/            across /əkrɒs/
       clue /klu/                                          proclaim /prəklem/
       try /traɪ/                                           attract /ətrakt/
       twig /twɪg/                                       matron /metrən/
       tune /tjun/

    d. atlas /atləs/       e. brew [bru]
       butler /bʌtlə/         drew [dru]
       Watney /wɒtnɪ/        glue [glu]

Based on the passage, first, complete the rule in (4) by filling in the blank with TWO words. Second, identify TWO data sets in (6) where devoicing of the sonorant occurs, using the number (6a)—(6e).

_____

_____

_____

_____

**68** **Read the passage and follow the directions.** [4 points]

In a *dynamic neutralization*, there is alternation: morphemes are actively changed in order to respect the pattern of contextually limited contrast. In English words, it is impossible for two final obstruents to disagree in their value for voicing.

The past tense suffix, which is analyzed as underlying /-d/, is actively devoiced (surfacing as [-t]) whenever this is necessary to avoid a disagreement in voicing between two _____ in the syllable final position as shown in (1).

(1) a. paid [peɪ-d]
     filled [fɪl-d]
     barred [bɑɹ-d]
     slammed [slæm-d]
  b. rubbed [ɹʌb-d]
     eased [iz-d]
     dragged [dɹæg-d]
     lived [lɪv-d]
  c. picked [pɪk-t]
     tapped [tæp-t]
     missed [mɪs-t]
     laughed [læf-t]

The usual analysis given for this pattern is to assume that a phonological rule of Voicing Assimilation changes the voicing of the /d/ where necessary to avoid a voicing conflict.

Consider now a case of *static neutralization* in (2), also from English. English words can end in two stops, but only under certain condition.

(2) a. concept [ˈkɑnsɛpt]      b. *[ˈkɑnsɛtp]
       contact [ˈkɑntækt]         *[ˈkɑntætk]
       milked [mɪlkt]             *[mɪltk]
       rubbed [ɹʌbd]              *[ɹʌdb]
       bagged [bægd]              *[bædg]

Speakers of English immediately recognize such hypothetical words in (2b) as ill-formed, and often regard them as hard to pronounce. Unlike Voicing Assimilation, however, there are no cases of repair in (2).

Based on the passage, first, fill in the blank with ONE word from the passage. Second, state the natural class of the second consonant where English words can end in two stops in (2).

_____

_____

_____

_____

_____

**69** Read the passage and fill in each blank with the ONE most appropriate word. Write your answers in the correct order. [2 points]

Deletion is a process that removes a segment from certain phonetic contexts. Deletion occurs in everyday rapid speech in many languages. In English, a schwa [ə] is often deleted when the next vowel in the word is _____①_____, as shown in (1). (Notice that in the first two words, the deletion of the schwa creates the environment for the [r] to become devoiced.)

(1) *Slow speech*    *Rapid speech*

    [pʰəred]        [pr̥ed]        parade

    [kʰərowd]     [kr̥owd]      corrode

    [səpʰowz]     [spowz]      suppose

Deletion also occurs as an alternative to dissimilation in words such as *fifths*. Many speakers delete the [θ] of the final consonant cluster and say [fɪfs]. In very rapid speech, both the second [f] and the [θ] are sometimes deleted, resulting in [fɪs].

Epenthesis is a process that inserts a syllabic or a non-syllabic segment within an existing string of segments. For example, in careful speech, the words *warmth* and *something* are pronounced [wɔrmθ] and [sʌ̃mθɪŋ]. It is common in casual speech for speakers to insert a [p] between the [m] and the [θ] and pronounce the words [wɔrmpθ] and [sʌ̃mpθɪŋ]. Consonant epenthesis of this type is another example of a coarticulation phenomenon. In English, the articulatory transition from a sonorant consonant to a non-sonorant appears to be eased by the insertion of a consonant that shares properties of both segments. Notice that the epenthesized consonants are all non-sonorant, have the same _____②_____ of articulation as the sonorant consonant to their left, and have the same voicing as the non-sonorant consonant to their right as shown in table 1.

| TABLE 1. Some examples of English consonant epenthesis | | |
|---|---|---|
| *Word* | *Non-epenthesized pronunciation* | *Epenthesized pronunciation* |
| something | [sʌ̃məɪ̃ŋ] | [sʌ̃mpəɪ̃ŋ] |
| warmth | [wɔrmə] | [wɔrmpə] |
| length | [lɛ̃ŋə] | [lɛ̃ŋkə] |
| prince | [prĩns] | [prĩnts] |
| tenth | [tɛ̃nə] | [tɛ̃ntə] |

## 70 Read the passage and follow the directions. [4 points]

Some of the alternation rules in English can be illustrated as follows:

(1) Velar softening: $\left\{ \begin{array}{l} \left\{ \begin{array}{l} k \\ t \end{array} \right\} \rightarrow s \\ d \rightarrow z \end{array} \right\} / \_\_ +\imath$

(2) Palatalization: $\left\{ \begin{array}{l} s \\ z \end{array} \right\} + \left\{ \begin{array}{l} \imath \\ j \end{array} \right\} \rightarrow \left\{ \begin{array}{l} \int \\ 3 \end{array} \right\} / \_\_ V$

(3) Z-devoicing: $z \rightarrow s / \_\_ + \imath v$

(4) Vowel lengthening: $V \rightarrow \left\{ \begin{array}{l} [V] / \_\_ [-voice] \\ [V'] \text{ elsewhere} \end{array} \right\}$

(5) Past tense: $+d \rightarrow \left\{ \begin{array}{l} \partial d / \left\{ \begin{array}{l} t \\ d \end{array} \right\} \_\_ \\ T / [-son.] \_\_ \\ d / [+son.] \_\_ \end{array} \right\}$

(6) Flapping: $\left\{ \begin{array}{l} t \\ d \end{array} \right\} \rightarrow [\mathfrak{r}] / \; 'V \_\_ V$

We shall illustrate the rules, and the ordering sequence, with some sample 'derivations' which proceed, step by step, from the underlying representation to an approximate pronunciation.

| (7) | corrosion | corroded |
|---|---|---|
| Input | /kə'roʊd+ɪən/ | /kə'roʊd+d/ |
| Output | [kə'roʊ·ʒən] | [kə'roʊ·ɾəd] |

*Note: · indicates lengthened vowel*

| (8) | delighted | corrosive |
|---|---|---|
| Input | /dɪ'laɪt+d/ | /kə'roʊd+ɪv/ |
| Output | [dɪ'laɪɾəd] | [kə'roʊsɪv] |

The derivations show that the ordering of these rules is quite important. The flapping rule (6) has to follow the past-tense rule (5), because the latter provides the unstressed vowel which is needed as (part of) the environment for the rule (6) (as in *delighted* in (8)). In the sequence, the flapping rule (6) has been put after the vowel length rule (4). The result is that a word with a 'voiceless' origin (*delighted*) is pronounced with a short vowel (/aɪ/ in terms of length) before the flap. If the rules had been put in the opposite order, we would have the output [dɪˈlaɪ·ɾəd].

**Based on the passage, in (7) state THREE rules applied to the words 'corrosion' AND 'corroded', respectively.**

_____

_____

_____

_____

_____

**71** **Read the passage and follow the directions.** [4 points]

In casual speech, assimilation frequently causes the breakdown of phonemic distinctions that are operative in citation forms.

(1) of  /ɒv/      Head of [əf] Spanish

Head of [əv] English

at  /æt/     stay at [ət] home

as  /æz/     good as [əz] gold

us  /ʌs/     give us [əz] a break

In (1), assimilation occurs in *of* [ɒf] *Spanish* vs. [ɒv] *English*. Similarly, compare the citation form us /ʌs/ with the weak form *give us* [ʌz] *a break*.

Here are some further examples in (2):

(2) ten pounds   /tɛnpaʊndz/

[tɛmpaʊndz]

in Crewe   /ɪnkru/

[ɪŋkru]

Assimilations such as these are extremely common in casual speech, illustrating once again the simplification—even the breakdown—of the phonological structure found in citation forms, [m] is not an allophone of [n]; but here we have [tɛm] as a realisation of *ten*.

To gain a final impression of just how much phonological information present in citation forms may be lost in casual speech, consider the examples given below. These are more complex than earlier ones in that they display reduction, elision as well as assimilation at the same time:

(3) grand piano    /ɡrændpɪæno/
                   [ɡræmpɪænə]
    hand Colin     /hændkɒlɪn/
                   [hæŋkɒlɪn]

In *grand piano*, /o/ is reduced to [ə], *grand* loses its final /d/, and then the /n/ assimilates to the following /p/.

Based on the passage, in (3) in *hand Colin*, explain how *hand* /hænd/ turns into [hæŋ] in order, as described in the passage.

_____

_____

_____

_____

_____

**72** Read the passage and fill in the blank ① with the ONE most appropriate word and the blank ② with the TWO most appropriate words. Write your answers in the correct order. [2 points]

A number of different processes, collectively known as assimilation, result from the influence of one segment on another. Assimilation always results in a sound becoming more like another nearby sound in terms of one or more of its phonetic characteristics.

Nasalization of a vowel before a nasal consonant (nasal assimilation) is caused by speakers expecting the lowering of the velum in advance of a nasal segment. The result is that the preceding segment takes on the nasality of the following consonant, as in [kʰæ̃nt] *can't*. (Nasality is marked with a tilde [~].) This type of assimilation is known as _____①_____ assimilation in terms of direction, since the nasalization is, in effect, moving backwards to a preceding segment.

Flapping is a process in which a dental or alveolar stop articulation changes to a flap [ɾ] articulation. In English, this process applies to [t] and [d] when they occur between vowels, the first of which is generally stressed. Flaps are heard in the casual speech pronunciation of words such as *butter, writer, fodder,* and *wading,* and even in phrases such as *I bought it* [ajbáɾɪt]. The alveolar flap is always voiced. Flapping is considered a type of assimilation because it involves a stop consonant being weakened and becoming less stop-like when it occurs between vowels, which involve no closure at all in the vocal tract.

Voicing assimilation is also widespread. For many speakers of English, voiceless liquids and glides occur after _____②_____ in words such as *please* [pl̥iz], *try* [tr̥aj], and *cure* [kj̊ur]. These sounds are said to be devoiced in this environment. Devoicing is a kind of assimilation since the vocal folds are not set in motion immediately after the release of the voiceless consonant closure.

Dissimilation, the opposite of assimilation, results in two sounds becoming less alike in articulatory or acoustic terms. The resulting sequence of sounds is easier to articulate and distinguish. It is a much rarer process than assimilation. One commonly heard example of dissimilation in English occurs in words ending with three consecutive fricatives, such as *fifths.* Many speakers dissimilate the final [fθs] sequence to [fts], apparently to break up the sequence of three fricatives with a stop.

**73** Read the passage and follow the directions. [4 points]

In connected speech, schwa can occur in positions in which corresponding citation forms have full vowels. Consider the following examples:

(1) veto /ˈviˌto/           veto the proposal [ˌvitəðəprəˈpozəɫ]

    potato /pəˈteˌto/     potato peeler [pəˈtetəˌpilə]

    uneven /ˌʌnˈivən/     rather uneven [ˌrɑðərənˈivən]

Similar variation between stressed and unstressed forms of the same word can be observed in function words. Below are some examples:

(2) and /ænd/     the king and [ənd] I           come and [ən] see

                  Fred and [n̩d]~[n̩] I         bread and [n̩] butter

    but /bʌt/     smart but [bət] casual

    them /ðɛm/     show them [ðəm]           give them [əm] a drink

Elision of schwa is common especially before sonorant consonants. Consider the following:

(3) police       a. /pəˈlis/       b. [pl̩is]       c. [plis]

    canoe         /kəˈnu/           [kn̩u]           [knu]

    balloon       /bəˈlun/          [bl̩un]          [blun]

    solicitor     /səˈlɪsɪtə/       [sl̩ɪsɪtə]       [slɪstə]

    catalyst      /ˈkatəlɪst/       [katl̩ɪst]       [katlɪst]

    botany        /ˈbɒtənɪ/         [bɒtn̩ɪ]         [bɒtnɪ]

In (3b) schwa is elided before sonorants; the syllable is maintained through syllabicity of the sonorant. In (3c) sonorant consonants are no longer syllabic; hence, the words in (3c) have monosyllabic pronunciations in fast speech.

Again, this kind of consonant elision and cluster simplification is not restricted to weak forms of words. Here are some more examples where the second consonant is elided in consonant clusters:

(4)  West Germany      /ˌwɛstˈdʒɜmənɪ/      [wɛsdʒɜmənɪ]

　　 thousand times     /ˈθaʊzəndˈtaɪmz/      [θaʊzn̩taɪmz]

　　 hold still          /holdˈstɪl/           [holstɪl]

In addition, certain consonants at word or morpheme boundaries are usually simplified in connected speech:

(5)  keenness /kinnəs/ [kinəs]        bus stop /bʌsstɒp/ [bʌstɒp]

　　 call Linda /kɔllɪndə/ [kɔlɪndə]    red dress /rɛddrɛs/ [rɛdrɛs]

　　 big glass /bɪgglæs/ [bɪglæs]      both things /boθθɪŋz/ [boθɪŋz]

Based on the passage, first, in (3c) identify ONE word that violates phonotactic constraints. Second, state the condition where consonant cluster simplification occurs in (5).

_____

_____

_____

_____

## 74 Read the passage and follow the directions. [4 points]

The sonority-based phonetic theory identifies peaks, slopes, and troughs in the sonority profiles of words, thereby predicting the analysis of these syllables into onsets, peaks and codas. It also predicts that syllable boundaries occur in the close vicinity of sonority troughs.

But this is all that our phonetic syllable theory is able to predict. It does not tell us where, precisely, a syllable boundary is located. We have to amend our theory by a rule for the placement of syllable boundaries.

(2) a. ma.ri.na     b. al.ti.tude     c. a.pri.cot

     a.ro.ma        nigh.tin.gale     re.flect

     pho.ne.         mica.gen.da     de.crease

     co.di.fy        stan.dard       ma.tron

Let us attempt to establish a general rule for the placement of syllable boundaries in polysyllabic words. In (2a), we have simple consonant-vowel sequences: (C)VCV(C), where each C constitutes a trough in sonority and each V a peak. The generalisation is a simple one: a single consonant between vowels is a syllable onset rather than the coda of the preceding syllable. In (2b) and (2c), we have examples of ...VCCV... sequences. In (2b), the first C is more sonorous than the second: in *altitude*, /l/ is more sonorous than /t/, and the second C /t/ constitutes the sonority trough. In (2c), however, the first C in a consonant cluster does not show the same pattern.

Drawing together our findings regarding (2), we can conclude that syllable boundaries occur immediately before the consonant that constitutes a sonority trough. And this trough is always part of the _____ rather than being the coda of the preceding syllable. But before we state this rule in its final form, let us consider a few more examples:

| (3) e.nig.ma | /gm/ | at.las | /tl/ |
| --- | --- | --- | --- |
| Ag.nes | /gn/ | hem.lock | /ml/ |
| Ed.na | /dn/ | de.cath.lon | /θl/ |

Just like those in (2c), the examples in (3) contain consonant clusters in which the leftmost consonant is less sonorous than the right one. The /tr/ in *matron* and the /gm/ in *enigma* have in common. While in (2c) the syllable boundary regularly precedes the cluster, the clusters in (3) are divided by the syllable boundary. None of the clusters listed in (3) are possible English syllable onsets. Accounting for all the facts discussed so far, the rule for the placement of syllable boundaries can be formulated like this:

(4) Syllable-Boundary Rule

Within words, syllable boundaries are placed in such a way that onsets are maximal (in accordance with the phonotactic constraints of the language).

**Based on the passage, first, fill in the blank with the ONE word from the passage. Second, identify the first C in a CC cluster in (2c) with the sonority profiles of words (i.e., a peak, a slope, or a trough).**

___

___

___

___

___

**75** Read the passage and fill in each blank with the ONE most appropriate word. Write your answers in the correct order. [2 points]

> Tense vowels are produced with greater vocal tract constriction than non-tense vowels and are longer in duration than non-tense vowels. Some vowels of English are made with roughly the same tongue position as the tense vowels but with a less constricted articulation; they are called *lax*.

> **TABLE 1. Tense and lax vowels in Canadian English**
>
> | Tense | | Lax | |
> |-------|------|--------|------|
> | heat | [i] | hit | [ɪ] |
> | mate | [ej] | met | [ɛ] |
> | — | — | mat | [æ] |
> | shoot | [u] | should | [ʊ] |
> | coat | [ow] | cut | [ʌ] |
> | — | — | Canada | [ə] |
> | — | — | — | — |
> | lock | [ɑ] | | |
> | lies | [aj] | | |
> | loud | [aw] | | |
> | boy | [oj] | | |

> Table 1 provides examples from English comparing tense and lax vowels. Note that not all the vowels come in tense/lax pairs. The difference between two of the vowels illustrated in table 1 is often not easy to hear at first. Both the vowel [ʌ] in *cut, dud, pluck,* and *Hun,* and the vowel [ə] of *Canada, about, tomahawk,* and *sofa* are mid, central(back), _____①_____ , and lax. The vowel of the second set of examples, called *schwa,* is referred to as a reduced vowel. In addition to being lax, its duration is briefer than that of any of the other vowels.

A simple test can help determine whether vowels are tense or lax. In English, _____②_____ words spoken in isolation do not end in lax vowels. We find *see* [si], *say* [sej], *Sue* [su], *so* [sow], and *saw* [sɑ] in English, but not *s[ɪ], *s[ɛ], *s[æ], *s[ʊ], or *s[ʌ]. Schwa, however, frequently appears in unstressed syllables in polysyllabic words like *sof[ə]* and *Can[ə]d[ə]*. It should be pointed out—especially for those who think their ears are deceiving them—that many speakers produce the final vowel in the last two examples as [ʌ], not as [ə].

Part 03

**76** **Read the passages and follow the directions.** [4 points]

─┤ A ├─

An interesting aspect of phonological systems is that some rules evidently apply in environments that are defined phonemically, rather than phonetically. The crucial mechanism for analyzing such cases is to apply the phonological rules in a particular order.

Our discussion of this phenomenon will be based on one phonological rule of North American English. It is found in a large number of dialects, especially in the northeastern US and throughout Canada. /aɪ/ is realized as [ʌɪ] when it precedes a/an _____ consonant.

(1) tripe /tɹaɪp/ [tɹʌɪp]         tribe /tɹaɪb/ [tɹaɪb]

    right /ɹaɪt/ [ɹʌɪt]            ride /ɹaɪd/ [ɹaɪd]

    hiker /haɪkɚ/ [hʌɪkɚ]        tiger /taɪgɚ/ [taɪgɚ]

    life /laɪf/ [lʌɪf]              live /laɪv/ [laɪv]

    rifle /ɹaɪfəl/ [ɹʌɪfəl]         rival /ɹaɪvəl/ [ɹaɪvəl]

    rice /ɹaɪs/ [ɹʌɪs]            rise /ɹaɪz/ [ɹaɪz]

                                  rye /ɹaɪ/ [ɹaɪ]

                                  ion /aɪɑn/ [aɪɑn]

The other rule we will need is the rule of Tapping, where the /t/ phoneme is realized as a tap [ɾ]. Tapping also affects /d/, converting it as well into a tap. The generalized version of Tapping can be stated as follows: an alveolar stop is realized as [ɾ] when it is preceded by a vowel or /ɹ/, and followed by a stressless vowel.

(2) | wet | wetting | wed | wedding |
|---|---|---|---|
| /ˈwɛt/ | /ˈwɛt-ɪŋ/ | /ˈwɛd/ | /ˈwɛd-ɪŋ/ |
| [ˈwɛt] | [ˈwɛɾɪŋ] | [ˈwɛd] | [ˈwɛɾɪŋ] |
| butt | butted | bud | budded |
| /ˈbʌt/ | /ˈbʌt-əd/ | /ˈbʌd/ | /ˈbʌd-əd/ |
| [ˈbʌt] | [ˈbʌɾəd] | [ˈbʌd] | [ˈbʌɾəd] |

---
**B**
---

   With the two rules of /aɪ/ Raising and Tapping in hand, we can now see how they might interact. Crucial words that would bear on the question are the following, which for the moment we give in spelled and phonemic form only:

(3) cite          cited          side          sided
    /ˈsaɪt/      /ˈsaɪt-əd/     /ˈsaɪd/      /ˈsaɪd-əd/
    white         whiter         wide          wider
    /ˈwaɪt/      /ˈwaɪt-ɚ/      /ˈwaɪd/      /ˈwaɪd-ɚ/

   A widely employed method of analyzing differences such as the one just shown is to suppose that phonological rules must be ordered. Under such a theory, the difference between the two dialects just described is a difference of rule ordering. While /aɪ/ Raising is ordered before Tapping in one dialect, Tapping is ordered before /aɪ/ Raising in the other dialect.

Based on the passages, first, in <A>, fill in the blank with the ONE most appropriate word. Second, state the order of the two rules of /aɪ/ Raising and Tapping in the dialect in which *writing* and *riding* are pronounced the same.

_____

_____

_____

_____

_____

**77** **Read the passages and follow the directions.** [4 points]

┤ A ├

A fully explicit phonological analysis of a language would use no phonetic symbols. Only the feature matrices have theoretical status, and the phonetic symbols are meant only as convenient abbreviations for particular feature matrices. Here are ways in which rules benefit by writing them with features.

We capture an assimilation by showing that the assimilating segment adopts a feature value already possessed by one of its neighbors. For example, in English, /k, g, ŋ/ become fronted [ḵ, g̱, ŋ̱] as in *keel* ['ḵil], *gale* ['ge͡ɪl], or *dinghy* ['dɪŋi]:

(1) Velar Fronting

    *Velars become fronted* _____.

(2) $\begin{bmatrix} + \text{dorsal} \\ + \text{consonantal} \end{bmatrix} \rightarrow \begin{bmatrix} + \text{front} \\ - \text{back} \end{bmatrix} / \underline{\quad} \begin{bmatrix} + \text{syllabic} \\ + \text{front} \end{bmatrix}$

Only one or two feature values show that a change is minor. For example, if a rule changes /p/ to [b], one would write p → [+ voice] rather than p → b, to show that nothing other than [voice] is changing.

There are good reasons to include only just as many features in a rule as are needed. Here is an example. In English, all voiced fricatives can be realized as voiceless when they precede a pause; that is to say, they are at the end of an utterance.

(3) save /seɪv/ [seɪf], [seɪv]        bathe /beɪð/ [beɪθ], [beɪð]

    maze /meɪz/ [meɪs], [meɪz]    rouge /ɹuʒ/ [ɹuʃ], [ɹuʒ]

Since there are four voiced fricatives in English, we could, in principle, write four rules. But phonological rules make reference to natural classes; certainly a more elegant approach would be to adopt a single rule:

(4) Final Fricative Devoicing

*Voiced fricatives are realized as voiceless at the end of an utterance.*

(5) $\left[ \quad \right] \rightarrow \left[ - \text{voice} / \underline{\quad} \right]_{\text{Utterance}}$ (optional)

---

## ⊣ B ⊢

A restrictive set of distinctive features keep sound distinct. Some distinctive features simply translate the phonetic parameters in a self-explanatory manner: [± sonorant], [± voice], [± nasal], [± lateral] and [± continuant].

**Based on the passage, first, considering the feature values in (2), complete Velar Fronting rule in (1) by filling in the blank with THREE words. Second, in (5), fill in the square bracket with THREE feature values to translate Final Fricative Devoicing rule in (4), using the distinctive features described in <B>.**

_____

_____

_____

_____

_____

**78** **Read the passage and follow the directions.** [4 points]

┤ A ├

One case of the interaction of morphology and phonology occurs in zero derivation, sometimes called conversion. This refers to a kind of derivational morphology in which there is no overt affix, but there is a change in category accompanied by a corresponding change in meaning. In English, the major cases involve a noun and a verb of identical phonological form and closely related meanings. Among disyllabic cases, there are some where stress remains the same for the noun and the verb in (1a), whereas, in (1b), the stress patterns are distinct.

(1) a. pattern, comfort, picture, focus

   b. torment, conflict, increase

Besides the stress, there are certain other differences between the pairs in groups (1a) and (1b). Semantically, verbs of the form (1a) mean 'to do something with N.' On the other hand, nouns of (1b) mean 'that which Vs' or 'that which is Ved,' as an *increase* is 'something which increases.'

We can explain this pattern by saying that the noun is basic in (1a), while the verb is basic in (1b). If we assign stress to the basic form, before the morphological conversion, we obtain exactly the right results. In (1a), stress is assigned to the noun, which is the basic form. When the zero derivation takes place, the noun's stress carries over to the verb, since no restressing occurs. In (1b), the noun has a remnant of the verb's stress in the form of a secondary stress on the second syllable.

As a further demonstration of the correctness of this approach, the model predicts zero derivations of the form V→N→V, but makes zero derivations N→V →N impossible. Some example words are given in (2).

(2) a. [protést]$_V$ → [prótèst]$_N$ → [prótèst]$_V$

　　'stage a protest'

　 b. [discóunt]$_V$ → [díscòunt]$_N$ → [díscòunt]$_V$

　　'sell at a discount'

　 c. [compóund]$_V$ → [cómpòund]$_N$ → [cómpòund]$_V$

　　'join or become joined in a compound'

　 d. [digést]$_V$ → [dígèst]$_N$ → [dígèst]$_V$

　　'make a digest'

In each case the verb derived from the noun has a meaning distinct from the verb that the noun was originally derived from.

─────────────────┤ B ├────────────

(a) import　　(b) permit　　(c) poison

(d) ransom　　(e) export

**Based on the passage, in <B>, identify TWO words that show the same stress pattern as the words in (1a), and then, state the basic form of each word (i.e., a verb or noun).**

_____

_____

_____

_____

_____

# 04

Morphology

**01** Read the passage, and fill in the blank ① with the ONE most appropriate word and the blank ② with ONE word from the passage. Write your answers in the correct order. [2 points]

Some morphological processes, inflection in particular, are productive, meaning that they can be used freely to form new words from the list of free and bound morphemes. Among derivational morphemes, the suffix *-able* can be conjoined with any verb to derive an adjective with the meaning of the verb and the meaning of *-able*, which is something like 'able to be' as in *accept + able, laugh + able, pass + able, change + able, breathe + able, adapt + able,* and so on. The productivity of this rule is illustrated by the fact that we find *-able* affixed to new verbs such as *downloadable* and *faxable*.

The prefix *un-* derives same-class words with an opposite meaning: *unafraid, unfit, un-American,* and so on. Additionally, *un-* can be added to derived adjectives that have been formed by morphological rules, resulting in perfectly acceptable words such as *un + believe + able* or *un + pick + up + able*.

Yet *un-* is not fully productive. We find *happy* and *unhappy, cowardly* and *uncowardly,* but not *sad* and **unsad*, *brave* and **unbrave*, or *obvious* and **unobvious*. It appears that the "un-Rule" is most productive for adjectives that are derived from verbs, such as *unenlightened, unsimplified, uncharacterized, unauthorized, undistinguished,* and so on. It also appears that most acceptable *un-* words have polysyllabic bases, and while we have *unfit, uncool, unread,* and *unclean,* many of the unacceptable *un-* forms have _____①_____ stems such as **unbig, *ungreat, *unred, *unsad, *unsmall, *untall*.

The rule that adds an *-er* to a/an _____②_____ in English to produce a noun meaning 'one who does' is a nearly productive morphological rule, giving us *examiner, exam-taker, analyzer, lover, hunter,* and so forth, but fails full productivity owing to "unwords" like **chairer*, which is not 'one who chairs.'

## 02 Read the passages and follow the directions. [4 points]

---
|  A  |
---

When examining words made up of only two morphemes, we know two facts about the ways in which the affixes attach to other morphemes.

Affixes attach to certain syntactic categories : *-able* attaches to verbs (but not to nouns or adjectives), but *-ish* attaches to nouns (and some adjectives, but not to verbs):

(1) a. readable, drivable, breakable but not *greenable, *catable
   b. girlish, selfish, longish but not *readish, *breakish

Affixes can determine the syntactic category of a word: words that end in *-able* are adjectives, words that end in *-ish* are also adjectives, but words that end in *-ness* are nouns (*happiness, attractiveness, hopelessness*). These two facts are important for determining the steps by which words with more than one affix must be formed. Let's look first at the word *reusable* and what we know about the affixes *re-* and *-able*. The prefix *re-* attaches to verbs and creates new verbs: *reword, redo, retype*. The affix *-able* attaches to verbs and forms adjectives: *washable, stoppable*. Crucially, *re-* does not attach to adjectives : *\*rehappy, \*regreen, \*retall*.

Now, let's consider how to draw a word formed in steps, such as *reusable*. The tree for this word requires different levels of structure if we are to represent how we store this word in our mental lexicon.

(2)

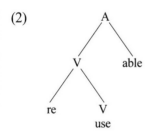

This is the only possible way to build this word: The prefix *re-* must attach first to the verb *use* to form the verb *reuse,* Then, the suffix *-able* attaches to the verb *reuse* to form the adjective *reusable*.

---

**B**

Now consider the following word in (3). Does *-ment* attach to the word *disengage*, or does *dis-* attach to *engagement*? Both *disengage* and *engagement* are words, so how do we decide?

(3) disengagement

---

In <B>, analyze the word in (3) by providing the order of derivation, identifying the types of affixes and the syntactic category (i.e., the part of speech), as shown in the passage <A>.

_____

_____

_____

_____

_____

## 03 Read the passages and follow the directions. [4 points]

┤ A ├

A word is not a simple sequence of morphemes. It has an internal structure. For example, the word *unsystematic* is composed of three morphemes: *un-, system,* and *-atic*. The order of derivation is shown in (1) below:

(1) First, the root is *system*, a noun, to which we add the suffix *-atic*, resulting in an adjective, *systematic*. Second, to this adjective, we add the prefix *un-* forming a new adjective, *unsystematic*.

In order to represent the hierarchical organization of words (and sentences), linguists use tree diagrams. The tree diagram for *unsystematic* is as follows:

(2)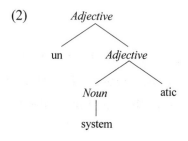

This tree represents the application of two morphological rules:

Rule 1. Noun + *atic* → Adjective
Rule 2. *un* + Adjective → Adjective

Rule 1 attaches the derivational suffix -atic to the root noun, forming an adjective. Rule 2 takes the adjective formed by rule 1 and attaches the derivational prefix *un-*. The diagram shows that the entire word—*unsystematic*—is an adjective that is composed of an adjective—*systematic*—plus *un*. The adjective is itself composed of a noun—*system*—plus the suffix *-atic*.

Hierarchical structure is an essential property of human language. Words (and sentences) have component parts, which relate to each other in specific, rule-governed ways. Although at first glance it may seem that, aside from order, the morphemes *un-* and *-atic* each relate to the root system in the same way, this is not the case. The root system is "closer" to *-atic* than it is to *un-*, and *un-* is actually connected to the adjective *systematic*, and not directly to *system*. Indeed, *\*unsystem* is not a word.

---

**B**

There is an example of a word with four morphemes in (3) below; try to determine for yourself the order in which the morphemes are put together.

(3) activation

Based on the description in <A>, analyze the word given in (3) in <B>. Provide the order of derivation, identifying the types of affixes and the grammatical form (part of speech) as in (1). Notice that write the exact affixes in your answer.

_____

_____

_____

_____

_____

## 04 Read the passage and follow the directions. [4 points]

┤ A ├

English orthography is not consistent in representing compounds, which are sometimes written as single words, sometimes with a hyphen, and sometimes as separate words. In terms of pronunciation, however, an important generalization can be made, as shown in (1) and (2): adjective-noun compounds are characterized by more prominent stress on their first component. In non-compounds consisting of an adjective and a noun, in contrast, the second element is generally stressed.

(1) Compound word

greénhouse                              'a glass-enclosed garden'

bláckboard                              'a chalkboard'

(2) Non-compound expressions

green hoúse                             'a house painted green'

black boárd                             'a board that is black'

A second distinguishing feature of compounds in English is that tense and plural markers can typically not be attached to the first element, although they can be added to the compound as a whole. There are some exceptions, however, such as *parks supervisor*.

(3) a. Compound noun with internal plural:

   *The [ducks hunter] didn't have a licence.

   b. Compound noun with external plural:

   The [duck hunter]s didn't have a licence.

---

**B**

(i) a. The craftsman beat the gold into rings.

   b. The film tells the story of a lonely swordsman.

   c. The player dropped kick the ball through the goal post.

   d. The player drop kicked the ball through the goal post.


(ii) a. wet suit: 'a suit that is wet'

   b. wet suit: 'a diver's costume'

---

Based on the description in <A>, in <B>, first, identify ONE ungrammatical sentence in (i), and explain why. Second, in (ii), specify each phrase *wet suit* in (iia) and (iib) (i.e., *Compound Word* or *Non-compound Expression*).

_____

_____

_____

_____

_____

**05** Read the passage and fill in the blank ① with the ONE most appropriate word and the blank ② with an appropriate natural class. Write your answers in the correct order. [2 points]

Derivation is often subject to special constraints and restrictions. For instance, the suffix ‑*ant* can combine with bases of Latin origin, such as *assistant* and *combat*, but not with those of native English origin, such as *help* and *fight*. Thus, we find words such as *assistant* and *combatant* but not *\*helpant* and *\*fightant*.

In other cases, derivation may be blocked by the existence of an alternative word. For instance, the word *cooker* (to mean 'one who cooks') is blocked by the existence of the word ____①____, which already has that meaning; *famosity* (from *famous*) is blocked by *fame*; and so on.

Sometimes, a derivational affix is able to attach only to bases with particular phonological properties. A good example of this involves the suffix *-en*, which can combine with some adjectives to create verbs with a causative meaning as shown in table 1 (*whiten* means roughly 'cause to become white').

| TABLE 1. Restrictions on the use of *-en* | |
|---|---|
| *Acceptable* | *Unacceptable* |
| whiten | *abstracten |
| soften | *bluen |
| madden | *angryen |
| quicken | *slowen |
| liven | *greenen |

The contrasts illustrated here reflect the fact that *-en* can be attached only to a monosyllabic base that ends in a consonant other than /l/, /r/, /m/, /n/, or /ŋ/. Thus, it can be added to *white, quick, mad,* and *live*, which are monosyllabic and end in a consonant of the right type. But it cannot be added to *abstract*, which has more than one syllable; to *slow* or *blue*, which end in a vowel; or to *green*, which ends in the wrong type of consonant. Therefore, the suffix *-en* can only combine with a monosyllabic base that ends in a/an ____②____.

# 05

Semantics

## 01 Read the passage <A> and the dialogue in <B>, and follow the directions.

[4 points]

┤ A ├

Although no theory of word meaning is complete, we know that speakers have considerable knowledge about the meaning relationships among different words in their mental lexicons, and any theory must take that knowledge into account. Words are semantically related to one another in a variety of ways. There are some lexical relations: homonyms, homophones, homographs, polysemy, and hyponyms.

Homonyms are words with the same sound and spelling but different, unrelated meanings. For example, the verb *bear* can mean 'to have children' or 'to tolerate'. So, *She can't bear children* is ambiguous because *bear* is a homonym. Homophones are words that do not share the same spellings or meanings but sound the same (e.g., sole/soul). Homographs are words that have the same spelling, different meanings, and different pronunciations (e.g., bow/bow).

When a word has multiple meanings that are related conceptually or historically, it is said to be polysemous. Polysemous senses are listed under the same lexical entry. For example, the word *diamond* referring to a jewel and also to a baseball field is polysemous.

Speakers of English know that the words *red, white,* and *blue* are color words. Similarly, *lion, tiger, leopard,* and *lynx* are all felines. Hyponymy is the relationship between the more general term such as *color* and the more specific instances of it, such as *red*. Thus *red* is a hyponym of *color*, and *lion* is a hyponym of *feline*; or equivalently, *color* has the hyponym *red* and *feline* has the hyponym *lion*.

---
**B**

Here is a passage from Alice's Adventures in Wonderland:

(1) "How is bread made?"
(2) "I know that!" Alice cried eagerly.
(3) "You take some flour."
(4) "Where do you pick the flower?" the White Queen asked. "In a garden, or in the hedges?"
(5) "Well, it isn't picked at all," Alice explained; "it's ground."
(6) "How many acres of ground?" said the White Queen.

---

In <B>, TWO pairs of words can create the humor. Identify each pair with the sentence number, and state the lexical relation of each pair, based on the passage in <A>.

_____

_____

_____

_____

_____

**02** Read the passage <A> and fill in each blank in <B> with ONE word from the passage <A>. Write your answers in the correct order. [2 points]

---

**⊢ A ⊢**

Two words are antonyms if their meanings differ only in the value for a single semantic feature. The following pairs are all antonyms: *dead* and *alive*, *hot* and *cold*, and *above* and *below*. The meanings of the members of each pair are presumably identical, except for opposite values of some semantic features. The meanings of *dead* and *alive*, for instance, are identical except that *dead* is marked [−living] and *alive* is marked [+living].

Antonyms, moreover, fall into at least three groups. *Binary antonyms* are pairs that exhaust all linguistic possibilities along some dimension. *Dead* and *alive* are examples of binary antonyms. Everything that can be dead or alive is, in fact, either dead or alive: there is no middle ground between the two. All people, for example, are either dead or alive.

*Gradable antonyms*, on the other hand, are pairs that describe opposite ends of a continuous dimension. *Hot* and *cold* are examples of gradable antonyms. Not everything that can be hot or cold is, in fact, either hot or cold. A liquid, for example, may be neither hot nor cold; it can be in between, say, warm or cool.

*Converse antonyms* are pairs that describe a single relationship between two items from opposite perspectives. *Above* and *below* are examples of converse antonyms. If a picture, for example, is above a sofa, then the sofa is necessarily below the picture.

---

**⊢ B ⊢**

Consider the following paraphrastic sentences:

(1) a. The dictionary is heavier than the novel.
   b. The novel is lighter than the dictionary.

Although *heavy* and *light* are _____①_____ antonyms, the comparative forms, *heavier* and *lighter* are _____②_____ antonyms.

---

## 03 Read the passage and fill in each blank with ONE word from the passage. Write your answers in the correct order. [2 points]

If you know that the sentence *Jack swims beautifully* is true, then you also know that the sentence *Jack swims* is true. This meaning relation is called entailment. We say that *Jack swims beautifully* entails *Jack swims*. More generally, one sentence entails another if whenever the first sentence is true the second one is also true in all conceivable circumstances.

Generally, entailment goes only in one direction. So while the sentence *Jack swims beautifully* entails *Jack swims*, the reverse is not true. Knowing merely that *Jack swims* is true does not necessitate the truth of *Jack swims beautifully*. Jack could be a poor swimmer. On the other hand, negating both sentences reverses the entailment. *Jack doesn't swim* entails *Jack doesn't swim beautifully*.

The notion of entailment can be used to reveal knowledge that we have about other meaning relations. For example, omitting tautologies and contradictions, two sentences are synonymous if they are both true or both false with respect to the same situations. Sentences like *Jack put off the meeting* and *Jack postponed the meeting* are synonymous, because when one is true the other must be true; and when one is false the other must also be false.

Two sentences are contradictory if, whenever one is true, the other is false or, equivalently, there is no situation in which they are both true or both false. For example, the sentences *Jack is alive* and *Jack is dead* are contradictory because if the sentence *Jack is alive* is true, then the sentence *Jack is dead* is false, and vice versa. In other words, *Jack is alive* and *Jack is dead* have opposite truth values.

We can describe these patterns in a more concise way by using the notion of entailment:

(1) Two sentences are _____①_____ if they entail each other.
(2) Two sentences are _____②_____ if one entails the negation of the other.

The notions of contradiction (always false) and contradictory (opposite in truth value) are related in that if two sentences are contradictory, their conjunction with *and* is a contradiction. Thus *Jack is alive and Jack is dead* is a contradiction; it cannot be true under any circumstances.

**04** Read the passage and fill in each blank with ONE word from the passage. Write your answers in the correct order. [2 points]

Words that are opposite in meaning are antonyms. There are several kinds of antonymy. There are complementary pairs:

(1) alive/dead      present/absent      pass/fail

They are complementary in that *alive* = *not dead* and *dead* = *not alive*, and so on. There are gradable pairs of antonyms:

(2) big/small      fast/slow      happy/sad

The meaning of adjectives in gradable pairs is related to the objects they modify. The words do not provide an absolute scale. For example, we know that "a small elephant" is much bigger than "a large mouse." *Fast* is faster when applied to an airplane than to a car. Another characteristic of certain pairs of gradable antonyms is that one is marked and the other unmarked. The unmarked member is the one used in questions of degree. We ask, ordinarily, "How high is the mountain?" (not "How low is it?"). We answer "Ten thousand feet high" but never "Ten thousand feet low," except humorously or ironically. Thus *high* is the unmarked member of *high/low*. Similarly, *tall* is the unmarked member of *tall/short*, *fast* the unmarked member of *fast/slow*, and so on.

Another kind of opposition involves pairs like:

(3) give/receive      buy/sell      teacher/pupil

They are called relational opposites, and they display symmetry in their meanings. If X gives Y to Z, then Z receives Y from X. If X is Y's teacher, then Y is X's pupil.

Now consider the following pairs:

(4) false/true      asleep/awake      lessor/lessee

     rude/polite      larger/smaller      legal/illegal

In (4), the pair *asleep/awake* belong to complementary opposites, the pair *larger/smaller* are _____①_____ opposites, and the pair *rude/polite* are the example of _____②_____ opposites.

**05** Read the passage <A> and the sentences in <B>, and follow the directions. [4 points]

---| A |---

There is an important difference between entailment and presupposition. If we negate an entailing sentence, then the entailment fails. However, negating a presupposing sentence allows the presupposition to survive. Take for example the entailment pair in (1):

(1) a. John killed the bear.
    b. The bear is dead.

If we negate (1a) to form (2a) then it no longer entails (1b), repeated as (2b):

(2) a. John didn't kill the bear.
    b. The bear is dead.

Now (2b) no longer automatically follows from the preceding sentence.
  However, negating the presupposing sentence does not affect the presupposition. Consider the presupposition pair in (3):

(3) a. I do regret leaving New York.
    b. I left New York.

If we negate (3a) to form (4a) the resulting sentence still has the presupposition, shown as (4b):

(4) a. I don't regret leaving New York.
    b. I left New York.

  Therefore, negating a presupposing sentence allows the presupposition to survive, whereas negating an entailing sentence destroys the entailment. So it seems that viewing presupposition as a truth relation allows us to capture one interesting difference between the behaviour of presupposition and entailment under negation.

---

┤ B ├

(i) a. I am sorry that the team lost.

b. The team lost.

(ii) a. The mayor of Liverpool is in town.

b. There is a mayor of Liverpool.

(iii) a. John has arrived in Edinburgh.

b. John is in Edinburgh.

(iv) a. Mary's sister has just got back from Boston.

b. Mary has a sister.

---

In <B>, identify ONE pair of sentences that shows the semantic relation of entailment, and explain why, based on the description in <A>.

_____

_____

_____

_____

_____

## 06 Read the passage <A> and the sentences in <B>, and follow the directions. [4 points]

─── A ───

Some types of presupposition are produced by particular words or constructions, which together are sometimes called presupposition triggers. Some of these triggers derive from syntactic structures, for example the cleft construction in (1) and the pseudo-cleft in (2) share the presupposition in (3), and a *wh*-question also serves as a presupposition trigger, but a *yes-no* question doesn't.

(1) It was his behavior with frogs that disgusted me.
(2) What disgusted me was his behavior with frogs.
(3) Something disgusted me.

Other forms of subordinate clauses may produce presuppositions, for example, time adverbial clauses and comparative clauses. In the following sentences, the (a) sentence has the presupposition in (b):

(4) a. I was riding motorcycles before you learned to walk.
    b. You learned to walk.

Many presuppositions are produced by the presence of certain words. Many of these lexical triggers are predicates. For example, some predicates like *realize* are called factive predicates (or verbs) because they presuppose the truth of their complement clause. Compare sentences (5) and (6) below: only the sentence with the factive verb *realize* presupposes (7). There is no such presupposition with the non-factive verb *think* in (6).

(5) Sean realized that Miranda had dandruff.
(6) Sean thought that Miranda had dandruff.
(7) Miranda had dandruff.

---

┤ B ├

(a) You didn't explain that your train was late.

(b) It is true that Jill had lent Ed her key.

(c) It matters that they lied to us.

(d) He's even more gullible than you are.

(e) Will you take out that trash?

(f) When will you take out that trash?

---

In <B>, identify TWO sentences which DO NOT produce presupposition, and explain why, specifying the type of presupposition triggers, based on the description in <A>.

_____

_____

_____

_____

_____

## 07 Read the passage and follow the directions. [4 points]

─┤ A ├─

Hyponymy is a relation of inclusion. A hyponym includes the meaning of a more general word, for example: *dog* and *cat* are hyponyms of *animal*, and *sister* and *mother* are hyponyms of *woman*. The more general term is called the superordinate or hypernym (alternatively hyperonym). Some taxonomies reflect the natural world, like (1) below:

(1)

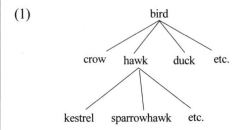

Here *kestrel* is a hyponym of *hawk*, and *hawk* a hyponym of *bird*. We assume the relationship is transitive so that *kestrel* is a hyponym of *bird*.

Meronymy is a term used to describe a part-whole relationship between lexical items. Thus *cover* and *page* are meronyms of *book*. The whole term, here *book*, is sometimes called the holonym. We can identify this relationship by using sentence frames like *X is part of Y*, or *Y has X*, as in *A page is part of a book*, or *A book has pages*. Meronymy reflects hierarchical classifications in the lexicon somewhat like taxonomies, as shown in (2).

(2)

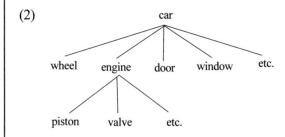

Meronymic hierarchies are less clear cut and regular than taxonomies. Meronyms vary for example in how necessary the part is to the whole. Some are necessary for normal examples, for example *nose* as a meronym of *face*; others are usual but not obligatory, like *collar* as a meronym of *shirt*.

Meronymy also differs from hyponymy in transitivity. _____①_____ is always transitive, as we saw, but _____②_____ may or may not be. A transitive example is: *nail* as a meronym of *finger*, and *finger* of *hand*. We can see that *nail* is a meronym of *hand*, for we can say *A hand has nails*. A non-transitive example is: *pane* is a meronym of *window* (*A window has a pane*), and *window* of *room* (*A room has a window*); but *pane* is not a meronym of *room*, for we cannot say *A room has a pane*.

---

| B |

(a) *hole* is a meronym of *button*.

(b) *button* is a meronym of *shirt*.

(c) *hole* is not a meronym of *shirt*.

(d) *cellar* is a meronym of *house*.

(e) *house* is a meronym of *building*.

(f) *saw* is a meronym of *tool*.

First, in <A>, fill in each blank with ONE word from the passage. Write your answers in the correct order. Second, identify TWO wrong sentences in <B>, and correct the sentences, replacing ONLY ONE word in the sentence.

_____

_____

_____

_____

_____

memo

# 06

Pragmatics

# Pragmatics

**01** Read the passage and fill in each blank with ONE word from the passage. Write your answers in the correct order. [2 points]

---

Here is a summary of the four conversational maxims, parts of the broad cooperative principle.

(1) **Name of Maxim**      **Description of Maxim**

  Quantity          Say neither more nor less than the discourse requires.
  Relevance         Be relevant.
  Manner            Be brief and orderly; avoid ambiguity and obscurity.
  Quality           Do not lie; do not make unsupported claims.

A maxim is violated when a speaker chooses to be uncooperative for whatever reason. A maxim is obeyed in a literal discourse devoid of implicature, as in (2).

(2) Dad : Very nice girl. What do you think, Hon?
  Mom : Not really.

_____①_____ arise when a maxim is flouted. To flout a maxim is to choose not to follow that maxim in order to implicate something. The discourse in (3), repeated below, is an example of the Maxim of _____②_____ being flouted.

(3) Dad : Very nice girl. What do you think, Hon?
  Mom : The turkey sure was moist.

---

Because Mom knows that the quality of the turkey isn't relevant to being a "very nice girl"—and because Dad is assuming that Mom knows it, too—Dad can pick up on the fact that Mom is implicating that she doesn't like the girl.

Because implicatures result from violations of one or more maxims, they can be easily cancelled by providing further, clarifying information. For example:

(4) Dad : Very nice girl. What do you think, Hon?
    Mom : The turkey sure was moist. Toni basted it every ten minutes.

The additional remark cancels, or at least weakens, the implicature that Mom dislikes Toni.

**02** Read the passage <A> and the sentences in <B>, and follow the directions. [4 points]

---| A |---

You can use language to do things. You can use language to make promises, lay bets, issue warnings, christen boats, place names in nomination, offer congratulations, or swear testimony. The theory of speech acts describes how this is done.

By saying *I warn you that there is a sheepdog in the closet*, you not only say something, you *warn* someone. Verbs like *bet, promise, warn,* and so on are performative verbs. Using them in a sentence (in the first person, present tense) adds something extra over and above the statement.

There are hundreds of performative verbs in every language. The following sentences illustrate their usage:

(1) a. I *bet* you five dollars the Yankees win.
　　 b. I *move* that we adjourn.
　　 c. I *nominate* Batman for mayor of Gotham City.
　　 d. I *resign*!

In all of these sentences, the speaker is the subject (i.e., the sentences are in the first person), who by uttering the sentence is accomplishing some additional action, such as nominating, resigning, etc. In addition, all of these sentences are affirmative, declarative, and in the present tense. They are typical performative sentences.

In studying speech acts, the importance of context is evident. In some situations *Band practice, my house, 6 to 8* is a reminder, but the same sentence may be a warning in a different context. We call this underlying purpose of the utterance —be it a reminder, a warning, a promise, a threat, or whatever—the illocutionary force of a speech act. Illocutionary force may accompany utterances without overt performative verbs, for example *I've got five bucks that says you're wrong* has the illocutionary force of a bet under appropriate circumstances. Because the illocutionary force of a speech act depends on the context of the utterance, speech act theory is a part of pragmatics.

```
┤ B ├
```

(a) I bequeath $1,000,000 to the IRS.

(b) I fine you $100 for possession of oregano.

(c) I dare you to step over this line.

(d) I owe the IRS $1 million.

(e) I swore I didn't do it.

(f) I challenge you to a match.

Identify TWO sentences which are NOT typical performative sentences in <B>, and explain why, based on the description in <A>.

_____

_____

_____

_____

_____

**03** Read the passage and fill in each blank with ONE word from the passage. Write your answers in the correct order. [2 points]

The British philosopher H. Paul Grice concluded that language users can calculate implicatures because they are all following some implicit principles (and each language user can therefore assume that others are following those principles). Grice called these principles "maxims" of discourse. We'll list them and then provide examples of each.

I.   Maxim of Quality: Do not say what you believe to be false, and Do not say that for which you lack adequate evidence.

II.  Maxim of Quantity: Make your contribution as informative as is required for the current purposes of the exchange, and Do not make your contribution more informative than is required.

III. Maxim of Relevance: Be relevant.

IV.  Maxim of Manner: Avoid obscurity of expression, Avoid ambiguity, Avoid unnecessary wordiness, and Be orderly.

The following discourse (Hamlet, Act II, Scene II), which gave rise to Polonius's famous remark, does not seem quite right—it is not coherent, for reasons that Grice's Maxims can explain.

POLONIUS : What do you read, my lord?

HAMLET : Words, words, words.

POLONIUS : What is the matter, my lord?

HAMLET : Between who?

POLONIUS : I mean, the matter that you read, my lord.

HAMLET : Slanders, sir : for the satirical rogue says here that old men have gray beards, that their faces are wrinkled, their eyes purging thick amber and plum-tree gum, and that they have a plentiful lack of wit, together with most weak hams: all which, sir, though I most powerfully and potently believe, yet I hold it not honesty to have it thus set down; for yourself, sir, should grow old as I am, if like a crab you could go backward.

Hamlet, who is feigning insanity, refuses to answer Polonius's questions "in good faith." He has violated the Maxim of Quantity, which states that a speaker's contribution to the discourse should be as informative as is required—neither more nor less. Hamlet has violated this maxim in both directions. In answering "Words, words, words" to the question of what he is reading, he is providing too little information. His final remark goes to the other extreme in providing too much information; this could also be seen as a violation of the Maxim of _____①_____. Hamlet also violates the Maxim of _____②_____ when he "misinterprets" the question about the reading matter as a matter between two individuals.

**04** Read the passage and fill in each blank with ONE word from the passage. Write your answers in the correct order. [2 points]

Tag questions are made up of a stem (statement) and a tag (short question form). In opposite polarity tag questions, the verb in the tag and the verb in the stem have opposite values.

In (1), rising intonation on the tag indicates that the speaker is asking for information, and in (2), falling intonation on the tag indicates that the speaker expects the listener will agree with the information in the stem.

(1) Rich will pay me back, won't he? ↗

(2) Sarah owns a car, doesn't she? ↘

In same polarity tag questions, both the stem and the tag are positive. A low pitch that jumps up on the tag, and indicates that the speaker has inferred or reached a conclusion that is expressed in the stem, as shown in (3). Same polarity tag questions don't ask for confirmation, but suggest an attitude such as surprise, disbelief, disapproval or the like.

(3) So they've read my book, have they? ↗ Amazing!

Now look at this part of the conversations in terms of old or new information.

(4) James : I'll be off to Australia soon, as usual.
    Tim : You go there every year, do you?

Tim realizes from James's words (*as usual*) that James goes every year. The information is new to him. He is expressing interest and inviting James to continue the conversation and give him more details. Tim's words mean 'Oh, so you go there every year.' Compare the following positive and negative tags:

(5) A : We can't move this cupboard.

　　B : It's heavy, isn't it? I tried to lift it, but I couldn't.

(6) A : We can't move this cupboard.

　　B : It's heavy, is it? I was afraid it might be.


In (5), the information that *it is heavy* is _____①_____ to the second speaker, but in (6) the information that *it is heavy* is _____②_____ to the second speaker.

**05** Read the passage and fill in each blank with ONE word from the passage. Write your answers in the correct order. [2 points]

> Philosophers use the term *speech acts* for things you can do with sentences of your language—things like making statements, asking questions, issuing commands, or uttering exclamations. Which of these you can do with a given sentence depends to a large extent on its syntactic form. The syntax of English distinguishes a set of clause types that are characteristically used to perform different kinds of speech acts. The major types are the five illustrated in (1):
>
> (1) a. declarative          You are very tactful.
>     b. closed interrogative  Are you very tactful?
>     c. open interrogative    How tactful are you?
>     d. exclamative           How tactful you are!
>     e. imperative            Be very tactful.
>
> Although the correspondence between these clause types and the speech acts they can be used to perform is not one-to-one, speech acts do have a characteristic correlation with clause types. We show the default correlation in (2):
>
> (2) CLAUSE TYPE            CHARACTERISTIC SPEECH ACT
>     a. declarative           making a statement
>     b. closed interrogative  asking a closed question
>     c. open interrogative    asking an open question
>     d. exclamative           making an exclamatory statement
>     e. imperative            issuing a directive
>
> Now consider the following examples:
>
> (3) a. Could you please open the door?
>     b. <u>Turn up late</u> and you'll be fired.

Example (3a) would normally be used and understood as a directive (specifically, a polite request); but it is of closed interrogative form. It's not an imperative. The underlined clause of (3b) has _____①_____ form, but would not be naturally interpreted as a/an _____②_____ : I'm not telling you to turn up late. The whole sentence is understood as if it had a conditional adjunct: it means "If you turn up late, you'll be fired". This of course implies that you should NOT turn up late, so the sentence does the opposite of telling you to turn up late!

_____

_____

**06** Read the passage and fill in the blank with ONE word from the passage.

[2 points]

The assumptions that hearers make about a speaker's conduct seemed to Grice to be of several different types, giving rise to different types of inference, or, from the speaker's point of view, implicatures. In identifying these, Grice called them maxims. Grice's four main maxims are as follows:

(1) The Maxim of Quality:

    a. Do not say what you believe is false

    b. Do not say that for which you lack adequate evidence

(2) The Maxim of Quantity:

    a. Make your contribution as informative as is required

    b. Do not make your contribution more informative than is required

(3) The Maxim of Relevance:

    a. Make your contributions relevant

(4) The Maxim of Manner:

    a. Avoid ambiguity and obscurity

    b. Be brief and orderly

How considerations of relevance can help make sense of a conversational turn is illustrated in (5).

(5) A: (picking up a book from a display in a bookshop)

    "Have you read *Long Walk to Freedom*?"

    B: "I find autobiographies fascinating."

A asked about *Long Walk to Freedom*. B talks about autobiographies. A asked whether B had read the book. B talks about what she finds fascinating. One might think that B had ignored the question, but the conversation can be read as co-operative and coherent by trying to work out how B's contribution could be relevant to A's question. If the book is an autobiography, then B has not switched topics.

Now consider the following conversation:

(6) A: "Can anyone use this car park?"
B: "It's for customers of the supermarket."

If the car park was for the use of everyone, then that would include the supermarket's customers and there would be no need to mention them; so B's utterance appears to offer superfluous information. An assumption that B is abiding by the maxim of _____ —and therefore not giving more information than needed—invites an implicature that it is necessary to specify supermarket customers—it is for them and not for other motorists.

_____

_____

2025
교원임용시험 전공영어 대비
최신 출제경향 반영

Mentor Linguistics

모범답안

# 멘토영어학 문제은행

LSI 영어연구소 앤드류 채 편저

박문각 임용   동영상강의 www.pmg.co.kr   박문각

Mentor Linguistics

모범답안

# 멘토영어학 문제은행

LSI 영어연구소 앤드류 채 편저

차 례
# CONTENTS

# PART 01 Syntax

## 01 Raising

본책 p.010

**01**

| 하위내용영역 | 배점 | 예상정답률 |
|---|---|---|
| 영어학 (통사론) B형 기입형 | 2점 | 90% |

**모범답안 ⤵**

① two  ② three

**채점기준 ⤵**

2점: ①, ② 모두 답안과 일치하면 2점을 준다.

1점: ①, ② 중 하나만 답안과 일치하면 1점을 준다.

0점: ①, ② 모두 답안과 일치하지 않으면 0점을 준다.

본책 p.012

**02**

| 하위내용영역 | 배점 | 예상정답률 |
|---|---|---|
| 영어학 (통사론) A형 서술형 | 4점 | 65% |

**모범답안 ⤵**

Sentence (c) is ungrammatical. The adjective 'free' belongs to *ready*-type; thus, it cannot allow an extraposed construction. Sentence (e) is ungrammatical. The adjective 'frosty' belongs to *ready*-type; thus, it cannot allow the construction with an infinitive clause subject.

**채점기준 ⤵**

내용학: 4점

(1) Sentence (c) is ungrammatical이 맞으면 1점을 준다.

(2) The adjective 'free' belongs to *ready*-type; thus, it cannot allow an extraposed construction의 내용이 맞으면 1점을 준다.

(3) Sentence (e) is ungrammatical이 맞으면 1점을 준다.

(4) The adjective 'frosty' belongs to *ready*-type; thus, it cannot allow the construction with an infinitive clause subject의 내용이 맞으면 1점을 준다.

## 02 Complements & Adjuncts

### 01
본책 p.014

| 하위내용영역 | 배점 | 예상정답률 |
|---|---|---|
| 영어학 (통사론) B형 기입형 | 2점 | 80% |

**모범답안**

function

**채점기준**

2점 : 답안과 일치하면 2점을 준다.

0점 : 답안과 일치하지 않으면 0점을 준다.

### 02
본책 p.016

| 하위내용영역 | 배점 | 예상정답률 |
|---|---|---|
| 영어학 (통사론) B형 서술형 | 4점 | 65% |

**모범답안**

Sentence (d) is ungrammatical because the verb 'place(d)' selects (or requires) an NP and a PP as its complements, (but this sentence lacks an NP). Sentence (e) is ungrammatical because the verb 'stay(ed)' selects (or requires) (only) a PP as its complement, (but this sentence contains the NP 'Kim' which is unnecessary).

**채점기준**

내용학 : 4점

(1) Sentence (d) is ungrammatical이 맞으면 1점을 준다.

(2) the verb 'place(d)' selects (or requires) an NP and a PP as its complements의 내용이 맞으면 1점을 준다.

(3) Sentence (e) is ungrammatical이 맞으면 1점을 준다.

(4) the verb 'stay(ed)' selects (or requires) (only) a PP as its complement의 내용이 맞으면 1점을 준다.

### 03
본책 p.018

| 하위내용영역 | 배점 | 예상정답률 |
|---|---|---|
| 영어학 (통사론) B형 기입형 | 2점 | 90% |

**모범답안**

① modifier  ② complement

2점: ①, ② 모두 답안과 일치하면 2점을 준다.

1점: ①, ② 중 하나만 답안과 일치하면 1점을 준다.

0점: ①, ② 모두 답안과 일치하지 않으면 0점을 준다.

---

## 04
본책 p.020

| 하위내용영역 | 배점 | 예상정답률 |
|---|---|---|
| 영어학 (통사론) B형 서술형 | 4점 | 50% |

모범답안 ⌁

Sentence (e) is ungrammatical because the adjunct NP 'The wrong way' do not become the subject of a passive sentence. Sentence (f) is ungrammatical because the adjunct NP 'All afternoon' do not become the subject of a passive sentence.

채점기준 ⌁

내용학 : 4점

(1) Sentence (e) is ungrammatical이 맞으면 1점을 준다.

(2) the adjunct NP 'The wrong way' do not become the subject of a passive sentence의 내용이 맞으면 1점을 준다.

(3) Sentence (f) is ungrammatical이 맞으면 1점을 준다.

(4) the adjunct NP 'All afternoon' do not become the subject of a passive sentence의 내용이 맞으면 1점을 준다.

---

## 05
본책 p.022

| 하위내용영역 | 배점 | 예상정답률 |
|---|---|---|
| 영어학 (통사론) B형 기입형 | 2점 | 80% |

모범답안 ⌁

① longer  ② so

채점기준 ⌁

2점: ①, ② 모두 답안과 일치하면 2점을 준다.

1점: ①, ② 중 하나만 답안과 일치하면 1점을 준다.

0점: ①, ② 모두 답안과 일치하지 않으면 0점을 준다.

| 하위내용영역 | 배점 | 예상정답률 |
|---|---|---|
| 영어학 (통사론) A형 서술형 | 4점 | 50% |

[모범답안]

Sentence (a) contains the PP which has the different function from the rest: the PP 'with a razor-blade' is an adjunct. Sentence (f) contains the PP which has the different function from the rest: the PP 'at the office' is an adjunct.

[채점기준]

내용학 : 4점

(1) Sentence (a) contains the PP which has the different function from the rest이 맞으면 1점을 준다.
(2) the PP 'with a razor-blade' is an adjunct이 맞으면 1점을 준다.
(3) Sentence (f) contains the PP which has the different function from the rest이 맞으면 1점을 준다.
(4) the PP 'at the office' is an adjunct이 맞으면 1점을 준다.

| 하위내용영역 | 배점 | 예상정답률 |
|---|---|---|
| 영어학 (통사론) B형 기입형 | 2점 | 90% |

[모범답안]

external complement

[채점기준]

2점 : 답안과 일치하면 2점을 준다.
0점 : 답안과 일치하지 않으면 0점을 준다.

| 하위내용영역 | 배점 | 예상정답률 |
|---|---|---|
| 영어학 (통사론) A형 서술형 | 4점 | 45% |

[모범답안]

**Version 1**

Sentence (b) is ambiguous. The clause 'when you are ready' can be interpreted as complement or adjunct. Sentence (f) is ambiguous. The phrase 'last night' can be interpreted as complement or adjunct.

**Version 2**

Sentences (b) and (f) are ambiguous. In (b), the clause 'when you are ready' can either be a complement or an adjunct. In (f), The phrase 'last night' can either be a complement or an adjunct.

채점기준

내용학: 4점

(1) Sentence (b) is ambiguous이 맞으면 1점을 준다.
(2) The clause 'when you are ready' can be interpreted as complement or adjunct의 내용이 맞으면 1점을 준다.
(3) Sentence (f) is ambiguous이 맞으면 1점을 준다.
(4) he phrase 'last night' can be interpreted as complement or adjunct의 내용이 맞으면 1점을 준다.

---

**09** 본책 p.028

| 하위내용영역 | 배점 | 예상정답률 |
|---|---|---|
| 영어학 (통사론) B형 기입형 | 2점 | 70% |

모범답안

① from  ② with

채점기준

2점: ①, ② 모두 답안과 일치하면 2점을 준다.

1점: ①, ② 중 하나만 답안과 일치하면 1점을 준다.

0점: ①, ② 모두 답안과 일치하지 않으면 0점을 준다.

---

**10** 본책 p.030

| 하위내용영역 | 배점 | 예상정답률 |
|---|---|---|
| 영어학 (통사론) A형 서술형 | 4점 | 60% |

모범답안

(b) is false. The correct statement is as follows: the underlined clause is the complement and is a sister of N. (e) is false: the underlined PP is the adjunct and is a sister of N' (N-bar).

채점기준

내용학: 4점

(1) (b) is false이 맞으면 1점을 준다.
(2) the underlined clause is the complement and is a sister of N이 맞으면 1점을 준다.
(3) (e) is false이 맞으면 1점을 준다.
(4) the underlined PP is the adjunct and is a sister of N' (N-bar)이 맞으면 1점을 준다.

| 하위내용영역 | 배점 | 예상정답률 |
|---|---|---|
| 영어학 (통사론) A형 서술형 | 4점 | 60% |

[모범답안]

### Version 1

The phrase (e) is ungrammatical because the noun 'ignorance' cannot select a CP complement. The phrase (f) is ungrammatical because the noun 'article' cannot select a CP complement.

### Version 2

(e) is ungrammatical. The noun 'ignorance' cannot combine with a CP complement, (indicating that they do not have CP in the value of COMPS). (f) is ungrammatical. The noun 'article' cannot combine with a CP complement, (indicating that they do not have CP in the value of COMPS).

[채점기준]

내용학 : 4점

(1) The phrase (e) is ungrammatical이 맞으면 1점을 준다.

(2) the noun 'ignorance' cannot select a CP complement의 내용이 맞으면 1점을 준다.

(3) The phrase (f) is ungrammatical이 맞으면 1점을 준다.

(4) the noun 'article' cannot select a CP complement의 내용이 맞으면 1점을 준다.

## 03 Substitution

| 하위내용영역 | 배점 | 예상정답률 |
|---|---|---|
| 영어학 (통사론) B형 서술형 | 4점 | 50% |

[모범답안]

First, the one word for the blank is 'complements'. Second, sentence (b) is ungrammatical because do-so replacement cannot be understood to leave out any complement which is the PP 'of the child'.

[채점기준]

내용학 : 4점

(1) First, the one word for the blank is 'complements'이 맞으면 2점을 준다.

(2) sentence (b) is ungrammatical이 맞으면 1점을 준다.

(3) because do-so replacement cannot be understood to leave out any complement which is the PP 'of the child'의 내용이 맞으면 1점을 준다.

(4) sentence (b) 외에 답을 추가로 기술한 경우 2점을 감점한다.

## 02

본책 p.036

| 하위내용영역 | 배점 | 예상정답률 |
|---|---|---|
| 영어학 (통사론) A형 서술형 | 4점 | 60% |

모범답안 ✍

**Version 1**

Sentence (d) is ungrammatical. The proform 'one' must replace an N' (N-bar), but 'one' in (d) is replacing the noun (N) 'claim'. A pro-N' 'one' cannot replace an N (by itself unless an N is the constituent of an N').

**Version 2**

Sentence (d) is ungrammatical. The proform 'one' in (d) is replacing the noun (N) 'claim'. A pro-N' 'one' cannot replace an N; it must replace an N' (N-bar).

채점기준 ✍

내용학 : 4점

(1) Sentence (d) is ungrammatical이 맞으면 2점을 준다.
(2) The proform 'one' in (d) is replacing the noun (N) 'claim'의 내용이 맞으면 1점을 준다.
(3) A pro-N' 'one' cannot replace an N; it must replace an N'의 내용이 맞으면 1점을 준다.

## 03

본책 p.038

| 하위내용영역 | 배점 | 예상정답률 |
|---|---|---|
| 영어학 (문법/통사론) B형 서술형 | 4점 | 35% |

모범답안 ✍

**Version 1**

Sentences (a) and (c) are ungrammatical. In (a) the antecedent for 'did so (do so)' is 'read all the reports'; we cannot add 'most of them' as another complement in the second clause. In (c) the antecedent for 'did so (do so)' is 'rode her bicycle'; we cannot add 'to school' as another complement (of the verb 'rode') in the second clause.

**Version 2**

Sentence (a) is ungrammatical because 'did so (do so)' must be interpreted as 'read all the reports'; thus, we can't add 'most of them' as another complement (object) in the second clause. Sentence (c) is ungrammatical. The antecedent for 'did so (do so)' is 'rode her bicycle'. The added phrase 'to school' can consist of another complement in the second clause; it cannot combine with *do so* (in the second clause).

채점기준 ↩

내용학 : 4점

(1) Sentence (a) is ungrammatical이 맞으면 1점을 준다.

(2) In (a) the antecedent for 'did so (do so)' is 'read all the reports'; we cannot add 'most of them' as another complement in the second clause의 내용이 맞으면 1점을 준다.

(3) Sentence (c) is ungrammatical이 맞으면 1점을 준다.

(4) In (c) the antecedent for 'did so (do so)' is 'rode her bicycle'; we cannot add 'to school' as another complement (of the verb 'rode') in the second clause의 내용이 맞으면 1점을 준다.

(5) (a)와 (c) 모두 답으로 선택하지 않은 경우나 그 외에 답을 추가 선택한 경우는 부분 점수 없이 0점을 준다.

---

| 04 | | 본책 p.040 |

| 하위내용영역 | 배점 | 예상정답률 |
| --- | --- | --- |
| 영어학 (통사론) A형 서술형 | 4점 | 60% |

모범답안 ↩

**Version 1**

First, in (4b) the word 'French' is an AP adjunct, and in (5a) the word 'French' is an NP complement. Second, in (4c) 'French' is an adjective, and in (5c) 'French' is a noun.

**Version 2**

First, in (4b) 'French' functions as an adjunct and its form is an (prenominal) AP. In (5b) 'French' functions as a complement and its form is an (prenominal) NP. Second, in (4c) 'French' is an adjective, and in (5c) 'French' is a noun.

채점기준 ↩

내용학 : 4점

(1) in (4b) the word 'French' is an AP adjunct이 맞으면 1점을 준다.

(2) in (5a) the word 'French' is an NP complement이 맞으면 1점을 준다.

(3) in (4c) 'French' is an adjective이 맞으면 1점을 준다.

(4) in (5c) 'French' is a noun이 맞으면 1점을 준다.

# 04 Case Theory

## 01

본책 p.042

| 하위내용영역 | 배점 | 예상정답률 |
|---|---|---|
| 영어학 (통사론) B형 서술형 | 4점 | 55% |

모범답안 ⊕

### Version 1

Sentence (6) in <B> is syntactically well-formed. The matrix subject 'The book' originates in the object position of the verb 'read' (in the embedded clause). The NP 'The book' gets a theta role from the verb 'read' in its original position. The NP 'The book' is assigned the subject Case by the tense inflection of the matrix clause.

### Version 2

Sentence (6) in <B> is syntactically well-formed. The matrix subject 'The book' originates in the object position of the verb 'read' (in the embedded clause). The NP 'The book' gets a theta role in its original position by the verb 'read', and then this NP moves to the subject position of the main clause. This NP is assigned the subject Case by the tense inflection of the matrix clause.

채점기준 ⊕

내용학: 4점

(1) Sentence (6) in <B> is syntactically well-formed이 맞으면 1점을 준다.

(2) The matrix subject 'The book' originates in the object position of the verb 'read' (in the embedded clause)의 내용이 맞으면 1점을 준다.

(3) The NP 'The book' gets a theta role from the verb 'read' in its original position의 내용이 맞으면 1점을 준다.

(4) The NP 'The book' is assigned the subject Case by the tense inflection of the matrix clause의 내용이 맞으면 1점을 준다.

## 02

본책 p.044

| 하위내용영역 | 배점 | 예상정답률 |
|---|---|---|
| 영어학 (통사론) A형 서술형 | 4점 | 65% |

모범답안 ⊕

### Version 1

Sentence (d) is ungrammatical. The adjective 'envious' is not a case assigner; the NP 'Mary' is the caseless NP. (It violates the case filter.) Sentence (e) is ungrammatical. The noun 'destruction' is not a case assigner; the NP 'the rainforests' is the caseless NP. (It violates the case filter.)

## Version 2

Sentence (d) is ungrammatical because the NP 'Mary' cannot be (accusative) case-assigned by the adjective 'envious', (violating the case filter). Sentence (e) is ungrammatical because the NP 'the rainforests' cannot be (accusative) case-assigned by the noun 'destruction', (violating the case filter).

[ 채점기준 ⊶ ]

내용학: 4점

(1) Sentence (d) is ungrammatical이 맞으면 1점을 준다.

(2) The adjective 'envious' is not a case assigner; the NP 'Mary' is the caseless NP의 내용이 맞으면 1점을 준다.

(3) Sentence (e) is ungrammatical이 맞으면 1점을 준다.

(4) The noun 'destruction' is not a case assigner; the NP 'the rainforests' is the caseless NP의 내용이 맞으면 1점을 준다.

## 05 Binding Theory

### 01 본책 p.046

| 하위내용영역 | 배점 | 예상정답률 |
|---|---|---|
| 영어학 (통사론) B형 서술형 | 4점 | 50% |

[ 모범답안 ⊶ ]

Sentence (b) is ungrammatical. The reflexive 'himself' does not have the antecedent 'Jack' within the same clause: its antecedent is the pronoun 'Jack', and 'Jack' is contained within the *believe*-clause, not within the *was*-clause.

[ 채점기준 ⊶ ]

내용학: 4점

(1) Sentence (b) is ungrammatical이 맞으면 2점을 준다.

(2) The reflexive 'himself' does not have the antecedent 'Jack' within the same clause: its antecedent is the pronoun 'Jack', and 'Jack' is contained within the *believe*-clause, not within the *was*-clause의 내용이 맞으면 2점을 준다.

## 02

본책 p.048

| 하위내용영역 | 배점 | 예상정답률 |
|---|---|---|
| 영어학 (통사론) A형 서술형 | 4점 | 60% |

**모범답안 ↱**

Sentence (b) is ungrammatical because the anaphor 'himself' is not bound by its antecedent 'Frank' within its smallest binding domain 'to behave himself'. Sentence (d) is ungrammatical because the anaphor 'himself' is not bound by its antecedent 'Frank' within its smallest binding domain 'to gather evidence about himself'.

**채점기준 ↱**

내용학 : 4점

(1) Sentence (b) is ungrammatical이 맞으면 1점을 준다.

(2) the anaphor 'himself' is not bound by its antecedent 'Frank' within its smallest binding domain 'to behave himself'의 내용이 맞으면 1점을 준다.

(3) Sentence (d) is ungrammatical이 맞으면 1점을 준다.

(4) the anaphor 'himself' is not bound by its antecedent 'Frank' within its smallest binding domain 'to gather evidence about himself'의 내용이 맞으면 1점을 준다.


## 03

본책 p.050

| 하위내용영역 | 배점 | 예상정답률 |
|---|---|---|
| 영어학 (통사론) A형 서술형 | 4점 | 60% |

**모범답안 ↱**

Sentence (a) is ungrammatical. The anaphor 'himself' is not bound by the potential antecedent 'John' in its binding domain; (it violates Binding Principle A). Sentence (e) is ungrammatical. The anaphor 'himself' is not bound by the potential antecedent 'Bill' in its binding domain; (it violates Binding Principle A).

**채점기준 ↱**

내용학 : 4점

(1) Sentence (a) is ungrammatical이 맞으면 1점을 준다.

(2) The anaphor 'himself' is not bound by the potential antecedent 'John' in its binding domain의 내용이 맞으면 1점을 준다.

(3) Sentence (e) is ungrammatical이 맞으면 1점을 준다.

(4) The anaphor 'himself' is not bound by the potential antecedent 'Bill' in its binding domain의 내용이 맞으면 1점을 준다.

## 06 Control Theory

### 01

본책 p.052

| 하위내용영역 | 배점 | 예상정답률 |
|---|---|---|
| 영어학 (통사론) B형 기입형 | 2점 | 80% |

모범답안 ↵

① object   ② subject

채점기준 ↵

2점: ①, ② 모두 답안과 일치하면 2점을 준다.

1점: ①, ② 중 하나만 답안과 일치하면 1점을 준다.

0점: ①, ② 모두 답안과 일치하지 않으면 0점을 준다.

## 07 Theta Theory

### 01

본책 p.054

| 하위내용영역 | 배점 | 예상정답률 |
|---|---|---|
| 영어학 (통사론) B형 기입형 | 2점 | 80% |

모범답안 ↵

① source   ② experiencer

채점기준 ↵

2점: ①, ② 모두 답안과 일치하면 2점을 준다.
1점: ①, ② 중 하나만 답안과 일치하면 1점을 준다.
0점: ①, ② 모두 답안과 일치하지 않으면 0점을 준다.

### 02

본책 p.056

| 하위내용영역 | 배점 | 예상정답률 |
|---|---|---|
| 영어학 (통사론) B형 기입형 | 2점 | 80% |

모범답안 ↵

① EXPERIENCER   ② GOAL

2점: ①, ② 모두 답안과 일치하면 2점을 준다.

1점: ①, ② 중 하나만 답안과 일치하면 1점을 준다.

0점: ①, ② 모두 답안과 일치하지 않으면 0점을 준다.

## 08 Constituency

### 01
본책 p.058

| 하위내용영역 | 배점 | 예상정답률 |
| --- | --- | --- |
| 영어학 (통사론) B형 기입형 | 2점 | 85% |

모범답안

① the mother  ② the girl

채점기준

2점: ①, ② 모두 답안과 일치하면 2점을 준다.

1점: ①, ② 중 하나만 답안과 일치하면 1점을 준다.

0점: ①, ② 모두 답안과 일치하지 않으면 0점을 준다.

### 02
본책 p.060

| 하위내용영역 | 배점 | 예상정답률 |
| --- | --- | --- |
| 영어학 (통사론) A형 서술형 | 4점 | 60% |

모범답안

Sentences (6a) and (7b) are ungrammatical. In (6a), the string (phrase) 'that book' is not a complete constituent. In (7b), the string (phrase) 'that book with her best friend' is not a single constituent; (the two constituents, the NP 'that book' and the PP 'with her best friend', occur in the focus position of a cleft sentence.)

채점기준

내용학: 4점

(1) Sentences (6a) and (7b) are ungrammatical이 맞으면 2점을 준다. (각 1점)

(2) In (6a), the string (phrase) 'that book' is not a complete constituent의 내용이 맞으면 1점을 준다.

(3) In (7b), the string (phrase) 'that book with her best friend' is not a single constituent; (the two constituents, the NP 'that book' and the PP 'with her best friend', occur in the focus position of a cleft sentence.)의 내용이 맞으면 1점을 준다.

## 03

본책 p.062

| 하위내용영역 | 배점 | 예상정답률 |
|---|---|---|
| 영어학 (통사론) B형 기입형 | 2점 | 90% |

**모범답안**

head

**채점기준**

2점: 답안과 일치하면 2점을 준다.

0점: 답안과 일치하지 않으면 0점을 준다.

## 04

본책 p.064

| 하위내용영역 | 배점 | 예상정답률 |
|---|---|---|
| 영어학 (통사론) A형 서술형 | 4점 | 60% |

**모범답안**

Sentence (c) is ungrammatical. The different functions cannot be conjoined: the PP 'to the park' is a complement and the PP 'for health reasons' is an adjunct. Sentence (f) is ungrammatical. The different functions cannot be conjoined: the PP 'of the riots' is a complement and the PP 'in the bar' is an adjunct.

**채점기준**

내용학: 4점

(1) Sentence (c) is ungrammatical이 맞으면 1점을 준다.

(2) The different functions cannot be conjoined: the PP 'to the park' is a complement and the PP 'for health reasons' is an adjunct의 내용이 맞으면 1점을 준다.

(3) Sentence (f) is ungrammatical이 맞으면 1점을 준다.

(4) The different functions cannot be conjoined: the PP 'of the riots' is a complement and the PP 'in the bar' is an adjunct의 내용이 맞으면 1점을 준다.

## 05

| 하위내용영역 | 배점 | 예상정답률 |
|---|---|---|
| 영어학 (통사론) A형 서술형 | 4점 | 60% |

【모범답안】

**Version 1**

Sentence (c) is ungrammatical. TP 'them to be conscientious' cannot be in the focus position of a *wh*-cleft sentence. Sentence (f) is ungrammatical. AP 'very pretty' cannot be in the focus position of a *it*-cleft sentence.

**Version 2**

Sentences (c) and (f) are ungrammatical. In (c) TP 'them to be conscientious' cannot be in the focus position of a Pseudocleft. In (f) AP 'very pretty' cannot be in the focus position of a Cleft.

【채점기준】

내용학: 4점

(1) Sentence (c) is ungrammatical이 맞으면 1점을 준다.

(2) TP 'them to be conscientious' cannot be in the focus position of a *wh*-cleft sentence의 내용이 맞으면 1점을 준다.

(3) Sentence (f) is ungrammatical이 맞으면 1점을 준다.

(4) AP 'very pretty' cannot be in the focus position of a *it*-cleft sentence의 내용이 맞으면 1점을 준다.

## 06

| 하위내용영역 | 배점 | 예상정답률 |
|---|---|---|
| 영어학 (통사론) A형 서술형 | 4점 | 60% |

【모범답안】

Sentence (d) is ungrammatical. The different categories cannot be coordinated (conjoined); (the clause) 'that John made a mistake' is the CP and 'him to be in great pain' is the TP. Sentence (e) is ungrammatical. The different categories cannot be coordinated (conjoined); 'there to be fried squid at the reception' is the TP and 'for John to stay' is the CP.

【채점기준】

내용학: 4점

(1) Sentence (d) is ungrammatical이 맞으면 1점을 준다.

(2) The different categories cannot be coordinated (conjoined); (the clause) 'that John made a mistake' is the CP and 'him to be in great pain' is the TP의 내용이 맞으면 1점을 준다.

(3) Sentence (e) is ungrammatical이 맞으면 1점을 준다.

(4) The different categories cannot be coordinated (conjoined); 'there to be fried squid at the reception' is the TP and 'for John to stay' is the CP의 내용이 맞으면 1점을 준다.

## 09 Verbs

본책 p.070

**01**

| 하위내용영역 | 배점 | 예상정답률 |
|---|---|---|
| 영어학 (통사론) A형 서술형 | 4점 | 60% |

**모범답안**

Sentence (a) is ungrammatical. The non-object NP 'a good friend' cannot be promoted to the subject (in the passive sentence). Sentence (d) is ungrammatical. When the DO 'a review copy of the book' follows the IO 'her', the DO cannot be passivized.

**채점기준**

내용학: 4점

(1) Sentence (a) is ungrammatical이 맞으면 1점을 준다.

(2) The non-object NP 'a good friend' cannot be promoted to the subject (in the passive sentence)의 내용이 맞으면 1점을 준다.

(3) Sentence (d) is ungrammatical이 맞으면 1점을 준다.

(4) When the DO 'a review copy of the book' follows the IO 'her', the DO cannot be passivized의 내용이 맞으면 1점을 준다.

**02**

본책 p.072

| 하위내용영역 | 배점 | 예상정답률 |
|---|---|---|
| 영어학 (통사론) B형 서술형 | 4점 | 50% |

**모범답안**

**Version 1**

Sentences (a) and (f) are ungrammatical. In (a), 'went out (go out)' is a prepositional verb and 'out' is a preposition, (forming a PP with the following NP 'the door'), but the NP 'the door' precedes the preposition 'out'. In (f), 'looked up' is a phrasal verb and 'up' is a particle; the particle 'up' does not form a constituent with the following NP 'Mary's number' (in the focus position of the cleft sentence).

**Version 2**

Sentence (a) is ungrammatical because 'went out (go out)' is a prepositional verb and 'out' is a preposition; thus, the NP 'the door' cannot precede the preposition 'out'. Sentence (f) is ungrammatical because 'looked up' is a phrasal verb and 'up' is a particle that forms no constituent with the following NP 'Mary's number' (in the focus position of the cleft construction).

채점기준

내용학 : 4점

(1) Sentences (a) and (f) are ungrammatical이 맞으면 2점을 준다. (각 1점)

(2) In (a), 'went out (go out)' is a prepositional verb and 'out' is a preposition, (forming a PP with the following NP 'the door'), but the NP 'the door' precedes the preposition 'out'의 내용이 맞으면 1점을 준다.

(3) In (f), 'looked up' is a phrasal verb and 'up' is a particle; the particle 'up' does not form a constituent with the following NP 'Mary's number' (in the focus position of the cleft sentence)의 내용이 맞으면 1점을 준다.

## 03

본책 p.074

| 하위내용영역 | 배점 | 예상정답률 |
|---|---|---|
| 영어학 (통사론) B형 서술형 | 4점 | 60% |

모범답안

### Version 1

Sentence (b) is ungrammatical because the verb 'tend(s)' cannot select (take) the infinitival CP (clause) 'for Mary to avoid confrontations' as the complement. Sentence (d) is ungrammatical because the verb 'hope(d)' cannot select the infinitival CP 'for Beth to find a solution' as the complement.

### Version 2

Sentences (b) and (d) are ungrammatical. The verbs 'tend(s)' in (b) and 'hope(d)' in (d) cannot select an infinitival CP (clause) as the complement.

<참고> an infinitival CP complement / an infinitive type of CP / a nonfinite CP 모두 가능한 표현이다.

채점기준

내용학 : 4점

(1) Sentence (b) is ungrammatical이 맞으면 1점을 준다.

(2) the verb 'tend(s)' cannot select (take) the infinitival CP (clause) 'for Mary to avoid confrontations' as the complement의 내용이 맞으면 1점을 준다.

(3) Sentence (d) is ungrammatical이 맞으면 1점을 준다.

(4) the verb 'hope(d)' cannot select the infinitival CP 'for Beth to find a solution' as the complement의 내용이 맞으면 1점을 준다.

## 04

본책 p.076

| 하위내용영역 | 배점 | 예상정답률 |
|---|---|---|
| 영어학 (통사론) B형 서술형 | 4점 | 60% |

**모범답안**

Sentence (d) is ungrammatical. The verb 'like(d)' cannot allow for passivizing the matrix clause. Sentence (f) is ungrammatical. The verb 'prove(d)' takes a TP complement ('Ashley to be an idiot'); TP cannot be in the focus position of a pseudo cleft sentence.

**채점기준**

내용학: 4점

(1) Sentence (d) is ungrammatical이 맞으면 1점을 준다.

(2) The verb 'like(d)' cannot allow for passivizing the matrix clause의 내용이 맞으면 1점을 준다.

(3) Sentence (f) is ungrammatical이 맞으면 1점을 준다.

(4) The verb 'prove(d)' takes a TP complement ('Ashley to be an idiot'); TP cannot be in the focus position of a pseudo cleft sentence의 내용이 맞으면 1점을 준다.

## 05

본책 p.078

| 하위내용영역 | 배점 | 예상정답률 |
|---|---|---|
| 영어학 (통사론) B형 서술형 | 4점 | 60% |

**모범답안**

Sentence (c) is ungrammatical. The (monotransitive or intransitive) verb 'haul(ed)' cannot take two objects, ('the boy' and 'the ball'). Sentence (f) is ungrammatical. The (intransitive or monotransitive) verb 'shriek(ed)' cannot take two objects, ('Helen' and 'the news').

**채점기준**

내용학: 4점

(1) Sentence (c) is ungrammatical이 맞으면 1점을 준다.

(2) The (monotransitive or intransitive) verb 'haul(ed)' cannot take two objects, ('the boy' and 'the ball')의 내용이 맞으면 1점을 준다.

(3) Sentence (f) is ungrammatical이 맞으면 1점을 준다.

(4) The (intransitive or monotransitive) verb 'shriek(ed)' cannot take two objects, ('Helen' and 'the news')의 내용이 맞으면 1점을 준다.

## 06
본책 p.080

| 하위내용영역 | 배점 | 예상정답률 |
|---|---|---|
| 영어학 (통사론) A형 서술형 | 4점 | 60% |

**모범답안** ◦→

Sentence (a) is ungrammatical. The verb 'pinch(ed)' cannot select the CP complement 'that he feels pain'. Sentence (b) is ungrammatical. The verb 'hope' cannot select the NP complement 'the availability of a new vaccine'.

**채점기준** ◦→

내용학 : 4점

(1) Sentence (a) is ungrammatical이 맞으면 1점을 준다.

(2) The verb 'pinch(ed)' cannot select the CP complement 'that he feels pain'의 내용이 맞으면 1점을 준다.

(3) Sentence (b) is ungrammatical이 맞으면 1점을 준다.

(4) The verb 'hope' cannot select the NP complement 'the availability of a new vaccine'의 내용이 맞으면 1점을 준다.


## 07
본책 p.082

| 하위내용영역 | 배점 | 예상정답률 |
|---|---|---|
| 영어학 (통사론) A형 서술형 | 4점 | 45% |

**모범답안** ◦→

Sentence (d) is ungrammatical. The subject 'the avalanche' is selected by the (matrix/main) verb 'tell (told)'; this sentence is semantically ill-formed. Sentence (f) is ungrammatical. The subject 'the key' is selected by the (matrix/main) verb 'ask (asked)'; this sentence is semantically ill-formed.

**채점기준** ◦→

내용학 : 4점

(1) Sentence (d) is ungrammatical이 맞으면 1점을 준다.

(2) The subject 'the avalanche' is selected by the (matrix/main) verb 'tell (told)'; this sentence is semantically ill-formed의 내용이 맞으면 1점을 준다.

(3) Sentence (f) is ungrammatical이 맞으면 1점을 준다.

(4) The subject 'the key' is selected by the (matrix/main) verb 'ask (asked)'; this sentence is semantically ill-formed의 내용이 맞으면 1점을 준다.

## 05

본책 p.096

| 하위내용영역 | 배점 | 예상정답률 |
|---|---|---|
| 영어학 (통사론) A형 서술형 | 4점 | 50% |

**모범답안**

Sentence (5a) is grammatical and (5b) is ungrammatical. In (5a), a (typical) *wh*-pronoun 'which' can function as the (immediately following) Complement of a Preposition 'for', whereas in (5b), 'that' is a complementiser (rather than a relative pronoun); thus, it ('that') cannot function as the Complement of a Preposition 'for'.

**채점기준**

내용학 : 4점

(1) Sentence (5a) is grammatical and (5b) is ungrammatical이 맞으면 2점을 준다. (각 1점)

(2) In (5a), a (typical) *wh*-pronoun 'which' can function as the (immediately following) Complement of a Preposition 'for'의 내용이 맞으면 1점을 준다.

(3) in (5b), 'that' is a complementiser (rather than a relative pronoun); thus, it ('that') cannot function as the Complement of a Preposition 'for'의 내용이 맞으면 1점을 준다.

## 06

본책 p.098

| 하위내용영역 | 배점 | 예상정답률 |
|---|---|---|
| 영어학 (통사론) B형 서술형 | 4점 | 50% |

**모범답안**

### Version 1

The two interpretations of sentence (4) are as follows: (i) How old is Sam?, and (ii) How is old Sam? On the first interpretation, in (i), 'old' goes (belongs) with 'how' to form the phrase 'how old'. On the second interpretation, in (ii), 'old' goes (belongs) with 'Sam' to form the phrase 'old Sam'.

### Version 2

On the first interpretation, 'old' goes (belongs) with 'how' to form the phrase 'how old'. The question is as follows: How old is Sam?. On the second interpretation, 'old' goes (belongs) with 'Sam' to form the phrase 'old Sam'. The question is as follows: How is old Sam?

**채점기준**

내용학 : 4점

(1) (i) How old is Sam?이 맞으면 1점을 준다.

(2) (ii) How is old Sam?이 맞으면 1점을 준다.

(3) in (i), 'old' goes (belongs) with 'how' to form the phrase 'how old'의 내용이 맞으면 1점을 준다.

(4) in (ii), 'old' goes (belongs) with 'Sam' to form the phrase 'old Sam'의 내용이 맞으면 1점을 준다.

# 10 Syntactic Structures

## 01

본책 p.084

| 하위내용영역 | 배점 | 예상정답률 |
|---|---|---|
| 영어학 (통사론) B형 기입형 | 2점 | 80% |

모범답안 ↴

① intermediate  ② specifiers

채점기준 ↴

2점: ①, ② 모두 답안과 일치하면 2점을 준다.

1점: ①, ② 중 하나만 답안과 일치하면 1점을 준다.

0점: ①, ② 모두 답안과 일치하지 않으면 0점을 준다.

## 02

본책 p.086

| 하위내용영역 | 배점 | 예상정답률 |
|---|---|---|
| 영어학 (통사론) B형 기입형 | 2점 | 80% |

모범답안 ↴

① tense  ② non-past

채점기준 ↴

2점: ①, ② 모두 답안과 일치하면 2점을 준다.

1점: ①, ② 중 하나만 답안과 일치하면 1점을 준다.

0점: ①, ② 모두 답안과 일치하지 않으면 0점을 준다.

## 03

본책 p.087

| 하위내용영역 | 배점 | 예상정답률 |
|---|---|---|
| 영어학 (통사론) B형 기입형 | 2점 | 90% |

모범답안 ↴

modal auxiliary

채점기준 ↴

2점: 답안과 일치하면 2점을 준다.

0점: 답안과 일치하지 않으면 0점을 준다.

## 11 Additional Tests

01 〔 본책 p.088

| 하위내용영역 | 배점 | 예상정답률 |
|---|---|---|
| 영어학 (통사론) B형 기입형 | 2점 | 80% |

**모범답안**

**head**

**채점기준**

2점: 답안과 일치하면 2점을 준다.

0점: 답안과 일치하지 않으면 0점을 준다.

02 〔 본책 p.090

| 하위내용영역 | 배점 | 예상정답률 |
|---|---|---|
| 영어학 (통사론) B형 서술형 | 4점 | 50% |

**모범답안**

Sentence (d) is ungrammatical because the adjective 'easy' cannot select a finite CP (complement) 'that we please him' (or cannot combine with a finite CP complement). Sentence (f) is ungrammatical because the adjective 'true' cannot select an infinitival CP (complement) 'for him to be a genius'.

**채점기준**

내용학: 4점

(1) Sentence (d) is ungrammatical이 맞으면 1점을 준다.

(2) because the adjective 'easy' cannot select a finite CP (complement) 'that we please him' (or cannot combine with a finite CP complement)의 내용이 맞으면 1점을 준다.

(3) Sentence (f) is ungrammatical이 맞으면 1점을 준다.

(4) because the adjective 'true' cannot select an infinitival CP (complement) 'for him to be a genius'의 내용이 맞으면 1점을 준다.

## 03

본책 p.092

| 하위내용영역 | 배점 | 예상정답률 |
|---|---|---|
| 영어학 (통사론) A형 서술형 | 4점 | 60% |

[ 모범답안 ]

Sentence (b) is ungrammatical and violates Tensed S Constraint. The NP 'Ed' is the subject of a tensed verb 'will be' and cannot be moved. Sentence (c) is ungrammatical and Unit Movement Constraint is violated. The string (phrase) 'The car into the garage' is not a constituent, and thus cannot be moved.

[ 채점기준 ]

내용학 : 4점

(1) Sentence (b) is ungrammatical and violates Tensed S Constraint이 맞으면 1점을 준다.

(2) The NP 'Ed' is the subject of a tensed verb 'will be' and cannot be moved의 내용이 맞으면 1점을 준다.

(3) Sentence (c) is ungrammatical and Unit Movement Constraint is violated이 맞으면 1점을 준다.

(4) The string (phrase) 'The car into the garage' is not a constituent, and thus cannot be moved의 내용이 맞으면 1점을 준다.

## 04

본책 p.094

| 하위내용영역 | 배점 | 예상정답률 |
|---|---|---|
| 영어학 (통사론) B형 서술형 | 4점 | 60% |

[ 모범답안 ]

Sentence (3) is ambiguous. This sentence has the two different D-structures as follows: (i) You did say to whom [that Mary was talking]? (ii) You did say [that Mary was talking to whom]?

[ 채점기준 ]

내용학 : 4점

(1) Sentence (3) is ambiguous이 맞으면 2점을 준다.

(2) (i) You did say to whom [that Mary was talking]?이 맞으면 1점을 준다.

(3) (ii) You did say [that Mary was talking to whom]?이 맞으면 1점을 준다.

본책 p.100

**07**

| 하위내용영역 | 배점 | 예상정답률 |
|---|---|---|
| 영어학 (통사론) B형 기입형 | 2점 | 90% |

[모범답안]

① object  ② subject

[채점기준]

2점: ①, ② 모두 답안과 일치하면 2점을 준다.

1점: ①, ② 중 하나만 답안과 일치하면 1점을 준다.

0점: ①, ② 모두 답안과 일치하지 않으면 0점을 준다.

본책 p.102

**08**

| 하위내용영역 | 배점 | 예상정답률 |
|---|---|---|
| 영어학 (통사론) B형 서술형 | 4점 | 50% |

[모범답안]

Sentence (b) is ungrammatical. (The verb) 'have' cannot cliticise onto (the pronoun) 'you' because the presence of the null infinitive particle 'to' intervening between 'you' and 'have' blocks cliticisation of 'have' onto 'you'.

[채점기준]

내용학: 4점

(1) Sentence (b) is ungrammatical이 맞으면 1점을 준다.

(2) (The verb) 'have' cannot cliticise onto (the pronoun) 'you'의 내용이 맞으면 1점을 준다.

(3) because the presence of the null infinitive particle 'to' intervening between 'you' and 'have' blocks cliticisation of 'have' onto 'you'의 내용이 맞으면 2점을 준다.

본책 p.104

**09**

| 하위내용영역 | 배점 | 예상정답률 |
|---|---|---|
| 영어학 (통사론) B형 기입형 | 2점 | 80% |

[모범답안]

① subject  ② object

2점: ①, ② 모두 답안과 일치하면 2점을 준다.

1점: ①, ② 중 하나만 답안과 일치하면 1점을 준다.

0점: ①, ② 모두 답안과 일치하지 않으면 0점을 준다.

---

## 10 본책 p.106

| 하위내용영역 | 배점 | 예상정답률 |
|---|---|---|
| 영어학 (통사론) B형 서술형 | 4점 | 50% |

모범답안 ↴

### Version 1

Sentence (d) is ungrammatical because the *wh*-phrase 'who' does not move to the closest potential landing site (which is already filled by the other *wh*-phrase 'what'); this movement violates the Minimal Link Condition.

### Version 2

Sentence (d) is ungrammatical. If the *wh*-phrase 'who' moves to the specifier of the higher CP, this movement does not meet MLC. Since the closest potential landing site is already occupied by the other *wh*-phrase 'what', this movement skips the first potential position, the lower (embedded) CP.

채점기준 ↴

내용학: 4점

(1) Sentence (d) is ungrammatical이 맞으면 2점을 준다.

(2) the *wh*-phrase 'who' does not move to the closest potential landing site (which is already filled by the other *wh*-phrase 'what')의 내용이 맞으면 1점을 준다.

(3) this movement violates the Minimal Link Condition의 내용이 맞으면 1점을 준다.

---

## 11 본책 p.108

| 하위내용영역 | 배점 | 예상정답률 |
|---|---|---|
| 영어학 (통사론) B형 기입형 | 2점 | 90% |

모범답안 ↴

① non-gradable   ② gradable

채점기준 ↴

2점: ①, ② 모두 답안과 일치하면 2점을 준다.

1점: ①, ② 중 하나만 답안과 일치하면 1점을 준다.

0점: ①, ② 모두 답안과 일치하지 않으면 0점을 준다.

## 12
본책 p.109

| 하위내용영역 | 배점 | 예상정답률 |
|---|---|---|
| 영어학 (통사론) B형 기입형 | 2점 | 80% |

모범답안

① verb  ② prepositions

채점기준

2점: ①, ② 모두 답안과 일치하면 2점을 준다.

1점: ①, ② 중 하나만 답안과 일치하면 1점을 준다.

0점: ①, ② 모두 답안과 일치하지 않으면 0점을 준다.

## 13
본책 p.111

| 하위내용영역 | 배점 | 예상정답률 |
|---|---|---|
| 영어학 (통사론) B형 기입형 | 2점 | 90% |

모범답안

① direct object  ② predicative complement

채점기준

2점: ①, ② 모두 답안과 일치하면 2점을 준다.

1점: ①, ② 중 하나만 답안과 일치하면 1점을 준다.

0점: ①, ② 모두 답안과 일치하지 않으면 0점을 준다.

## 14
본책 p.113

| 하위내용영역 | 배점 | 예상정답률 |
|---|---|---|
| 영어학 (통사론) B형 기입형 | 2점 | 80% |

모범답안

① adjunct  ② predicative

채점기준

2점: ①, ② 모두 답안과 일치하면 2점을 준다.

1점: ①, ② 중 하나만 답안과 일치하면 1점을 준다.

0점: ①, ② 모두 답안과 일치하지 않으면 0점을 준다.

## 15

본책 p.115

| 하위내용영역 | 배점 | 예상정답률 |
|---|---|---|
| 영어학 (통사론) A형 서술형 | 4점 | 50% |

모범답안 ↩

### Version 1

Sentence (a) is ungrammatical because no constituent can be moved out of a sentential subject 'for Mary to kiss (whom)'; it violates a subject condition. Sentence (e) is ungrammatical because once you move the *wh*-phrase 'what' into the specifier of the embedded CP, then that CP becomes an island for further extraction, the other *wh*-phrase 'who' into the main CP specifier; it violates a *wh*-island.

### Version 2

Sentences (a) and (e) are ungrammatical. In (a), in the sentential subject 'for Mary to kiss whom', the *wh*-phrase 'whom' cannot be moved into the main CP specifier because no constituent can be moved out of a sentential subject; it violates a subject condition. In (e), when the *wh*-phrase 'what' is moved into the embedded specifier, the other *wh*-phrase 'who' cannot be moved into the main CP specifier; it violates a *wh*-island.

채점기준 ↩

내용학 : 4점

(1) Sentence (a) is ungrammatical이 맞으면 1점을 준다.

(2) because no constituent can be moved out of a sentential subject 'for Mary to kiss whom'; it violates a subject condition의 내용이 맞으면 1점을 준다.

(3) Sentence (e) is ungrammatical이 맞으면 1점을 준다.

(4) because once you move the *wh*-phrase 'what' into the specifier of the embedded CP, then that CP becomes an island for further extraction, the other *wh*-phrase 'who' into the main CP specifier; it violates a *wh*-island의 내용이 맞으면 1점을 준다.

## 16

본책 p.117

| 하위내용영역 | 배점 | 예상정답률 |
|---|---|---|
| 영어학 (통사론) B형 기입형 | 2점 | 80% |

모범답안 ↩

① adverb  ② adjective

채점기준 ↩

2점 : ①, ② 모두 답안과 일치하면 2점을 준다.

1점 : ①, ② 중 하나만 답안과 일치하면 1점을 준다.

0점 : ①, ② 모두 답안과 일치하지 않으면 0점을 준다.

## 17

본책 p.119

| 하위내용영역 | 배점 | 예상정답률 |
|---|---|---|
| 영어학 (통사론) B형 기입형 | 2점 | 90% |

【모범답안】

① verb  ② noun

【채점기준】

2점: ①, ② 모두 답안과 일치하면 2점을 준다.

1점: ①, ② 중 하나만 답안과 일치하면 1점을 준다.

0점: ①, ② 모두 답안과 일치하지 않으면 0점을 준다.

## 18

본책 p.121

| 하위내용영역 | 배점 | 예상정답률 |
|---|---|---|
| 영어학 (통사론) B형 기입형 | 2점 | 90% |

【모범답안】

head

【채점기준】

2점: 답안과 일치하면 2점을 준다.

0점: 답안과 일치하지 않으면 0점을 준다.

# Grammar

---

## PART 02

## 01

본책 p.126

| 하위내용영역 | 배점 | 예상정답률 |
|---|---|---|
| 영어학 (문법) A형 서술형 | 4점 | 60% |

**모범답안**

Sentences (a) and (d) are infelicitous. In (a) the indefinite NP 'A hole' denotes an abstract entity; the non-existential is infelicitous. (The existential is required.) In (d) the indefinite NP 'An accident' (also) denotes an abstract entity; the non-existential is infelicitous.

**채점기준**

내용학 : 4점

(1) Sentences (a) and (d) are infelicitous이 맞으면 2점을 준다. (각 1점)

(2) In (a) the indefinite NP 'A hole' denotes an abstract entity; the non-existential is infelicitous의 내용이 맞으면 1점을 준다.

(3) In (d) the indefinite NP 'An accident' (also) denotes an abstract entity; the non-existential is infelicitous의 내용이 맞으면 1점을 준다.

---

## 02

본책 p.128

| 하위내용영역 | 배점 | 예상정답률 |
|---|---|---|
| 영어학 (문법) A형 서술형 | 4점 | 50% |

**모범답안**

**Version 1**

Sentences (a) and (d) are ungrammatical. The correct forms are as follows: (a) He pointed out that not once had she complained, and (d) Only two of them did he find useful.

**Version 2**

Sentence (a) is ungrammatical. The correct form is "He pointed out that not once had she complained". Sentence (d) is ungrammatical. The correct form is "Only two of them did he find useful".

**채점기준**

내용학 : 4점

(1) Sentences (a) and (d) are ungrammatical이 맞으면 2점을 준다. (각 1점)

(2) (a) He pointed out that not once had she complained이 맞으면 1점을 준다.

(3) (d) Only two of them did he find useful이 맞으면 1점을 준다.

## 03

본책 p.130

| 하위내용영역 | 배점 | 예상정답률 |
|---|---|---|
| 영어학 (문법) B형 서술형 | 4점 | 50% |

**모범답안**

Sentence (a) is ungrammatical. This sentence (The main clause) is the positive clause; it does not allow a continuation with 'not even'. Sentence (b) is ungrammatical. This sentence is the positive clause; thus, it cannot take the positive confirmation tag. (It requires (or needs) the negative confirmation tag (doesn't she?)).

**채점기준**

내용학: 4점

(1) Sentence (a) is ungrammatical이 맞으면 1점을 준다.

(2) This sentence (The main clause) is the positive clause; it does not allow a continuation with 'not even'의 내용이 맞으면 1점을 준다.

(3) Sentence (b) is ungrammatical이 맞으면 1점을 준다.

(4) This sentence is the positive clause; thus, it cannot take the positive confirmation tag의 내용이 맞으면 1점을 준다.

## 04

본책 p.132

| 하위내용영역 | 배점 | 예상정답률 |
|---|---|---|
| 영어학 (문법) A형 서술형 | 4점 | 50% |

**모범답안**

Sentence (b) is ungrammatical. *Get* passives cannot occur with the verb 'comprehend(ed)' that describes cognition. Sentence (e) is ungrammatical. Insertion of the expression 'more' is not possible with a passive sentence (*get* passives).

**채점기준**

내용학: 4점

(1) Sentence (b) is ungrammatical이 맞으면 1점을 준다.

(2) *Get* passives cannot occur with the verb 'comprehend(ed)' that describes cognition의 내용이 맞으면 1점을 준다.

(3) Sentence (e) is ungrammatical이 맞으면 1점을 준다.

(4) Insertion of the expression 'more' is not possible with a passive sentence (*get* passives)의 내용이 맞으면 1점을 준다.

본책 p.134

## 05

| 하위내용영역 | 배점 | 예상정답률 |
|---|---|---|
| 영어학 (문법) A형 서술형 | 4점 | 50% |

[모범답안]

Sentence (b) is ungrammatical because the achievement expression 'reach the summit' cannot occur as complement to the (lexical aspectual) verb 'begin'. Sentence (d) is ungrammatical. The verb 'dying' belongs to achievements (which has the natural endpoint); the *for*-phrase 'for an hour' is not acceptable (in situations in which such endpoints do not exist).

[채점기준]

내용학: 4점

(1) Sentence (b) is ungrammatical이 맞으면 1점을 준다.

(2) because the achievement expression 'reach the summit' cannot occur as complement to the (lexical aspectual) verb 'begin'의 내용이 맞으면 1점을 준다.

(3) Sentence (d) is ungrammatical이 맞으면 1점을 준다.

(4) The verb 'dying' belongs to achievements (which has the natural endpoint); the *for*-phrase 'for an hour' is not acceptable (in situations in which such endpoints do not exist)의 내용이 맞으면 1점을 준다.

본책 p.136

## 06

| 하위내용영역 | 배점 | 예상정답률 |
|---|---|---|
| 영어학 (문법) A형 서술형 | 4점 | 40% |

[모범답안]

Sentence (b) is ungrammatical because the verb 'allude(d)' does not license (require) an object 'the letter'; it belongs to intransitive verbs. Sentence (d) is ungrammatical because the verb 'peruse(d)' does not have an object (does not belong to intransitive verbs), but it belongs to monotransitive verbs; (it requires an object).

transitive도 맞게

[채점기준]

내용학: 4점

(1) Sentence (b) is ungrammatical이 맞으면 1점을 준다.

(2) because the verb 'allude(d)' does not license (require) an object 'the letter'; it belongs to intransitive verbs의 내용이 맞으면 1점을 준다.

(3) Sentence (d) is ungrammatical이 맞으면 1점을 준다.

(4) because the verb 'peruse(d)' does not have an object (does not belong to intransitive verbs), but it belongs to monotransitive verbs; (it requires an object)의 내용이 맞으면 1점을 준다.

(5) Sentence (b)와 sentence (d) 외에 다른 문장을 추가로 기술하거나 둘 중 하나만 기술한 경우 0점을 준다.

| 하위내용영역 | 배점 | 예상정답률 |
|---|---|---|
| 영어학 (문법) A형 서술형 | 4점 | 65% |

**모범답안**

### Version 1

Sentence (c) is ungrammatical. The negative feature in the verb 'doubt(s)' doesn't allow the positive polarity item, 'sometimes', but needs the negative polarity item 'ever'. Sentence (d) is unnatural. The stative verb 'like(s)' cannot occur with the manner adverb 'deliberately'.

### Version 2

Sentence (c) is ungrammatical. The verb 'doubt(s)' may be analyzed as 'think that not.' The negative feature in the verb needs the negative polarity item ever (to occur grammatically without the overt presence of *not*), but it doesn't allow the positive polarity item, 'sometimes'. Sentence (d) is unnatural. This stative sentence sounds unnatural with the manner adverb 'deliberately'.

**채점기준**

내용학: 4점

(1) Sentence (c) is ungrammatical이 맞으면 1점을 준다.

(2) The negative feature in the verb 'doubt(s)' doesn't allow the positive polarity item, 'sometimes', but needs the negative polarity item 'ever'의 내용이 맞으면 1점을 준다.

(3) Sentence (d) is unnatural이 맞으면 1점을 준다.

(4) The stative verb 'like(s)' cannot occur with the manner adverb 'deliberately'의 내용이 맞으면 1점을 준다.

| 하위내용영역 | 배점 | 예상정답률 |
|---|---|---|
| 영어학 (문법) A형 서술형 | 4점 | 50% |

**모범답안**

The appropriate tag for the blank is 'hadn't you'. Sentences (d) and (e) are ungrammatical. The correct sentences are as follows: (d) The others were taken by her, weren't they?, and (e) The others she took, didn't she?

**채점기준**

내용학: 4점

(1) The appropriate tag for the blank is 'hadn't you'이 맞으면 2점을 준다.

(2) (d) The others were taken by her, weren't they?이 맞으면 1점을 준다.

(3) (e) The others she took, didn't she?이 맞으면 1점을 준다.

## 09

본책 p.142

| 하위내용영역 | 배점 | 예상정답률 |
|---|---|---|
| 영어학 (문법) A형 서술형 | 4점 | 60% |

**모범답안**

Sentence (e) is ungrammatical. The correct form is as follows: Her mother's not coming, either. Sentence (f) is ungrammatical. The correct form is as follows: I hardly have any friends, and neither do you.

**채점기준**

내용학 : 4점

(1) Sentence (e) is ungrammatical이 맞으면 1점을 준다.
(2) Her mother's not coming, either이 맞으면 1점을 준다.
(3) Sentence (f) is ungrammatical이 맞으면 1점을 준다.
(4) I hardly have any friends, and neither do you이 맞으면 1점을 준다.

## 10

본책 p.144

| 하위내용영역 | 배점 | 예상정답률 |
|---|---|---|
| 영어학 (문법) A형 서술형 | 4점 | 70% |

**모범답안**

The phrase (d) is ungrammatical. 'His' is a central determiner and 'both' is a predeterminer; switching the order (→predeterminer, central determiner, postdeterminer→) results in ungrammaticality. The phrase (e) is ungrammatical. 'All' and 'twice' belong to a predeterminer; determiners belonging to the same category (class) cannot be combined with each other.

**채점기준**

내용학 : 4점

(1) The phrase (d) is ungrammatical이 맞으면 1점을 준다.
(2) 'His' is a central determiner and 'both' is a predeterminer; switching the order (→predeterminer, central determiner, postdeterminer→) results in ungrammaticality의 내용이 맞으면 1점을 준다.
(3) The phrase (e) is ungrammatical이 맞으면 1점을 준다.
(4) 'All' and 'twice' belong to a predeterminer; determiners belonging to the same category (class) cannot be combined with each other의 내용이 맞으면 1점을 준다.

11 본책 p.146

| 하위내용영역 | 배점 | 예상정답률 |
|---|---|---|
| 영어학 (문법) A형 서술형 | 4점 | 50% |

채점기준 ⊙

### Version 1

First, sentence (c) is ambiguous. (c) can be interpreted in either way, deontically (as authorising her to speak French) or dynamically (as reporting her ability to do so). Second, sentence (a) has the deontic interpretation, while sentence (b) has the dynamic interpretation.

### Version 2

Sentence (c) is ambiguous. (c) can be interpreted in either way, deontically (as authorising her to speak French) or dynamically (as reporting her ability to do so). Sentence (a) gives (or reports) permission: [deontic], while sentence (b) is concerned with her ability: [dynamic].

채점기준 ⊙

내용학 : 4점

(1) sentence (c) is ambiguous이 맞으면 1점을 준다.

(2) (c) can be interpreted in either way, deontically or dynamically이 맞으면 1점을 준다.

(3) sentence (a) has the deontic interpretation이 맞으면 1점을 준다.

(4) sentence (b) has the dynamic interpretation이 맞으면 1점을 준다.

12 본책 p.148

| 하위내용영역 | 배점 | 예상정답률 |
|---|---|---|
| 영어학 (문법) B형 서술형 | 4점 | 60% |

모범답안 ⊙

### Version 1

In (a), (the NP) 'a fool' functions as a predicative complement. There is only a single person involved, the one referred to by the subject NP 'I'. In (b) 'a fool' functions as an object. There are two people involved, the subject NP 'I' and the object NP 'a fool'.

### Version 2

In (a), (the NP) 'a fool' functions as a predicative complement, and in (b) 'a fool' functions as an object. In (a) there is only a single person involved, the one referred to by the subject NP 'I'. Sentence (b) refers to two people: me, and the fool I could feel pushing in front of me on the platform.

**채점기준**

내용학 : 4점

(1) In (a), (the NP) 'a fool' functions as a predicative complement이 맞으면 1점을 준다.

(2) There is only a single person involved, the one referred to by the subject NP 'I'의 내용이 맞으면 1점을 준다.

(3) In (b) 'a fool' functions as an object이 맞으면 1점을 준다.

(4) There are two people involved, the subject NP 'I' and the object NP 'a fool'의 내용이 맞으면 1점을 준다.

---

## 13

본책 p.150

| 하위내용영역 | 배점 | 예상정답률 |
|---|---|---|
| 영어학 (문법) B형 서술형 | 4점 | 60% |

**모범답안**

**Version 1**

Sentence (b) is unambiguous and indicates the segregatory meaning (interpretation). Phrase (c) is unambiguous and indicates the segregatory meaning.

**Version 2**

Sentence (b) is unambiguous and has only the segregatory interpretation (meaning). Phrase (c) is unambiguous and has only the segregatory interpretation.

<참고> Only the segregatory meaning is ordinarily possible when the coordinated modifiers denote mutually exclusive properties.

**채점기준**

내용학 : 4점

(1) Sentence (b) is unambiguous and indicates the segregatory meaning (interpretation)이 맞으면 2점을 준다. (각 1점)

(2) Phrase (c) is unambiguous and indicates the segregatory meaning이 맞으면 2점을 준다. (각 1점)

| 하위내용영역 | 배점 | 예상정답률 |
|---|---|---|
| 영어학 (문법) B형 서술형 | 4점 | 70% |

[ 모범답안 ]

### Version 1

Sentence (c) is ungrammatical. After a positive clause ('He was unkind'), we cannot add a constituent introduced by 'not even'. Sentence (e) is ungrammatical. The negative tag (didn't they?) cannot attach to the negative clause ('Few of them realised it was a hoax'); (the positive tag (did they?) can attach to the negative clause.)

### Version 2

Sentence (c) is ungrammatical. We cannot add a constituent introduced by 'not even' to the positive clause ('He was unkind'). Sentence (e) is ungrammatical. The main clause ('Few of them realised it was a hoax') is the negative clause; thus, it cannot have the negative tag (didn't they?).

[ 채점기준 ]

내용학 : 4점

(1) Sentence (c) is ungrammatical이 맞으면 1점을 준다.

(2) After a positive clause ('He was unkind'), we cannot add a constituent introduced by 'not even'의 내용이 맞으면 1점을 준다.

(3) Sentence (e) is ungrammatical이 맞으면 1점을 준다.

(4) The negative tag (didn't they?) cannot attach to the negative clause ('Few of them realised it was a hoax')의 내용이 맞으면 1점을 준다.

| 하위내용영역 | 배점 | 예상정답률 |
|---|---|---|
| 영어학 (문법) B형 서술형 | 4점 | 50% |

[ 모범답안 ]

### Version 1

Sentence (c) is ungrammatical. The nonrestrictive relative clause 'which doesn't surprise me at all' modifies the entire main clause; thus, it must be set off from the main clause by a comma. Sentence (d) is ungrammatical. The two clauses, 'whose books have sold well' and 'who everyone likes', are nonrestrictive relative clauses; they cannot be stacked.

### Version 2

Sentence (c) is ungrammatical. The nonrestrictive relative clause 'which doesn't surprise me at all', which modifies the entire main clause (the main clause), must be set off from it by a comma. Sentence (d) is ungrammatical. The nonrestrictive relative clauses, ('whose books have sold well, who everyone likes',) cannot be stacked.

내용학 : 4점

(1) Sentence (c) is ungrammatical이 맞으면 1점을 준다.

(2) The nonrestrictive relative clause 'which doesn't surprise me at all' modifies the entire main clause; thus, it must be set off from the main clause by a comma의 내용이 맞으면 1점을 준다.

(3) Sentence (d) is ungrammatical이 맞으면 1점을 준다.

(4) The two clauses, 'whose books have sold well' and 'who everyone likes', are nonrestrictive relative clauses; they cannot be stacked의 내용이 맞으면 1점을 준다.

## 16

본책 p.156

| 하위내용영역 | 배점 | 예상정답률 |
|---|---|---|
| 영어학 (문법) B형 서술형 | 4점 | 50% |

모범답안 ↩

### Version 1

Sentence (a) is ungrammatical. The PP 'under what circumstances' is in adjunct function; the stranding construction to be avoided in adjuncts. Sentence (b) is ungrammatical. The clause (containing the preposition) 'for which grant we should apply' is (a subordinate interrogative clause) functioning as complement to a preposition 'on'; fronting is impossible (or stranding is obligatory).

### Version 2

Sentence (a) is ungrammatical because with the adjunct PP 'under what circumstances' stranding is prohibited. Sentence (b) is ungrammatical. The (interrogative) clause 'for which grant we should apply' is complement of 'on'; fronting is impossible.

채점기준 ↩

내용학 : 4점

(1) Sentence (a) is ungrammatical이 맞으면 1점을 준다.

(2) The PP 'under what circumstances' is in adjunct function; the stranding construction to be avoided in adjuncts의 내용이 맞으면 1점을 준다.

(3) Sentence (b) is ungrammatical이 맞으면 1점을 준다.

(4) The clause (containing the preposition) 'for which grant we should apply' is (a subordinate interrogative clause) functioning as complement to a preposition 'on'; fronting is impossible의 내용이 맞으면 1점을 준다.

## 17

본책 p.158

| 하위내용영역 | 배점 | 예상정답률 |
|---|---|---|
| 영어학 (문법) B형 서술형 | 4점 | 65% |

**모범답안**

Sentence (d) is ungrammatical. The verb 'insist' cannot license (or accept) interrogatives. Sentence (e) is ungrammatical. The verb 'inquire' cannot license declaratives.

**채점기준**

내용학: 4점

(1) Sentence (d) is ungrammatical이 맞으면 1점을 준다.

(2) The verb 'insist' cannot license (or accept) interrogatives의 내용이 맞으면 1점을 준다.

(3) Sentence (e) is ungrammatical이 맞으면 1점을 준다.

(4) The verb 'inquire' cannot license declaratives의 내용이 맞으면 1점을 준다.

## 18

본책 p.160

| 하위내용영역 | 배점 | 예상정답률 |
|---|---|---|
| 영어학 (문법) B형 서술형 | 4점 | 65% |

**모범답안**

**Version 1**

Sentence (a) is ungrammatical. The degree adverb 'nearly' cannot occur sentence finally. Sentence (e) is ungrammatical. The negative frequency adverb 'seldom' in sentence-initial position requires subject-aux inversion.

**Version 2**

Sentence (a) is ungrammatical. Degree adverbs like 'nearly' appear before but not after verbs. Sentence (e) is ungrammatical. When the negative frequency adverb 'seldom' appears sentence initially, the rule of subject-aux inversion must be applied.

**채점기준**

내용학: 4점

(1) Sentence (a) is ungrammatical이 맞으면 1점을 준다.

(2) The degree adverb 'nearly' cannot occur sentence finally의 내용이 맞으면 1점을 준다.

(3) Sentence (e) is ungrammatical이 맞으면 1점을 준다.

(4) The negative frequency adverb 'seldom' in sentence-initial position requires subject-aux inversion의 내용이 맞으면 1점을 준다.

## 19

본책 p.162

| 하위내용영역 | 배점 | 예상정답률 |
|---|---|---|
| 영어학 (문법) B형 서술형 | 4점 | 50% |

모범답안 ⊸

### Version 1

The underlined word (owing) in (4) belongs to the verb category. The word 'owing' is predicator (in a gerund-participial clause); this clause itself has no overt subject, but an understood subject is retrievable from the subject of the main clause 'farmers'. The underlined word (owing) in (5) belongs to the preposition category. This word does not have a predicational relationship to the subject 'many farms'.

### Version 2

The underlined word (owing) in (4) is a verb. 'Owing' is interpreted as follows: we understand that it is farmers who owe so much to the bank. The understood subject is retrievable from the subject of the main clause 'farmers'. The underlined word (owing) in (5) is a preposition. This word does not have a predicational relationship to the subject 'many farms'; 'owing to X' means 'because of X'.

채점기준 ⊸

내용학: 4점

(1) The underlined word (owing) in (4) belongs to the verb category이 맞으면 1점을 준다.

(2) The word 'owing' is predicator (in a gerund-participial clause); this clause itself has no overt subject, but an understood subject is retrievable from the subject of the main clause 'farmers'의 내용이 맞으면 1점을 준다.

(3) The underlined word (owing) in (5) belongs to the preposition category이 맞으면 1점을 준다.

(4) This word does not have a predicational relationship to the subject 'many farms'의 내용이 맞으면 1점을 준다.

## 20

본책 p.164

| 하위내용영역 | 배점 | 예상정답률 |
|---|---|---|
| 영어학 (문법) B형 서술형 | 4점 | 55% |

모범답안 ⊸

### Version 1

Sentence (b) is ungrammatical because the adjective 'lawful' cannot be used predicatively. The phrase (d) is ungrammatical because the adjective 'content' cannot be used attributively.

### Version 2

Sentence (b) is ungrammatical. The adjective 'lawful' is attributive-only. The phrase (d) is ungrammatical because the adjective 'content' is a never-attributive adjective.

채점기준 ↴

내용학 : 4점

(1) Sentence (b) is ungrammatical이 맞으면 1점을 준다.

(2) the adjective 'lawful' cannot be used predicatively의 내용이 맞으면 1점을 준다.

(3) The phrase (d) is ungrammatical이 맞으면 1점을 준다.

(4) the adjective 'content' cannot be used attributively의 내용이 맞으면 1점을 준다.

21     본책 p.166

| 하위내용영역 | 배점 | 예상정답률 |
|---|---|---|
| 영어학 (문법) B형 서술형 | 4점 | 65% |

모범답안 ↴

Discourse (a) is inappropriate. In the clause 'John had saved a seat for her', the new information 'a seat' comes before the old information '(for) her'; it should put the old information 'her' before the new information 'a seat'. Sentence (d) is inappropriate. The heavy direct object NP 'an alternative solution~the dispute' in the middle of the sentence is inappropriate; (it should move the heavy direct object NP to the end of the sentence.)

채점기준 ↴

내용학 : 4점

(1) Discourse (a) is inappropriate이 맞으면 1점을 준다.

(2) In the clause 'John had saved a seat for her', the new information 'a seat' comes before the old information '(for) her'; it should put the old information 'her' before the new information 'a seat'의 내용이 맞으면 1점을 준다.

(3) Sentence (d) is inappropriate이 맞으면 1점을 준다.

(4) The heavy direct object NP 'an alternative solution~the dispute' in the middle of the sentence is inappropriate의 내용이 맞으면 1점을 준다.

22     본책 p.168

| 하위내용영역 | 배점 | 예상정답률 |
|---|---|---|
| 영어학 (문법) B형 서술형 | 4점 | 60% |

모범답안 ↴

**Version 1**

First, in (i), sentence (d) is ungrammatical. This sentence has a semantic affinity with negation because of the adjective 'unaware'; 'some', which has positive orientation, cannot occur in (d). Second, verbal negation forms are as follows: (iia) We didn't know either of them, and (iib) He doesn't ever apologise (apologize).

## Version 2

In (i) sentence (d) is ungrammatical. 'Some' is a positive polarity item and cannot occur in the sentence which has a negative meaning (due to the adjective 'unaware').

(iia) We didn't know either of them.

(iib) He doesn't ever apologise (apologize).

[채점기준 ↵]

내용학 : 4점

(1) in (i), sentence (d) is ungrammatical이 맞으면 1점을 준다.

(2) This sentence has a semantic affinity with negation because of the adjective 'unaware'; 'some', which has positive orientation, cannot occur in (d)의 내용이 맞으면 1점을 준다.

(3) (iia) We didn't know either of them이 맞으면 1점을 준다.

(4) (iib) He doesn't ever apologise (apologize)이 맞으면 1점을 준다.

---

| 23 | | 본책 p.170 |

| 하위내용영역 | 배점 | 예상정답률 |
|---|---|---|
| 영어학 (문법) B형 서술형 | 4점 | 65% |

[모범답안 ↵]

## Version 1

Sentence (d) is inappropriate. When it is natural to expect change to occur (i.e., physical laws seem to be involved), the ergative sentence is needed. Sentence (f) is inappropriate. The verb 'broke' used ergatively does not permit an agent; thus, it cannot be used with a by-phrase.

## Version 2

Sentence (d) is inappropriate because it is natural to expect change to occur; thus, the verb 'melt(ed)' used with a passive form is inappropriate. Sentence (f) is inappropriate. The verb 'broke' used ergatively cannot be used with a by-phrase.

[채점기준 ↵]

내용학 : 4점

(1) Sentence (d) is inappropriate이 맞으면 1점을 준다.

(2) When it is natural to expect change to occur (i.e., physical laws seem to be involved), the ergative sentence is needed의 내용이 맞으면 1점을 준다.

(3) Sentence (f) is inappropriate이 맞으면 1점을 준다.

(4) The verb 'broke' used ergatively does not permit an agent; thus, it cannot be used with a by-phrase의 내용이 맞으면 1점을 준다.

## 24

| 하위내용영역 | 배점 | 예상정답률 |
|---|---|---|
| 영어학 (문법) B형 서술형 | 4점 | 65% |

[모범답안]

### Version 1

The phrase (iic) is ungrammatical. In the fronted preposition construction, fossilisation doesn't allow any departure from the fixed order of verb + preposition 'let + off'.

### Version 2

(iic) is ungrammatical. The fronted preposition construction is not permitted in (iic) because 'let + off' is fossilised in that the preposition must follow the verb, with only the object intervening.

[채점기준]

내용학: 4점

(1) The phrase (iic) is ungrammatical이 맞으면 2점을 준다.

(2) fossilisation doesn't allow any departure from the fixed order of verb + preposition 'let + off'의 내용이 맞으면 2점을 준다.

## 25

| 하위내용영역 | 배점 | 예상정답률 |
|---|---|---|
| 영어학 (문법) B형 서술형 | 4점 | 55% |

[모범답안]

First, in (ia), (the phrase or word) 'dead' is used as a predicative complement (Predicative Complement), and in (ib), 'long' is used as a adverb phrase complement (ADVP Complement). Second, the phrase 'two weeks ago' is the prepositional phrase. In (iia), the phrase 'two weeks ago' functions as predicative complement to the verb 'was (be)'. In (iib), 'two weeks ago' modifies the noun phrase 'his behaviour'.

[채점기준]

내용학: 4점

(1) in (ia), (the phrase or word) 'dead' is used as a predicative complement (Predicative Complement)이 맞으면 1점을 준다.

(2) in (ib), 'long' is used as a adverb phrase complement (ADVP Complement)이 맞으면 1점을 준다.

(3) the phrase 'two weeks ago' is the prepositional phrase이 맞으면 1점을 준다.

(4) In (iia), the phrase 'two weeks ago' functions as predicative complement to the verb 'was (be)'. In (iib), 'two weeks ago' modifies the noun phrase 'his behaviour'의 내용이 맞으면 1점을 준다.

# Phonetics & Phonology

## 01

본책 p.178

| 하위내용영역 | 배점 | 예상정답률 |
|---|---|---|
| 영어학 (음운론) A형 기입형 | 2점 | 80% |

【모범답안 ↵】

① stressed   ② phonemes

【채점기준 ↵】

2점: ①, ② 모두 답안과 일치하면 2점을 준다.

1점: ①, ② 중 하나만 답안과 일치하면 1점을 준다.

0점: ①, ② 모두 답안과 일치하지 않으면 0점을 준다.

## 02

본책 p.180

| 하위내용영역 | 배점 | 예상정답률 |
|---|---|---|
| 영어학 (음운론) A형 서술형 | 4점 | 65% |

【모범답안 ↵】

### Version 1

First, the two words are 'mirage' and 'bush'. Second, the rule is as follows: (insert a [ə] before the plural morpheme /z/ when) a (regular) noun ends with a sibilant, (giving [əz].)

### Version 2

'mirage' and 'bush'

(Insert a [ə] before the plural morpheme /z/ when) the last sound of (the singular) nouns is a sibilant.

【채점기준 ↵】

내용학: 4점

(1) First, the two words are 'mirage' and 'bush'가 맞으면 2점을 준다. (각 1점)

(2) a regular noun ends with a sibilant, (giving [əz])의 내용이 맞으면 2점을 준다.

## 03

본책 p.182

| 하위내용영역 | 배점 | 예상정답률 |
|---|---|---|
| 영어학 (음운론) B형 서술형 | 4점 | 50% |

[ 모범답안 ]

First, the one word for the blank is 'unstressed'. Second, alveolar stops (between vowels) cannot be flapped in a stressed syllable. (including (the) secondary stress)

[ 채점기준 ]

내용학 : 4점

(1) unstressed가 맞으면 2점을 준다.

(2) alveolar stops (between vowels) cannot be flapped in a stressed syllable의 내용이 맞으면 2점을 준다.

## 04

본책 p.184

| 하위내용영역 | 배점 | 예상정답률 |
|---|---|---|
| 영어학 (음운론) A형 기입형 | 2점 | 80% |

[ 모범답안 ]

① distinctive  ② nondistinctive

[ 채점기준 ]

2점 : ①, ② 모두 답안과 일치하면 2점을 준다.

1점 : ①, ② 중 하나만 답안과 일치하면 1점을 준다.

0점 : ①, ② 모두 답안과 일치하지 않으면 0점을 준다.

## 05

본책 p.185

| 하위내용영역 | 배점 | 예상정답률 |
|---|---|---|
| 영어학 (음운론) A형 서술형 | 4점 | 55% |

[ 모범답안 ]

### Version 1

The words 'discipline' and 'narrow' are ambisyllabic in (3). First, for the word 'discipline', [s] belongs simultaneously in the coda of the first syllable and the onset of the second syllable. Second, the word 'narrow' is another case of ambisyllabicity. [r] belongs simultaneously in the coda of the first syllable and the onset of the second syllable.

## Version 2

The words 'discipline' and 'narrow' are ambisyllabic. [s] in 'discipline' and [r] in 'narrow' contribute to the weight of the initial, stressed syllable, but its phonetic realisation will typically reflect the fact that it is also in the onset of the second syllable.

채점기준

내용학 : 4점

(1) The words 'discipline' and 'narrow' are ambisyllabic이 맞으면 2점을 준다. (각 1점)

(2) for the word 'discipline', [s] belongs simultaneously in the coda of the first syllable and the onset of the second syllable의 내용이 맞으면 1점을 준다.

(3) the word 'narrow' is another case of ambisyllabicity. [r] belongs simultaneously in the coda of the first syllable and the onset of the second syllable의 내용이 맞으면 1점을 준다.

---

## 06

본책 p.187

| 하위내용영역 | 배점 | 예상정답률 |
|---|---|---|
| 영어학 (음운론) B형 서술형 | 4점 | 50% |

모범답안

### Version 1

First, /d/ becomes [ð] between vowels in (2a). Second, /s/ becomes [ʃ] either before or after [ɪ] in (2b).

### Version 2

First, the allophone [ð] occurs between vowels in (2a). Second, the allophone [ʃ] occurs before or after the high front lax vowel [ɪ] in (2b).

채점기준

내용학 : 4점

(1) First, /d/ becomes [ð] between vowels in (2a)의 내용이 맞으면 2점을 준다.

(2) Second, /s/ becomes [ʃ] either before or after [ɪ] in (2b)의 내용이 맞으면 2점을 준다.

---

## 07

본책 p.189

| 하위내용영역 | 배점 | 예상정답률 |
|---|---|---|
| 영어학 (음운론) A형 서술형 | 4점 | 50% |

모범답안

First, the blank ① is 'fricatives' and the blank ② is 'stressed'. Second, an elided vowel followed by /n, 1/ or /r/ does not result in a reduction in the number of syllables. (When elision is compensated for with syllabic consonants,) the number of syllables remains the same because syllabic consonants function as the nucleus of the syllable.

내용학: 4점

(1) the blank ① is 'fricatives' and the blank ② is 'stressed'이 맞으면 2점을 준다. (각 1점)

(2) an elided vowel followed by /n, 1/ or /r/ does not result in a reduction in the number of syllables의 내용이 맞으면 1점을 준다.

(3) (When elision is compensated for with syllabic consonants,) the number of syllables remains the same because syllabic consonants function as the nucleus of the syllable의 내용이 맞으면 1점을 준다.

---

## 08

본책 p.191

| 하위내용영역 | 배점 | 예상정답률 |
|---|---|---|
| 영어학 (음운론) B형 서술형 | 4점 | 65% |

모범답안

First, in (4), the velar stops /k, g/ are fronted through the influence of a following front vowel. Second, in (5), the velar stops /k, g/ are retracted through the influence of a following back vowel.

채점기준

내용학: 4점

(1) in (4), the velar stops /k, g/ are fronted through the influence of a following front vowel이 맞으면 2점을 준다.

(2) in (5), the velar stops /k, g/ are retracted through the influence of a following back vowel이 맞으면 2점을 준다.

---

## 09

본책 p.193

| 하위내용영역 | 배점 | 예상정답률 |
|---|---|---|
| 영어학 (음운론) A형 기입형 | 2점 | 90% |

모범답안

① allophones   ② voiced

채점기준

2점: ①, ② 모두 답안과 일치하면 2점을 준다.

1점: ①, ② 중 하나만 답안과 일치하면 1점을 준다.

0점: ①, ② 모두 답안과 일치하지 않으면 0점을 준다.

## 10

| 하위내용영역 | 배점 | 예상정답률 |
|---|---|---|
| 영어학 (음운론) A형 서술형 | 4점 | 40% |

모범답안 ↴

First, the word for the blank is "bisyllabic". Second, in <B>, the phrase (a) *phone ya* (*phone you*) rhymes with the word (b) *pneumonia*. They (the phrase (a) and the word (b)) both contain the metrical foot of the shape ['əʊnje] (the same metrical foot structure ['əʊnje]).

채점기준 ↴

내용학 : 4점

(1) the word for the blank is "bisyllabic"이 맞으면 1점을 준다.

(2) the phrase (a) *phone ya* (*phone you*) rhymes with the word (b) *pneumonia*이 맞으면 1점을 준다.

(3) They both contain the metrical foot of the shape ['əʊnje]의 내용이 맞으면 2점을 준다.

## 11

| 하위내용영역 | 배점 | 예상정답률 |
|---|---|---|
| 영어학 (음운론) B형 서술형 | 4점 | 55% |

모범답안 ↴

**Version 1**

In (4) the two possible utterances are "that stuff" or "that's tough". In "that stuff", the /t/ after the word-initial /s/ (in "stuff") is unaspirated. In "that's tough", on the other hand, the word-initial /t/ (in "tough") is aspirated.

**Version 2**

In (4) the two possible utterances are "that stuff" or "that's tough". In "that stuff", the word-initial /s/ (in "stuff") is articulated with its usual fortis intensity, and the following /t/ is unaspirated. In "that's tough", the word-final /s/ is articulated with less intensity, and the word-initial /t/ (in "tough") is aspirated.

채점기준 ↴

내용학 : 4점

(1) In (4) the two possible utterances are "that stuff" or "that's tough"이 맞으면 2점을 준다. (각 1점)

(2) In "that stuff", the /t/ after the word-initial /s/ (in "stuff") is unaspirated의 내용이 맞으면 1점을 준다.

(3) In "that's tough", on the other hand, the word-initial /t/ (in "tough") is aspirated의 내용이 맞으면 1점을 준다.

## 12

본책 p.198

| 하위내용영역 | 배점 | 예상정답률 |
| --- | --- | --- |
| 영어학 (음운론) A형 기입형 | 2점 | 45% |

**모범답안**

[− continuant]

**채점기준**

2점: 답안과 일치하면 2점을 준다.

0점: 답안과 일치하지 않으면 0점을 준다.

## 13

본책 p.199

| 하위내용영역 | 배점 | 예상정답률 |
| --- | --- | --- |
| 영어학 (음운론) B형 서술형 | 4점 | 50% |

**모범답안**

First, the one word for the blank is 'consonants'. Second, the word 'Lesley' in <B> has clear [l]. Both the first [l] and the second [l] in 'Lesley' occur before a vowel.

**채점기준**

내용학: 4점

(1) First, the one word for the blank is 'consonants'이 맞으면 1점을 준다.
(2) Second, the word 'Lesley' has clear [l]이 맞으면 1점을 준다.
(3) Both the first [l] and the second [l] in 'Lesley' occur before a vowel이 맞으면 2점을 준다. (각 1점)
(4) <B>에 제시된 문장에서 'Lesley' 외 다른 단어를 추가로 쓴 경우 3점을 감점한다.

## 14

본책 p.201

| 하위내용영역 | 배점 | 예상정답률 |
| --- | --- | --- |
| 영어학 (음운론) A형 기입형 | 2점 | 90% |

**모범답안**

same syllable

**채점기준**

2점: 답안과 일치하면 2점을 준다.

0점: 답안과 일치하지 않으면 0점을 준다.

**15**

본책 p.203

| 하위내용영역 | 배점 | 예상정답률 |
|---|---|---|
| 영어학 (음운론) A형 서술형 | 4점 | 60% |

[모범답안]

First, both (2a) and (2b) sentences have the same number of stressed words; each sentence has four stressed words (content words). In (2a) the content words are 'Jimmy', 'bought', 'house', and 'Glasgow'. In (2b) the content words are 'Alastair', 'claimed', 'selling', and 'company'. Second, in (2a) the tonic syllable is the first syllable of the last content word 'Glasgow', and in (2b) the tonic syllable is the first syllable of the last content word 'company'.

[채점기준]

내용학: 4점

(1) both (2a) and (2b) sentences have the same number of stressed words; each sentence has four stressed words (content words)이 맞으면 1점을 준다.

(2) In (2a) the content words are 'Jimmy', 'bought', 'house', and 'Glasgow'이 맞으면 1점을 준다.

(3) In (2b) the content words are 'Alastair', 'claimed', 'selling', and 'company'이 맞으면 1점을 준다.

(4) in (2a) the tonic syllable is the first syllable of the last content word 'Glasgow', and in (2b) the tonic syllable is the first syllable of the last content word 'company'의 내용이 맞으면 1점을 준다. (둘 중 하나만 맞으면 1점을 감점한다.)

**16**

본책 p.205

| 하위내용영역 | 배점 | 예상정답률 |
|---|---|---|
| 영어학 (음운론) B형 서술형 | 4점 | 50% |

[모범답안]

(c) is the example of energy assimilation and (d) is the example of manner assimilation. In (c) a lenis /z/ in 'was' has been replaced by a fortis /s/ under the influence of a fortis /s/ in 'spectacular'. In (d) a (voiced dental) fricative /ð/ in 'they' may be replaced by a lateral /l/ under the influence of a lateral /l/ in 'till'.

[채점기준]

내용학: 4점

(1) (c) ('it was spectacular') is the example of energy assimilation and (d) ('till they meet again') is the example of manner assimilation이 맞으면 2점을 준다. (각 1점)

(2) In (c) a lenis /z/ in 'was' has been replaced by a fortis /s/ under the influence of a fortis /s/ in 'spectacular'의 내용이 맞으면 1점을 준다.

(3) In (d) a (voiced dental) fricative /ð/ in 'they' may be replaced by a lateral /l/ under the influence of a lateral /l/ in 'till'의 내용이 맞으면 1점을 준다.

## 17

본책 p.207

| 하위내용영역 | 배점 | 예상정답률 |
|---|---|---|
| 영어학 (음운론) A형 기입형 | 2점 | 80% |

모범답안 ⌐

① second  ② directions

채점기준 ⌐

2점: ①, ② 모두 답안과 일치하면 2점을 준다.

1점: ①, ② 중 하나만 답안과 일치하면 1점을 준다.

0점: ①, ② 모두 답안과 일치하지 않으면 0점을 준다.

## 18

본책 p.208

| 하위내용영역 | 배점 | 예상정답률 |
|---|---|---|
| 영어학 (음운론) A형 서술형 | 4점 | 60% |

모범답안 ⌐

First, the one word for the blank is 'obstruents'. Second, the lenis lateral and the three lenis approximants in (2) and (3) are fully devoiced when they follow any one of the fortis plosives (stops) /p, t, k/ (in stressed syllables).

채점기준 ⌐

내용학: 4점

(1) the one word for the blank is 'obstruents'이 맞으면 2점을 준다.

(2) the lenis lateral and the three lenis approximants in (2) and (3) are fully devoiced when they follow any one of the fortis plosives (stops) /p, t, k/ (in stressed syllables)이 맞으면 2점을 준다.

## 19

본책 p.210

| 하위내용영역 | 배점 | 예상정답률 |
|---|---|---|
| 영어학 (음운론) B형 서술형 | 4점 | 50% |

모범답안 ⌐

First, the word for the blank is 'unstressed'. Second, the one shared phonetic environment (of [i] in (2b)−(2c) and [u] in (3c)) is that the intermediate [i] and [u] occur before a vowel.

채점기준

내용학: 4점

(1) the word for the blank is 'unstressed'이 맞으면 2점을 준다.

(2) the one shared phonetic environment (of [i] in (2b)−(2c) and [u] in (3c)) is that the intermediate [i] and [u] occur before a vowel의 내용이 맞으면 2점을 준다.

## 20
본책 p.212

| 하위내용영역 | 배점 | 예상정답률 |
|---|---|---|
| 영어학 (음운론) A형 기입형 | 2점 | 60% |

모범답안

syllable-final nasal

채점기준

2점: 답안과 일치하면 2점을 준다.

0점: 답안과 일치하지 않으면 0점을 준다.

## 21
본책 p.213

| 하위내용영역 | 배점 | 예상정답률 |
|---|---|---|
| 영어학 (음운론) A형 서술형 | 4점 | 60% |

모범답안

An alveolar nasal /n/ does not change its place of articulation if the root-initial segment is an alveolar consonant (as in (1) and (2)) or a vowel (as in (3) and (4)).

채점기준

내용학: 4점

(1) (An alveolar nasal) /n/ does not change its place of articulation if the root-initial segment is an alveolar consonant (as in (1) and (2))이 맞으면 2점을 준다.

(2) (An alveolar nasal) /n/ does not change its place of articulation if the root-initial segment is a vowel (as in (3) and (4))이 맞으면 2점을 준다.

## 22
본책 p.215

| 하위내용영역 | 배점 | 예상정답률 |
|---|---|---|
| 영어학 (음운론) B형 서술형 | 4점 | 40% |

**모범답안**

The phoneme /ʌʊ/ is realized as [ɒʊ] when it is followed by an /l/ which is in the same syllable (i.e. when followed by a tautosyllabic /l/). The /ʌʊ/ phoneme is realized as [ʌʊ] elsewhere.

**채점기준**

내용학: 4점

(1) The phoneme /ʌʊ/ is realized as [ɒʊ] when it is followed by an /l/ which is in the same syllable (i.e. when followed by a tautosyllabic /l/)이 맞으면 2점을 준다.

(2) The /ʌʊ/ phoneme is realized as [ʌʊ] elsewhere이 맞으면 2점을 준다.

## 23
본책 p.217

| 하위내용영역 | 배점 | 예상정답률 |
|---|---|---|
| 영어학 (음운론) A형 기입형 | 2점 | 70% |

**모범답안**

① morpheme  ② onset

**채점기준**

2점: ①, ② 모두 답안과 일치하면 2점을 준다.

1점: ①, ② 중 하나만 답안과 일치하면 1점을 준다.

0점: ①, ② 모두 답안과 일치하지 않으면 0점을 준다.

## 24
본책 p.219

| 하위내용영역 | 배점 | 예상정답률 |
|---|---|---|
| 영어학 (음운론) B형 서술형 | 4점 | 40% |

**모범답안**

In (2), the words 'antimatter' and 'antihero' can be considered as compounds. In these two words, 'anti-' has primary stress.

**채점기준**

내용학: 4점

(1) In (2), the words 'antimatter' and 'antihero' can be considered as compounds이 맞으면 2점을 준다. (각 1점)

(2) In these two words, 'anti-' has primary stress의 내용이 맞으면 2점을 준다.

## 25

본책 p.221

| 하위내용영역 | 배점 | 예상정답률 |
|---|---|---|
| 영어학 (음운론) A형 기입형 | 2점 | 80% |

**모범답안**

ambisyllabic

**채점기준**

2점: 답안과 일치하면 2점을 준다.

0점: 답안과 일치하지 않으면 0점을 준다.

## 26

본책 p.222

| 하위내용영역 | 배점 | 예상정답률 |
|---|---|---|
| 영어학 (음운론) A형 서술형 | 4점 | 60% |

**모범답안**

First, the two processes are (a) Assimilation and (c) Elision. Second, the syllabic [r] can occur when /r/ is preceded by two consonants (and followed by a vowel) in unstressed syllables.

**채점기준**

내용학: 4점

(1) the two processes are (a) Assimilation and (c) Elision의 내용이 맞으면 2점을 준다.

(2) the syllabic [r] can occur when /r/ is preceded by two consonants (and followed by a vowel) in unstressed syllables의 내용이 맞으면 2점을 준다.

## 27

본책 p.224

| 하위내용영역 | 배점 | 예상정답률 |
|---|---|---|
| 영어학 (음운론) B형 서술형 | 4점 | 40% |

**모범답안**

The words 'consensus' and 'lemonade' do not have primary stress on the antepenultimate syllable. The word 'consensus' (is a noun which has consonant clusters after the penultimate vowel and) has penultimate stress. The word 'lemonade'(, which was borrowed from French,) has ultimate primary stress (has primary stress on the ultimate syllable).

**채점기준**

내용학 : 4점

(1) The words 'consensus' and 'lemonade' do not have primary stress on the antepenultimate syllable이 맞으면 2점을 준다. (각 1점)

(2) The word 'consensus' (is a noun which has consonant clusters after the penultimate vowel and) has penultimate stress이 맞으면 1점을 준다.

(3) The word 'lemonade'(, which was borrowed from French,) has ultimate primary stress (has primary stress on the ultimate syllable)이 맞으면 1점을 준다.

---

## 28 본책 p.226

| 하위내용영역 | 배점 | 예상정답률 |
|---|---|---|
| 영어학 (음운론) A형 기입형 | 2점 | 90% |

**모범답안**

① onsets  ② codas

**채점기준**

2점: ①, ② 모두 답안과 일치하면 2점을 준다.

1점: ①, ② 중 하나만 답안과 일치하면 1점을 준다.

0점: ①, ② 모두 답안과 일치하지 않으면 0점을 준다.

---

## 29 본책 p.228

| 하위내용영역 | 배점 | 예상정답률 |
|---|---|---|
| 영어학 (음운론) A형 서술형 | 4점 | 60% |

**모범답안**

First, /h/-deletion occurs in the words 'her' and 'his' in (2). Second, (between a nasal consonant and a voiceless fricative,) a voiceless stop with the same place of articulation as the nasal can be inserted.

**채점기준**

내용학 : 4점

(1) /h/-deletion occurs in the words 'her' and 'his' in (2)의 내용이 맞으면 2점을 준다. (각 1점)

(2) a voiceless stop with the same place of articulation as the nasal can be inserted의 내용이 맞으면 2점을 준다.

## 30

본책 p.230

| 하위내용영역 | 배점 | 예상정답률 |
|---|---|---|
| 영어학 (음운론) B형 서술형 | 4점 | 50% |

**모범답안**

First, the order in (3b) gives the correct phonetic form [ɹəɪɾəɹ]. Second, since flapping changes /t/ from a voiceless sound to a voiced one, if flapping were to apply first, then /ɑɪ/ would no longer be before a voiceless sound, and diphthong-raising should not apply. (If diphthong-raising were to apply first, however, flapping would not be affected.)

**채점기준**

내용학: 4점

(1) the order in (3b) gives the correct phonetic form [ɹəɪɾəɹ]의 내용이 맞으면 2점을 준다.

(2) since flapping changes /t/ from a voiceless sound to a voiced one, if flapping were to apply first, then /ɑɪ/ would no longer be before a voiceless sound, and (diphthong-)raising should not apply의 내용이 맞으면 2점을 준다.

## 31

본책 p.232

| 하위내용영역 | 배점 | 예상정답률 |
|---|---|---|
| 영어학 (음운론) A형 기입형 | 2점 | 80% |

**모범답안**

① [+ consonantal]　② [− syllabic]

**채점기준**

2점: ①, ② 모두 답안과 일치하면 2점을 준다.

1점: ①, ② 중 하나만 답안과 일치하면 1점을 준다.

0점: ①, ② 모두 답안과 일치하지 않으면 0점을 준다.

## 32

본책 p.234

| 하위내용영역 | 배점 | 예상정답률 |
|---|---|---|
| 영어학 (음운론) B형 서술형 | 4점 | 70% |

[모범답안]

First, the one word for the blank is 'approximant'. Second, [w] cannot follow a [labial] consonant (in initial CC clusters).

[채점기준]

내용학: 4점

(1) the one word for the blank is 'approximant'이 맞으면 2점을 준다.

(2) [w] cannot follow a [labial] consonant (in initial CC clusters)이 맞으면 2점을 준다.

## 33

본책 p.236

| 하위내용영역 | 배점 | 예상정답률 |
|---|---|---|
| 영어학 (음운론) A형 기입형 | 2점 | 90% |

[모범답안]

syllable

[채점기준]

2점: 답안과 일치하면 2점을 준다.

0점: 답안과 일치하지 않으면 0점을 준다.

## 34

본책 p.237

| 하위내용영역 | 배점 | 예상정답률 |
|---|---|---|
| 영어학 (음운론) A형 서술형 | 4점 | 70% |

[모범답안]

First, the distinction between [ɾ] and [l] is contrastive in Scottish English. Second, (/l/ is realized as [ɾ]) between vowels.

[채점기준]

내용학: 4점

(1) the distinction between [ɾ] and [l] is contrastive in Scottish English이 맞으면 2점을 준다. (각 1점)

(2) (/l/ is realized as [ɾ]) between vowels이 맞으면 2점을 준다.

## 35

본책 p.239

| 하위내용영역 | 배점 | 예상정답률 |
|---|---|---|
| 영어학 (음운론) B형 서술형 | 4점 | 70% |

**모범답안 ☞**

First, the words in sentences (a) and (b) have the same stress pattern. The verbs 'pervert' in (a) and 'subject' in (b) have the stress on the ult.

**채점기준 ☞**

내용학 : 4점

(1) the words in sentences (a) and (b) have the same stress pattern이 맞으면 2점을 준다.

(2) The verbs 'pervert' in (a) and 'subject' in (b) have the stress on the ult의 내용이 맞으면 2점을 준다.

## 36

본책 p.241

| 하위내용영역 | 배점 | 예상정답률 |
|---|---|---|
| 영어학 (음운론) A형 기입형 | 2점 | 80% |

**모범답안 ☞**

① [− consonantal]   ② [− syllabic]

**채점기준 ☞**

2점 : ①, ② 모두 답안과 일치하면 2점을 준다.

1점 : ①, ② 중 하나만 답안과 일치하면 1점을 준다.

0점 : ①, ② 모두 답안과 일치하지 않으면 0점을 준다.

## 37

본책 p.242

| 하위내용영역 | 배점 | 예상정답률 |
|---|---|---|
| 영어학 (음운론) A형 서술형 | 4점 | 70% |

**모범답안 ☞**

First, the tonic is on the word 'gave' in (a) because 'gave' is the last lexical item (LLI). Second, the tonic falls on the word 'camera' in (b). The word 'camera' is the last lexical item (LLI) in (b).

**채점기준 ☞**

내용학 : 4점

(1) the tonic is on the word 'gave' in (a)이 맞으면 1점을 준다.

(2) because 'gave' is the last lexical item (LLI)의 내용이 맞으면 1점을 준다.

(3) the tonic falls on the word 'camera' in (b)이 맞으면 1점을 준다.

(4) The word 'camera' is the last lexical item (LLI) in (b)의 내용이 맞으면 1점을 준다.

## 38

본책 p.244

| 하위내용영역 | 배점 | 예상정답률 |
|---|---|---|
| 영어학 (음운론) B형 서술형 | 4점 | 70% |

모범답안 ↵

First, the word for both blanks is 'free'. Second, unreleased stops occur before other (oral) stops in (1).

채점기준 ↵

내용학 : 4점

(1) the words for both blanks are 'free'이 맞으면 2점을 준다.

(2) unreleased stops occur before other (oral) stops in (1)의 내용이 맞으면 2점을 준다.

## 39

본책 p.246

| 하위내용영역 | 배점 | 예상정답률 |
|---|---|---|
| 영어학 (음운론) A형 기입형 | 2점 | 70% |

모범답안 ↵

① front   ② complementary

채점기준 ↵

2점 : ①, ② 모두 답안과 일치하면 2점을 준다.

1점 : ①, ② 중 하나만 답안과 일치하면 1점을 준다.

0점 : ①, ② 모두 답안과 일치하지 않으면 0점을 준다.

## 40

본책 p.248

| 하위내용영역 | 배점 | 예상정답률 |
|---|---|---|
| 영어학 (음운론) A형 서술형 | 4점 | 60% |

모범답안 ↵

In (2), underlined stops in Object noun are aspirated. In Object noun, when the (primary) stress shifts from the root to the suffix vowel, the preceding stop changes to become aspirated.

채점기준 ↵

내용학 : 4점

(1) In (2), underlined stops in Object noun are aspirated의 내용이 맞으면 2점을 준다.

(2) In Object noun, when the (primary) stress shifts from the root to the suffix vowel, the preceding stop changes to become aspirated의 내용이 맞으면 2점을 준다.

## 41

본책 p.250

| 하위내용영역 | 배점 | 예상정답률 |
|---|---|---|
| 영어학 (음운론) B형 서술형 | 4점 | 60% |

**모범답안**

First, the ONE word is 'Mary'. Second, (/ɹ/ is resyllabified as an onset of the following syllable) when /ɹ/ is followed by a syllable without onset consonant.

**채점기준**

내용학: 4점

(1) the ONE word is 'Mary'이 맞으면 2점을 준다.

(2) (/ɹ/ is resyllabified as an onset of the following syllable) when /ɹ/ is followed by a syllable without onset consonant이 맞으면 2점을 준다.

## 42

본책 p.252

| 하위내용영역 | 배점 | 예상정답률 |
|---|---|---|
| 영어학 (음운론) A형 기입형 | 2점 | 80% |

**모범답안**

① consonants  ② − continuant

**채점기준**

2점: ①, ② 모두 답안과 일치하면 2점을 준다.

1점: ①, ② 중 하나만 답안과 일치하면 1점을 준다.

0점: ①, ② 모두 답안과 일치하지 않으면 0점을 준다.

## 43

본책 p.253

| 하위내용영역 | 배점 | 예상정답률 |
|---|---|---|
| 영어학 (음운론) A형 서술형 | 4점 | 65% |

**모범답안**

### Version 1

First, Iambic Reversal occurs in the phrase 'champagne cocktails'. Second, it occurs to avoid clashes. The clashing sequences of WSSW change into the sequences of SWSW (i.e., the sequence of two trochaic feet).

## Version 2

First, Iambic Reversal occurs in the phrase 'champagne cocktails' to avoid clashes. Second, the clashing sequences of WSSW change into the sequences of SWSW (, the sequence of two trochaic feet).

채점기준

내용학: 4점

(1) Iambic Reversal occurs in the phrase 'champagne cocktails'이 맞으면 1점을 준다.
(2) it occurs to avoid clashes의 내용이 맞으면 1점을 준다.
(3) The clashing sequences of WSSW change into the sequences of SWSW의 내용이 맞으면 2점을 준다. (각 1점)

---

**44** 본책 p.255

| 하위내용영역 | 배점 | 예상정답률 |
| --- | --- | --- |
| 영어학 (음운론) B형 서술형 | 4점 | 50% |

모범답안

### Version 1

Vowel Nasalization occurs only if a nasal sound is in the same stem.

### Version 2

Vowels are nasalized before a nasal consonant if it is in the same stem (or within the same stem).

### Version 3

Vowel nasalization is stem-bounded.

채점기준

내용학: 4점

Vowel Nasalization occurs only if a nasal sound is in the same stem의 내용이 맞으면 4점을 준다.

---

**45** 본책 p.257

| 하위내용영역 | 배점 | 예상정답률 |
| --- | --- | --- |
| 영어학 (음운론) A형 기입형 | 2점 | 90% |

모범답안

① bearing  ② heavy

2점: ①, ② 모두 답안과 일치하면 2점을 준다.

1점: ①, ② 중 하나만 답안과 일치하면 1점을 준다.

0점: ①, ② 모두 답안과 일치하지 않으면 0점을 준다.

## 46
본책 p.258

| 하위내용영역 | 배점 | 예상정답률 |
|---|---|---|
| 영어학 (음운론) A형 서술형 | 4점 | 65% |

모범답안

### Version 1

First, the phonological form of a word 'notable' is ['norəbəl]. It is eligible for Tapping. Second, the phonological form of a word 'notation' is [noˈtʰeʃən]. Aspiration rule is applied (in this word).

### Version 2

First, the phonological form of a word 'notable' is [nórəbəl]. It is eligible for Tapping. Second, the phonological form of a word 'notation' is [notʰéʃən]. Aspiration rule is applied (in this word).

채점기준

내용학: 4점

(1) the phonological form of a word 'notable' is ['norəbəl]이 맞으면 1점을 준다.

(2) It is eligible for Tapping의 내용이 맞으면 1점을 준다.

(3) the phonological form of a word 'notation' is [noˈtʰeʃən]의 내용이 맞으면 1점을 준다.

(4) Aspiration rule is applied의 내용이 맞으면 1점을 준다.

## 47
본책 p.260

| 하위내용영역 | 배점 | 예상정답률 |
|---|---|---|
| 영어학 (음운론) B형 서술형 | 4점 | 20% |

모범답안

(a) and (b) show the same internal structure. The internal structure of this group is (1e) ([A['BC]D]).
(c) and (d) are the other pair. They belong to (1d) ([[AB] ['CD]]).

채점기준

내용학: 4점

(1) (a) and (b) show the same internal structure이 맞으면 1점을 준다.

(2) The internal structure of this group is (1e)의 내용이 맞으면 1점을 준다.

(3) (c) and (d) are the other pair이 맞으면 1점을 준다.

(4) They belong to (1d)의 내용이 맞으면 1점을 준다.

**48**
본책 p.262

| 하위내용영역 | 배점 | 예상정답률 |
|---|---|---|
| 영어학 (음운론) A형 기입형 | 2점 | 80% |

**모범답안**

① [− anterior]  ② [− lateral]

**채점기준**

2점: ①, ② 모두 답안과 일치하면 2점을 준다.

1점: ①, ② 중 하나만 답안과 일치하면 1점을 준다.

0점: ①, ② 모두 답안과 일치하지 않으면 0점을 준다.

**49**
본책 p.263

| 하위내용영역 | 배점 | 예상정답률 |
|---|---|---|
| 영어학 (음운론) B형 서술형 | 4점 | 60% |

**모범답안**

First, (/t/ is deleted when) it occurs between /n/ and a stressless (or unstressed) vowel. Second, the two interpretations are as follows: 'They are planting a garden' or 'They are planning a garden'.

**채점기준**

내용학: 4점

(1) (/t/ is deleted when) it occurs between /n/ and a stressless vowel이 맞으면 2점을 준다.

(2) 'They are planting a garden' or 'They are planning a garden'이 맞으면 2점을 준다. (각 1점)

**50**
본책 p.265

| 하위내용영역 | 배점 | 예상정답률 |
|---|---|---|
| 영어학 (음운론) A형 기입형 | 2점 | 80% |

**모범답안**

① different  ② same

**채점기준**

2점: ①, ② 모두 답안과 일치하면 2점을 준다.

1점: ①, ② 중 하나만 답안과 일치하면 1점을 준다.

0점: ①, ② 모두 답안과 일치하지 않으면 0점을 준다.

## 51

본책 p.266

| 하위내용영역 | 배점 | 예상정답률 |
|---|---|---|
| 영어학 (음운론) A형 서술형 | 4점 | 60% |

**모범답안**

First, the word 'envelope' is an example of phonological doublets: one word has two different phonemic forms (, either [ˈɛnvəˌloʊp] or [ˈɑnvəˌloʊp]). Second, the word 'ban' is a case of free variation: a single phonemic representation /bæn/ gives rise to two phonetic forms (of [bɛ̃ən] and [bæ̃n]).

**채점기준**

내용학 : 4점

(1) the word 'envelope' is an example of phonological doublets이 맞으면 1점을 준다.

(2) one word has two different phonemic forms (, either [ˈɛnvəˌloʊp] or [ˈɑnvəˌloʊp])의 내용이 맞으면 1점을 준다.

(3) the word 'ban' is a case of free variation이 맞으면 1점을 준다.

(4) a single phonemic representation /bæn/ gives rise to two phonetic forms (of [bɛ̃ən] and [bæ̃n])의 내용이 맞으면 1점을 준다.

## 52

본책 p.268

| 하위내용영역 | 배점 | 예상정답률 |
|---|---|---|
| 영어학 (음운론) B형 서술형 | 4점 | 45% |

**모범답안**

First, the two words are 'logician' and 'presidential'. In (the word) 'logician', /k/ changes to /ʃ/ before a suffix which begins with /ɪ/, followed immediately by a vowel. In 'presidential', /t/ changes to /ʃ/ before a suffix which begins with /ɪ/, followed immediately by a vowel.

**채점기준**

내용학 : 4점

(1) the two words are 'logician' and 'presidential'이 맞으면 2점을 준다. (각 1점)

(2) In 'logician', /k/ changes to /ʃ/ before a suffix which begins with /ɪ/, followed immediately by a vowel의 내용이 맞으면 1점을 준다.

(3) In 'presidential', /t/ changes to /ʃ/ before a suffix which begins with /ɪ/, followed immediately by a vowel의 내용이 맞으면 1점을 준다.

## 53

본책 p.270

| 하위내용영역 | 배점 | 예상정답률 |
|---|---|---|
| 영어학 (음운론) A형 기입형 | 2점 | 80% |

【모범답안】

① place  ② manner

【채점기준】

2점: ①, ② 모두 답안과 일치하면 2점을 준다.

1점: ①, ② 중 하나만 답안과 일치하면 1점을 준다.

0점: ①, ② 모두 답안과 일치하지 않으면 0점을 준다.

## 54

본책 p.271

| 하위내용영역 | 배점 | 예상정답률 |
|---|---|---|
| 영어학 (음운론) A형 서술형 | 4점 | 65% |

【모범답안】

First, the blank ① is 'word', and the blank ② is 'morphological'. Second, tense-vowel phonemes are realised as long before voiced fricatives.

【채점기준】

내용학: 4점

(1) the blank ① is 'word', and the blank ② is 'morphological'이 맞으면 2점을 준다. (각 1점)

(2) tense-vowel phonemes are realised as long before voiced fricatives의 내용이 맞으면 2점을 준다.

## 55

본책 p.273

| 하위내용영역 | 배점 | 예상정답률 |
|---|---|---|
| 영어학 (음운론) B형 서술형 | 4점 | 45% |

【모범답안】

First, the two words are 'camomile' and 'convoy'. Second, secondary stress occurs on the first syllable in (1) only where that syllable is heavy.

【채점기준】

내용학: 4점

(1) the two words are 'camomile' and 'convoy'가 맞으면 2점을 준다. (각 1점)

(2) secondary stress occurs on the first syllable in (1) only where that syllable is heavy의 내용이 맞으면 2점을 준다.

## 56

본책 p.275

| 하위내용영역 | 배점 | 예상정답률 |
|---|---|---|
| 영어학 (음운론) A형 기입형 | 2점 | 70% |

모범답안

① antepenultimate　② penultimate

채점기준

2점: ①, ② 모두 답안과 일치하면 2점을 준다.

1점: ①, ② 중 하나만 답안과 일치하면 1점을 준다.

0점: ①, ② 모두 답안과 일치하지 않으면 0점을 준다.

## 57

본책 p.277

| 하위내용영역 | 배점 | 예상정답률 |
|---|---|---|
| 영어학 (음운론) B형 서술형 | 4점 | 55% |

모범답안

First, the one word for the blank is 'plural'. Second, nasal assimilation optionally occurs across morpheme boundaries in (2) and across word boundaries in (3).

채점기준

내용학: 4점

(1) the one word for the blank is 'plural'이 맞으면 2점을 준다.

(2) nasal assimilation optionally occurs across morpheme boundaries in (2) and across word boundaries in (3) 의 내용이 맞으면 2점을 준다. (각 1점)

## 58

본책 p.279

| 하위내용영역 | 배점 | 예상정답률 |
|---|---|---|
| 영어학 (음운론) A형 서술형 | 4점 | 50% |

모범답안

**Version 1**

First, nasal stops belong to (fit into) (3a) and oral stops belong to (3b). Second, the feature combination (3d) refers to approximants.

## Version 2

First, the feature combination of [− continuant] and [+ sonorant] in (3a) belongs to nasal stops, and oral stops have the feature combination of [− continuant] and [− sonorant] in (3b). Second, the feature combination (3d) refers to approximants.

채점기준 ↦

내용학: 4점

(1) nasal stops belong to (3a) and oral stops belong to (3b)이 맞으면 2점을 준다. (각 1점)
(2) the feature combination (3d) refers to approximants의 내용이 맞으면 2점을 준다.

---

**59** 본책 p.281

| 하위내용영역 | 배점 | 예상정답률 |
|---|---|---|
| 영어학 (음운론) B형 서술형 | 4점 | 60% |

모범답안 ↦

First, while /ɛlm/ is well-formed, /silm/ is not well-formed. Well-formed syllables should contain no more than three X-positions in the rhyme. /ɛlm/ has three X-positions in the rhyme. However, /silm/ has four X-positions in the rhyme.

채점기준 ↦

내용학: 4점

(1) while /ɛlm/ is well-formed, /silm/ is not well-formed이 맞으면 1점을 준다.
(2) Well-formed syllables should contain no more than three X-positions in the rhyme의 내용이 맞으면 1점을 준다.
(3) /ɛlm/ has three X-positions in the rhyme의 내용이 맞으면 1점을 준다.
(4) /silm/ has four X-positions in the rhyme의 내용이 맞으면 1점을 준다.

---

**60** 본책 p.283

| 하위내용영역 | 배점 | 예상정답률 |
|---|---|---|
| 영어학 (음운론) A형 기입형 | 2점 | 70% |

모범답안 ↦

Alveolar obstruents

채점기준 ↦

2점: 답안과 일치하면 2점을 준다.

0점: 답안과 일치하지 않으면 0점을 준다.

## 61

본책 p.284

| 하위내용영역 | 배점 | 예상정답률 |
|---|---|---|
| 영어학 (음운론) B형 서술형 | 4점 | 45% |

[모범답안 ↵]

### Version 1

First, the words are 'globes' and 'coax'. Second, coronal obstruents can be appended to the core syllable.

### Version 2

First, the words, 'globes' and 'coax', violate both of the two constraints, Three-X exceeded and Sonority violated. Second, coronal obstruents can be appended to the core syllable.

[채점기준 ↵]

내용학: 4점

(1) the words are 'globes' and 'coax'이 맞으면 2점을 준다. 정답 단어 2개 중 하나만 쓴 경우나 그 외에 단어를 추가로 선택한 경우 0점을 준다.

(2) coronal obstruents can be appended to the core syllable의 내용이 맞으면 2점을 준다.

## 62

본책 p.286

| 하위내용영역 | 배점 | 예상정답률 |
|---|---|---|
| 영어학 (음운론) A형 기입형 | 2점 | 70% |

[모범답안 ↵]

① + consonantal   ② − continuant

[채점기준 ↵]

2점: ①, ② 모두 답안과 일치하면 2점을 준다.

1점: ①, ② 중 하나만 답안과 일치하면 1점을 준다.

0점: ①, ② 모두 답안과 일치하지 않으면 0점을 준다.

## 63

본책 p.287

| 하위내용영역 | 배점 | 예상정답률 |
|---|---|---|
| 영어학 (음운론) A형 서술형 | 4점 | 60% |

**모범답안**

First, derivational suffixes in (1b) are stress-neutral whereas those in (1c) are stress-shifting. Second, the stress-shifting suffixes in (2) are '-ette', '-ese', and '-esque'.

**채점기준**

내용학 : 4점

(1) derivational suffixes in (1b) are stress-neutral whereas those in (1c) are stress-shifting이 맞으면 2점을 준다. (각 1점)

(2) the stress-shifting suffixes in (2) are '-ette', '-ese', and '-esque'의 내용이 맞으면 2점을 준다. (정답과 다른 접미사를 쓰거나 정답 중 일부만 쓴 경우는 0점을 준다.)

## 64

본책 p.289

| 하위내용영역 | 배점 | 예상정답률 |
|---|---|---|
| 영어학 (음운론) B형 서술형 | 4점 | 50% |

**모범답안**

First, in (5), the word 'students' is the strongest stress of the noun phrase and the word 'regularly' is the strongest stress in the higher verb phrase. Second, the word 'regularly' is the strongest stress of the whole construction in (5).

**채점기준**

내용학 : 4점

(1) the word 'students' is the strongest stress of the noun phrase in (5) and the word 'regularly' is the strongest stress in the higher verb phrase이 맞으면 2점을 준다. (각 1점)

(2) the word 'regularly' is the strongest stress of the whole construction in (5)의 내용이 맞으면 2점을 준다.

## 65

본책 p.291

| 하위내용영역 | 배점 | 예상정답률 |
|---|---|---|
| 영어학 (음운론) A형 기입형 | 2점 | 90% |

**모범답안**

① unrounded   ② rounded

【채점기준】

2점: ①, ② 모두 답안과 일치하면 2점을 준다.

1점: ①, ② 중 하나만 답안과 일치하면 1점을 준다.

0점: ①, ② 모두 답안과 일치하지 않으면 0점을 준다.

---

## 66
본책 p.293

| 하위내용영역 | 배점 | 예상정답률 |
| --- | --- | --- |
| 영어학 (음운론) B형 서술형 | 4점 | 50% |

【모범답안】

The feature for the blank ① is '− continuant', and the blank ② is '+ consonantal'.
The redundancy statement for liquids is as follows: If [+ sonorant, + consonantal, + continuant], then [− syllabic].

【채점기준】

내용학: 4점

(1) The feature for the blank ① is '− continuant', and the blank ② is '+ consonantal'이 맞으면 2점을 준다. (각 1점)

(2) If [+ sonorant, + consonantal, + continuant], then [− syllabic]이 맞으면 2점을 준다.

---

## 67
본책 p.295

| 하위내용영역 | 배점 | 예상정답률 |
| --- | --- | --- |
| 영어학 (음운론) A형 서술형 | 4점 | 65% |

【모범답안】

First, (aspiration also occurs in) unstressed syllables. Second, the two data sets are (6a) and (6c).

【채점기준】

내용학: 4점

(1) unstressed syllables의 내용이 맞으면 2점을 준다.

(2) the two data sets are (6a) and (6c)이 맞으면 2점을 준다. (각 1점)

본책 p.297

## 68

| 하위내용영역 | 배점 | 예상정답률 |
|---|---|---|
| 영어학 (음운론) B형 서술형 | 4점 | 60% |

**모범답안**

First, the one word for the blank is 'obstruents'. Second, (English words can end in two stops when) the second consonant is an alveolar stop.

**채점기준**

내용학 : 4점

(1) the one word for the blank is 'obstruents'이 맞으면 2점을 준다.

(2) the second consonant is an alveolar stop의 내용이 맞으면 2점을 준다.

본책 p.299

## 69

| 하위내용영역 | 배점 | 예상정답률 |
|---|---|---|
| 영어학 (음운론) A형 기입형 | 2점 | 80% |

**모범답안**

① stressed   ② place

**채점기준**

2점 : ①, ② 모두 답안과 일치하면 2점을 준다.

1점 : ①, ② 중 하나만 답안과 일치하면 1점을 준다.

0점 : ①, ② 모두 답안과 일치하지 않으면 0점을 준다.

본책 p.301

## 70

| 하위내용영역 | 배점 | 예상정답률 |
|---|---|---|
| 영어학 (음운론) A형 서술형 | 4점 | 50% |

**모범답안**

First, in the word 'corrosion', three rules are as follows: Rule 1 (Velar softening), Rule 2 (Palatalization) and Rule 4 (Vowel lengthening). Second, in the word 'corroded', three rules are as follows: Rule 4 (Vowel lengthening), Rule 5 (Past tense) and Rule 6 (Flapping).

내용학: 4점

(1) in the word 'corrosion', three rules are as follows: Rule 1 (Velar softening), Rule 2 (Palatalization) and Rule 4 (Vowel lengthening)이 맞으면 2점을 준다.

(2) in the word 'corroded', three rules are as follows: Rule 4 (Vowel lengthening), Rule 5 (Past tense) and Rule 6 (Flapping)이 맞으면 2점을 준다.

## 71 본책 p.303

| 하위내용영역 | 배점 | 예상정답률 |
|---|---|---|
| 영어학 (음운론) B형 서술형 | 4점 | 65% |

모범답안 ○

### Version 1

In (3), in 'hand', the final /d/ of *hand* is elided, and then the /n/ assimilates to the following /k/.

### Version 2

In (3), in 'hand', 'hand' loses its final /d/, and then the /n/ assimilates to the following /k/.

채점기준 ○

내용학: 4점

The final /d/ of *hand* is elided and the /n/ assimilates to the (now) following /k/의 내용이 맞으면 4점을 준다.

## 72 본책 p.305

| 하위내용영역 | 배점 | 예상정답률 |
|---|---|---|
| 영어학 (음운론) A형 기입형 | 2점 | 90% |

모범답안 ○

① regressive  ② voiceless stops

채점기준 ○

2점: ①, ② 모두 답안과 일치하면 2점을 준다.

1점: ①, ② 중 하나만 답안과 일치하면 1점을 준다.

0점: ①, ② 모두 답안과 일치하지 않으면 0점을 준다.

## 73

본책 p.306

| 하위내용영역 | 배점 | 예상정답률 |
|---|---|---|
| 영어학 (음운론) A형 서술형 | 4점 | 60% |

**모범답안**

First, the word 'canoe' ([knu]) violates phonotactic constraints. Second, consonant cluster simplification occurs when there are sequences of identical ('geminate') consonants (at word or morpheme boundaries in connected speech).

**채점기준**

내용학 : 4점

(1) the word 'canoe' ([knu]) violates phonotactic constraints이 맞으면 2점을 준다.

(2) there are sequences of identical ('geminate') consonants의 내용이 맞으면 2점을 준다.

## 74

본책 p.308

| 하위내용영역 | 배점 | 예상정답률 |
|---|---|---|
| 영어학 (음운론) B형 서술형 | 4점 | 55% |

**모범답안**

First, the one word is 'onset'. Second, the first C in a CC cluster in (2c) is the (sonority) trough (or the trough in sonority).

**채점기준**

내용학 : 4점

(1) the one word is 'onset'이 맞으면 2점을 준다.

(2) The first C in a CC cluster in (2c) is the (sonority) trough (or the trough in sonority)의 내용이 맞으면 2점을 준다.

## 75

본책 p.310

| 하위내용영역 | 배점 | 예상정답률 |
|---|---|---|
| 영어학 (음운론) A형 기입형 | 2점 | 80% |

[모범답안]

① unrounded   ② monosyllabic

[채점기준]

2점: ①, ② 모두 답안과 일치하면 2점을 준다.

1점: ①, ② 중 하나만 답안과 일치하면 1점을 준다.

0점: ①, ② 모두 답안과 일치하지 않으면 0점을 준다.

## 76

본책 p.312

| 하위내용영역 | 배점 | 예상정답률 |
|---|---|---|
| 영어학 (음운론) B형 서술형 | 4점 | 60% |

[모범답안]

**Version 1**

First, the one word for the blank is 'voiceless'. Second, Tapping is ordered before /aɪ/ Raising (in the dialect in which 'writing' and 'riding' are pronounced the same).

**Version 2**

First, the one word is 'voiceless'. Second, Tapping is applied before /aɪ/ Raising (in the dialect in which 'writing' and 'riding' are pronounced the same).

[채점기준]

내용학: 4점

(1) the one word is 'voiceless'이 맞으면 2점을 준다.

(2) Tapping is ordered before /aɪ/ Raising의 내용이 맞으면 2점을 준다.

**77**
본책 p.314

| 하위내용영역 | 배점 | 예상정답률 |
|---|---|---|
| 영어학 (음운론) A형 서술형 | 4점 | 60% |

**모범답안**

First, (velars become fronted) before front vowels. Second, the three feature values are [− sonorant], [+ continuant], and [+ voice].

**채점기준**

내용학: 4점

(1) before front vowels이 맞으면 1점을 준다.

(2) the three feature values are [− sonorant], [+ continuant], and [+ voice]이 맞으면 3점을 준다. (각 1점)

**78**
본책 p.316

| 하위내용영역 | 배점 | 예상정답률 |
|---|---|---|
| 영어학 (음운론) B형 서술형 | 4점 | 55% |

**모범답안**

First, the two words are (c) 'poison' and (d) 'ransom'. In (c) 'poison', the noun is basic, and in (d) 'ransom', the noun is basic.

**채점기준**

내용학: 4점

(1) the two words are (c) 'poison' and (d) 'ransom'이 맞으면 2점을 준다. (각 1점)

(2) In (c) 'poison', the noun is basic, and in (d) 'ransom', the noun is basic의 내용이 맞으면 2점을 준다. (각 1점)

# Morphology

## 01

본책 p.320

| 하위내용영역 | 배점 | 예상정답률 |
|---|---|---|
| 영어학 (형태론) B형 기입형 | 2점 | 80% |

**모범답안**

① monosyllabic   ② verb

**채점기준**

2점: ①, ② 모두 답안과 일치하면 2점을 준다.

1점: ①, ② 중 하나만 답안과 일치하면 1점을 준다.

0점: ①, ② 모두 답안과 일치하지 않으면 0점을 준다.

## 02

본책 p.321

| 하위내용영역 | 배점 | 예상정답률 |
|---|---|---|
| 영어학 (형태론) A형 서술형 | 4점 | 60% |

**모범답안**

The prefix 'dis-' must attach first to the verb 'engage' to form the verb 'disengage'. Then, the suffix '-ment' attaches to the verb 'disengage' to form the noun 'disengagement'.

**채점기준**

내용학: 4점

(1) The prefix 'dis-' must attach first to the verb 'engage' to form the verb 'disengage'의 내용이 맞으면 2점을 준다.

(2) the suffix '-ment' attaches to the verb 'disengage' to form the noun 'disengagement'의 내용이 맞으면 2점을 준다.

| 하위내용영역 | 배점 | 예상정답률 |
|---|---|---|
| 영어학 (형태론) A형 서술형 | 4점 | 40% |

[ 모범답안 ❧ ]

### Version 1

The root is 'act', a verb, to which we add the suffix '-ive', resulting in an adjective, 'active'. To this adjective, we add the suffix '-ate' forming a verb 'activate'. Finally, the suffix '-ion' attaches to this verb and converts it into the noun 'activation'.

### Version 2

First, the suffix (the affix) '-ive' attaches to the verbal base 'act' to give an adjective 'active'. Second, the suffix '-ate' attaches to this adjective and converts it into a verb 'activate'. Finally, the suffix '-ion' is added, converting the verb into the noun 'activation'.

### Version 3

First, the suffix '-ive' attaches to the verb 'act' to form the adjective 'active'. Second, the suffix '-ate' attaches to the adjective 'active' to form the verb 'activate'. Lastly, the suffix '-ion' attaches to the verb 'activate' to form the noun 'activation'.

[ 채점기준 ❧ ]

내용학: 4점

(1) The root is 'act', a verb, to which we add the suffix '-ive', resulting in an adjective, 'active'의 내용이 맞으면 1점을 준다.

(2) To this adjective, we add the suffix '-ate' forming a verb 'activate'의 내용이 맞으면 2점을 준다.

(3) the suffix '-ion' attaches to this verb and converts it into the noun 'activation'의 내용이 맞으면 1점을 준다.

| 하위내용영역 | 배점 | 예상정답률 |
|---|---|---|
| 영어학 (형태론) A형 서술형 | 4점 | 65% |

[ 모범답안 ❧ ]

### Version 1

First, (ic) is ungrammatical. In 'dropped kick', the tense marker '-ed' cannot be attached to the first element. Second, (iia) is Non-compound Expression, and (iib) is Compound Word.

### Version 2

First, (ic) is ungrammatical because in the phrase 'dropped kick', the compound verb with internal tense is not possible. Second, in (iia) 'wet suit' belongs to Non-compound Expression, and in (iib) 'wet suit' belongs to Compound Word.

내용학 : 4점

(1) (ic) is ungrammatical이 맞으면 1점을 준다.

(2) In 'dropped kick', the tense marker '-ed' cannot be attached to the first element의 내용이 맞으면 1점을 준다.

(3) (iia) is Non-compound Expression이 맞으면 1점을 준다.

(4) (iib) is Compound Word이 맞으면 1점을 준다.

---

## 05 본책 p.327

| 하위내용영역 | 배점 | 예상정답률 |
| --- | --- | --- |
| 영어학 (형태론) A형 기입형 | 2점 | 80% |

모범답안 ↝

① cook  ② obstruent

채점기준 ↝

2점: ①, ② 모두 답안과 일치하면 2점을 준다.

1점: ①, ② 중 하나만 답안과 일치하면 1점을 준다.

0점: ①, ② 모두 답안과 일치하지 않으면 0점을 준다.

본책 p.330

## 01

| 하위내용영역 | 배점 | 예상정답률 |
|---|---|---|
| 영어학 (의미론) A형 서술형 | 4점 | 50% |

모범답안

The words, 'flour' in (3) and 'flower' in (4), are homophones. The words, 'ground' in (5) and 'ground' in (6), are homonyms.

채점기준

내용학: 4점

(1) The words, 'flour' in (3) and 'flower' in (4), are homophones이 맞으면 2점을 준다.

(2) The words, 'ground' in (5) and 'ground' in (6), are homonyms이 맞으면 2점을 준다.

## 02

본책 p.332

| 하위내용영역 | 배점 | 예상정답률 |
|---|---|---|
| 영어학 (의미론) B형 기입형 | 2점 | 70% |

모범답안

① gradable   ② converse

채점기준

2점: ①, ② 모두 답안과 일치하면 2점을 준다.

1점: ①, ② 중 하나만 답안과 일치하면 1점을 준다.

0점: ①, ② 모두 답안과 일치하지 않으면 0점을 준다.

## 03

본책 p.333

| 하위내용영역 | 배점 | 예상정답률 |
|---|---|---|
| 영어학 (의미론) B형 기입형 | 2점 | 80% |

모범답안

① synonymous   ② contradictory

채점기준

2점: ①, ② 모두 답안과 일치하면 2점을 준다.

1점: ①, ② 중 하나만 답안과 일치하면 1점을 준다.

0점: ①, ② 모두 답안과 일치하지 않으면 0점을 준다.

## 04

본책 p.335

| 하위내용영역 | 배점 | 예상정답률 |
|---|---|---|
| 영어학 (의미론) B형 기입형 | 2점 | 80% |

### 모범답안 ↵

① relational  ② gradable

### 채점기준 ↵

2점: ①, ② 모두 답안과 일치하면 2점을 준다.

1점: ①, ② 중 하나만 답안과 일치하면 1점을 준다.

0점: ①, ② 모두 답안과 일치하지 않으면 0점을 준다.

## 05

본책 p.337

| 하위내용영역 | 배점 | 예상정답률 |
|---|---|---|
| 영어학 (의미론) A형 서술형 | 4점 | 70% |

### 모범답안 ↵

**Version 1**

A pair of sentences in (iii) shows the semantic relation of entailment. If we negate (iiia) 'John hasn't arrived in Edinburgh', then it no longer entails (iiib) 'John is in Edinburgh'. (Negating an entailing sentence destroys the entailment / If we negate an entailing sentence, then the entailment fails.)

**Version 2**

A pair of sentences in (iii) shows the semantic relation of entailment. If we negate (iiia) 'John hasn't arrived in Edinburgh', then it no longer entails (iiib) 'John is in Edinburgh'. (If we negate an entailing sentence 'John hasn't arrived in Edinburgh', we don't know about whether John is in Edinburgh.)

### 채점기준 ↵

내용학: 4점

(1) A pair of sentences in (iii) shows the semantic relation of entailment이 맞으면 2점을 준다.

(2) If we negate (iiia), then it no longer entails (iiib)의 내용이 맞으면 2점을 준다.

## 06

| 하위내용영역 | 배점 | 예상정답률 |
|---|---|---|
| 영어학 (의미론) A형 서술형 | 4점 | 65% |

**모범답안**

Sentence (b) does not produce presupposition. The non-factive predicate 'is true' does not presuppose the truth of the complement clause ('Jill had lent Ed her key'). Sentence (e) does not produce presupposition because a *yes-no* question doesn't serve as a presupposition trigger.

**채점기준**

내용학: 4점

(1) Sentence (b) does not produce presupposition이 맞으면 1점을 준다.

(2) The non-factive predicate 'is true' does not presuppose the truth of the complement clause의 내용이 맞으면 1점을 준다.

(3) Sentence (e) does not produce presupposition이 맞으면 1점을 준다.

(4) a *yes-no* question doesn't serve as a presupposition trigger의 내용이 맞으면 1점을 준다.

## 07

| 하위내용영역 | 배점 | 예상정답률 |
|---|---|---|
| 영어학 (의미론) A형 서술형 | 4점 | 70% |

**모범답안**

**Version 1**

The blank ① is 'Hyponymy' and the blank ② is 'meronymy'.
The sentence (e) is wrong: house is a hyponym of building. The sentence (f) is wrong: saw is a hyponym of tool.

**Version 2**

① Hyponymy  ② meronymy

The sentences (e) and (f) are wrong. The correct forms are as follows: (e) house is a hyponym of building and (f) saw is a hyponym of tool.

**채점기준**

내용학: 4점

(1) The blank ① is 'Hyponymy' and the blank ② is 'meronymy'이 맞으면 2점을 준다. (각 1점)

(2) The sentence (e) is wrong: house is a hyponym of building이 맞으면 1점을 준다.

(3) The sentence (f) is wrong: saw is a hyponym of tool이 맞으면 1점을 준다.

# Pragmatics

## 01

본책 p.346

| 하위내용영역 | 배점 | 예상정답률 |
|---|---|---|
| 영어학 (화용론) A형 기입형 | 2점 | 80% |

[모범답안]

① Implicatures  ② Relevance

[채점기준]

2점: ①, ② 모두 답안과 일치하면 2점을 준다.

1점: ①, ② 중 하나만 답안과 일치하면 1점을 준다.

0점: ①, ② 모두 답안과 일치하지 않으면 0점을 준다.

## 02

본책 p.348

| 하위내용영역 | 배점 | 예상정답률 |
|---|---|---|
| 영어학 (화용론) A형 서술형 | 4점 | 70% |

[모범답안]

**Version 1**

Sentence (d) is not a (typical) performative sentence. The verb 'owe' does not accomplish some additional action. Sentence (e) is not a (typical) performative sentence because this sentence is not in the present tense; the verb 'swore' is the past tense (of the verb 'swear').

**Version 2**

Sentence (d) is not a (typical) performative sentence. The verb 'owe' does not denote an (additional) action. Sentence (e) is not a (typical) performative sentence. The verb 'swore' is the past tense (of the verb 'swear'); this sentence is not in the present tense.

[채점기준]

내용학: 4점

(1) Sentence (d) is not a (typical) performative sentence이 맞으면 1점을 준다.

(2) The verb 'owe' does not accomplish some additional action의 내용이 맞으면 1점을 준다.

(3) Sentence (e) is not a (typical) performative sentence이 맞으면 1점을 준다.

(4) because this sentence is not in the present tense; the verb 'swore' is the past tense (of the verb 'swear').의 내용이 맞으면 1점을 준다.

## 03
본책 p.350

| 하위내용영역 | 배점 | 예상정답률 |
|---|---|---|
| 영어학 (화용론) B형 기입형 | 2점 | 70% |

모범답안

① Manner   ② Relevance

채점기준

2점: ①, ② 모두 답안과 일치하면 2점을 준다.

1점: ①, ② 중 하나만 답안과 일치하면 1점을 준다.

0점: ①, ② 모두 답안과 일치하지 않으면 0점을 준다.

## 04
본책 p.352

| 하위내용영역 | 배점 | 예상정답률 |
|---|---|---|
| 영어학 (화용론) B형 기입형 | 2점 | 90% |

모범답안

① old   ② new

채점기준

2점: ①, ② 모두 답안과 일치하면 2점을 준다.

1점: ①, ② 중 하나만 답안과 일치하면 1점을 준다.

0점: ①, ② 모두 답안과 일치하지 않으면 0점을 준다.

## 05
본책 p.354

| 하위내용영역 | 배점 | 예상정답률 |
|---|---|---|
| 영어학 (화용론) A형 기입형 | 2점 | 80% |

모범답안

① imperative   ② directive

채점기준

2점: ①, ② 모두 답안과 일치하면 2점을 준다.

1점: ①, ② 중 하나만 답안과 일치하면 1점을 준다.

0점: ①, ② 모두 답안과 일치하지 않으면 0점을 준다.

**06**
본책 p.356

| 하위내용영역 | 배점 | 예상정답률 |
|---|---|---|
| 영어학 (화용론) A형 기입형 | 2점 | 90% |

**모범답안**

quantity (Quantity)

**채점기준**

2점: 답안과 일치하면 2점을 준다.

0점: 답안과 일치하지 않으면 0점을 준다.

Mentor Linguistics

# 멘토영어학
# 문제은행

**모범답안**

---

**초판인쇄** | 2024. 7. 10.　**초판발행** | 2024. 7. 15.

**편저자** | 앤드류 채　**발행인** | 박 용　**발행처** | (주)박문각출판

**표지디자인** | 박문각 디자인팀　**등록** | 2015년 4월 29일 제2019-000137호

**주소** | 06654 서울특별시 서초구 효령로 283 서경 B/D　**팩스** | (02)584-2927

**전화** | 교재 문의 (02)6466-7202, 동영상 문의 (02)6466-7201

저자와의
협의하에
인지생략

ISBN 979-11-7262-093-6

**Mentor
Linguistics
Series**

전공영어 멘토영어학
멘토영어학 기출분석
멘토영어학 문제은행

**Mentor Linguistics**

# 멘토영어학
# 문제은행

www.pmg.co.kr

교재관련 문의 02-6466-7202
학원관련 문의 02-816-2030
온라인강의 문의 02-6466-7201

ISBN 979-11-7262-093-6